BROTHERS FOREVER

BROTHERS
FOREVER

•————————•

THE ENDURING BOND BETWEEN
A MARINE AND A NAVY SEAL THAT
TRANSCENDED THEIR ULTIMATE SACRIFICE

Tom Sileo and Colonel Tom Manion, USMC (Ret.)

Foreword by General John Allen, USMC (Ret.)

DA CAPO PRESS
A Member of the Perseus Books Group

Designed by Trish Wilkinson
Set in 11.5 point Goudy Oldstyle by The Perseus Books Group

First Da Capo Press edition 2014

Library of Congress Cataloging-in-Publication Data

Sileo, Tom.
    Brothers forever : the enduring bond between a Marine and a Navy
SEAL that transcended their ultimate sacrifice / Tom Sileo and Col. Tom
Manion, USMCR (Ret.) ; foreword by Gen. John Allen, USMC (Ret.).
        pages   cm
    Includes bibliographical references and index.
    ISBN 978-0-306-82237-7 (hardcover) — ISBN 978-0-306-82238-4
(e-book) 1. Manion, Travis, 1980-2007. 2. Looney, Brendan, 1981-
2010. 3. Iraq War, 2003-2011—Casualties—United States. 4. Iraq
War, 2003-2011—Campaigns—Iraq—Fallujah. 5. Afghan War,
2001—Casualties—United States. 6. United States. Marine Corps—
Biography 7. United States. Navy. SEALs—Biography. 8. United States
Naval Academy—Alumni and alumnae—Biography. I. Title.
    DS79.766.M36S55 2014
    956.7044'34509730922—dc23
    [B]   2013043846

Published by Da Capo Press
A Member of the Perseus Books Group
www.dacapopress.com

Da Capo Press books are available at special discounts for bulk purchases
in the US by corporations, institutions, and other organizations. For more
information, please contact the Special Markets Department at the Perseus
Books Group, 2300 Chestnut Street, Suite 200, Philadelphia, PA 19103, or
call (800) 810-4145, ext. 5000, or e-mail special.markets@perseusbooks.com.

10 9 8 7 6 5 4 3 2

*For Brendan, Travis, and all the selfless patriots
of yesterday, today, and tomorrow
who define the "If not me, then who . . ." spirit.*

Contents

Foreword

"Sir, casualties are inbound. One of the MiTTs [military transition teams] has been hit hard, and we have casualties headed to 'Fallujah surgical.'" My head snapped up from my work; I quickly strapped on my 9mm and headed off to "Fallujah surgical," the Level Two trauma and surgical facility on Camp Fallujah servicing the casualty and medical needs of the eastern portion of the Al Anbar Province in Iraq. I had made a habit of going to the operating rooms to see and encourage the wounded whenever I was in the command post of II Marine Expeditionary Force (MEF) (Fwd) at Fallujah.

As my aide, Ben Carruthers, and I made our way through the maze of buildings and walls of the camp, something told me to hurry. I quickened my pace, then began to run. I hadn't done this before, and I'm sure my aide was wondering what was up. As we rounded the corner of the hospital I could see the up-armored HMMWVs (Humvees) of the MiTT team and the Marines themselves, standing near the entrance. They had their hands on their hips, and their heads were down. "This is bad," I thought. One of the Marines was lifting a set of body armor from the floor of a HMMWV, and it was covered with and dripping blood.

I quickly cleared my weapon at the clearing barrel and stepped into the facility. The medical personnel had become accustomed to my presence on these occasions and quickly briefed me on the situation: several wounded, one very seriously, and the survivors were down the corridor in an office. I hustled down to the office and quickly got a situation report from the team leader and others, one of whom was wounded and awaiting treatment. It had been a bad ambush, and the Marines had fought for their lives alongside the Iraqi troops they were advising. Then, looking up at me with an anguish you can only find in combat, the team leader said to me in a hushed tone: "We think Travis is dead." I didn't immediately connect the name, but knew I needed to get down the corridor right away to the ORs where the incredible surgical teams were working frantically on the wounded.

As I stepped into the first OR the surgical team were just finishing their work. One of the nurses was crying openly. They'd been unable to save this Marine, and he had died just seconds before I stepped into the OR. As I walked to the end of the gurney, I was stunned to see Travis Manion, the wonderful youngster I'd known as one of my midshipmen while I was commandant at the Naval Academy. I had known his family: his dad, Tom, a Marine colonel himself, and his mom, Janet, a stalwart of the family. Travis had selected the Corps from Annapolis, and though I had not seen him during this tour in Fallujah, I'd heard repeatedly of his courage and bravery as an advisor. One by one the doctors and nurses left the OR, leaving me alone with Travis. I don't think I had ever prayed so hard for anyone or anything in my life as I did while alone with him in that empty OR. His loss was very personal to me.

Three years later, while I was deputy commander at CENTCOM and headed ultimately to command the US forces in Afghanistan, I learned of an incident the previous night that had taken the lives of some of our magnificent special operators,

SEALs from SEAL Team 3. They had been operating in the Zabul Province south of the Hindu Kush in Afghanistan and had generally made the lives of the Taliban miserable the entire time they had served there. One of the finest of the young leaders in this SEAL Team, Brendan Looney, looked and lived every aspect of the ethos of being a SEAL, this now-legendary strata of the American special ops community. That night we lost Brendan Looney. As with Travis, Brendan's death was not simply a loss to their respective units and missions. Losing them was a terrible blow to America, which would now never benefit from the extraordinary qualities of these two men.

The irony of their relationship and their seemingly unrelated deaths was nearly as tragic. They had been roommates at the United States Naval Academy, growing up together at this most hallowed institution of our naval service. They had faced the challenges of Navy and had emerged committed in ways few can understand without experiencing the powerful formative forces of Annapolis. And in their intense sense of duty and their desire to serve, one sought to be a Marine, the other a SEAL. Remembering the times, it didn't take a fortune-teller to guess where this would lead them both: to war in Iraq, or Afghanistan, or both. And to war it did lead them, extracting from them long separations from their families as they grew into the full realization of their roles as combat leaders. But it also extracted from them their last full measure—their young lives—willingly sacrificed for their country and these causes.

Tom Manion has done us a great service in initiating the effort to tell this story. Yes, it's about war, but it's less a history of two wars than it is about the human experience of war and what this newest generation of American warriors has experienced. It ties together these precious young lives and their growth together as warriors, as leaders, and . . . as brothers. This book celebrates what we hear more and more frequently: that these young

Americans, on whose broad, strong shoulders we have fought two wars and who have kept the wolf from the door in innumerable other places, are the new "Greatest Generation." The reader sees all of this unfold in the maturing of these young lives, their interactions with their Annapolis classmates, and in the units in which they served, but very importantly as well in their interaction with their loving families, and in Brendan's case his wonderful young wife, Amy. Then the authors, Tom Sileo and Tom Manion, bring these two wars home for all Americans to understand what this country has really sacrificed in these causes. With less than 1 percent of our population in uniform, fewer and fewer Americans bear the brunt of the responsibility for military service, and fewer and fewer understand the sacrifices made by men like Travis and Brendan and their precious troops. In that context, we are given a glimpse of the impact of that sacrifice as the authors describe in heart-wrenching detail how two families navigate the grief and pain of losing their sons and a husband.

All of us who fought in these wars now pray that in the end the outcomes will justify the cost to America and its allies. Those of us left behind must ensure these sacrifices were not in vain, and that these lives lost will have meaning and purpose, now and in the future.

Within Arlington National Cemetery there is a portion, Section 60, which has taken on an iconic meaning, for here in this very small spot can be found the entire sweep of American sacrifice in the modern wars of the Republic. One can find the graves of the World War II generation and those of our Korean and Vietnam war veterans, but now, and poignantly, Section 60 is the final resting place of our most recent honored dead, those young American warriors who have perished in Iraq and Afghanistan. It should come as no surprise, then, that the families decided to inter Travis and Brendan side by side in Section 60. And there they lie. Roommates at Annapolis, they shared so much . . . their sense of duty . . .

their courage . . . their willingness to give their all for something bigger than themselves. And beneath this hallowed ground they lie shoulder to shoulder, the ultimate symbol of American selfless sacrifice and the ultimate emblem of the courage of their age. In virtually every sense, they had become brothers in life, and now in death they rest together . . . brothers forever. No regrets.

—General John Allen, USMC (Ret.)

Prologue

JUST ANOTHER DAY

Around every corner was a possible ambush. Beneath every roadway or garbage pile was a potential roadside bomb. Atop every roof or mosque tower was a possible sniper. In April 2007, Fallujah, Iraq, was arguably the most dangerous city in the world.

Stationed on a small forward operating base inside the war-ravaged terrorist haven was Travis Manion, a US Marine officer from Doylestown, Pennsylvania, near Philadelphia. At twenty-six, Travis was already on his second deployment to Fallujah, where American troops had fought some of the bloodiest battles since Vietnam.

Before heading out for another perilous patrol aimed at capturing and killing members of al Qaeda in Iraq, Travis, the son of a Marine Corps colonel, was finishing an e-mail to his friends and family back home. Eagerly awaiting his updates from the front lines was his close friend and US Naval Academy roommate, Brendan Looney, who was about to start training to become a Navy SEAL.

"We are a little over the halfway point of deployment," Travis began. "We have been pretty busy and working hard."

After explaining that times were tough in Fallujah, Travis, who was leading American and Iraqi troops into battle on a daily basis, closed his e-mail on an upbeat note.

"I'm excited to see the deployment end strong and leave the Iraqi battalion at a higher level than when we arrived," the Marine Corps first lieutenant wrote. "I miss you guys and I'm looking forward to seeing you soon."

Just a few days after sending the e-mail, Travis wasn't sure if he'd ever see his friends or family again. Surrounded by earsplitting rocket-propelled grenade (RPG) explosions and machine gun fire from enemy insurgents, a joint combat patrol on April 23, 2007, was quickly becoming a disaster for US and Iraqi forces. If the patrol couldn't quickly mount an effective counterattack, every US Marine and Iraqi Army soldier was in danger of not making it out of Fallujah's notorious industrial sector.

Most of the industrial area's streets were narrow and strewn with trash. Low-hanging electrical wires were everywhere, making it difficult to see rooftops, where the enemy would usually hide. On these joint patrols, the question wasn't if American and Iraqi troops would be attacked, but when.

Everyone, including Travis, was sweating and breathing heavily as the fierce battle's intensifying chaos exacerbated Iraq's already brutal heat. Enemy gunfire was raining down from multiple rooftops, making it difficult to hear and even harder to see. Bullets were smashing into buildings, creating a choking mixture of dust and concrete in the air as debris fell all around Travis's endangered patrol.

Several months into his second deployment, Travis knew Fallujah's streets almost as well as Philadelphia's. Shouting over enemy AK-47 and RPG fire, he told his Marines and their Iraqi partners where to go and how to get there. If the patrol was going to survive this attack, it was imperative that they get into proper fighting position.

Two Marines had already been wounded during the firefight, which made the situation even more urgent. They were lying behind a nearby Humvee, and Travis's first priority was reaching them. Braving enemy gunfire, Travis and his Marines made a beeline toward their injured comrades.

As Travis reached the most severely wounded American, he knelt over the Marine while continuing to direct his teammates.

"Keep moving!" Travis shouted to his men. "I've got to help this guy, or we're going to lose him."

After taking out his first aid kit, Travis pressed down and tried to stop the Marine's bleeding.

"You're going to be alright, brother," Travis said. "Just breathe."

Travis was still keeping tabs on his Marines. When he saw one teammate take a step in the wrong direction, he yelled out "LEFT!" to make sure the Marine stayed out of enemy crosshairs.

After a few minutes, the wounded Marine's bleeding was under control. Travis was confident he would survive and passed him off to a Marine from an adjacent unit before turning back toward the bullet-riddled street.

Like a lion let out of its cage, Travis burst onto the street and began firing at enemy positions with his M-4 rifle and attached M-203 grenade launcher. Punishing gunfire from Travis and his Marines quickly silenced one rooftop, and in just a few moments, the momentum was with the Americans.

Then a massive blast rocked the city's industrial sector. The force shook buildings and sent a huge cloud of dust billowing above Fallujah's buildings and electrical wires. Travis had been encountering roadside bombs since his first deployment, but this was the loudest explosion he had ever heard.

Travis and his fellow Marines watched as—in what seemed like slow motion—two Americans flew out of an armored Humvee and landed on the street. The US vehicle from the adjacent unit had struck an improvised explosive device (IED) while trying to move out of the kill zone, sending pieces of the Humvee flying so high into the air that Marines stationed several blocks away could see the blast's terrifying impact.

"MOVE!" Travis yelled as he took off running toward the two wounded Americans.

Upon arriving at what was left of the devastated Humvee, Travis found the first Marine pinned under a piece of the damaged vehicle. He asked a teammate to work on freeing the man while he ran toward the Humvee's turret gunner, who was the second casualty.

During the explosion, a huge piece of the vehicle had hit the Marine's head. The heavy chunk of metal had shattered his jaw and made it nearly impossible for him to breathe. He lay motionless in the street while Travis lifted a piece of the turret off his face and lifted him up.

"I've got you!" Travis said, carrying the Marine to safety. Travis and his teammates had already eliminated enemy gunfire from one rooftop, but sporadic shots were still ringing out from another.

Quickly recognizing that the gagging Marine's airway was blocked, Travis reached into his first aid kit and pulled out a nasopharyngeal tube. Pushing the device into the Marine's bloody nose, Travis comforted the frightened young American as he struggled to breathe.

"You're going to make it," Travis said. "I'm with you, man."

After a few tense moments, the wounded Marine's gasps for air became normal breaths, which allowed Travis to turn his attention to helping the adjacent unit organize a medevac to transport the wounded to hospitals on nearby bases. Eventually it became clear that all the injured Americans would survive.

For Travis, the day wasn't over when the medevac was complete or the enemy gunfire subsequently died down. Furious after seeing fellow Marines shot and nearly crushed by debris, Travis ran toward the crater left by the massive IED and found the command wire that enemy forces had used to detonate it. He organized a team, which carefully followed the wire to the inside of a nearby building, then rounded up several suspected terrorists and took them in for questioning.

Less than a week later, that harrowing patrol would pale in comparison to another vicious battle on the war-torn streets of Iraq's Al Anbar province. For the warriors of Fallujah, April 23, 2007, was just another day.

1

CALL TO ARMS

Brendan Looney was heading out to football practice at the US Naval Academy in the spring of 2001 when he heard the quiet strumming of a guitar as he walked by a room. Travis Manion was playing the opening chords to the Dave Matthews Band song "What Would You Say."

"Hey, man, that's pretty good," Brendan said. "I saw them at Nissan Pavilion—it was one hell of a show."

"That's in Virginia, right?" Travis asked, laying the guitar on his lap while looking up at Brendan. "You from around here?"

"Yep, Owings, Maryland, and now Silver Spring," Brendan said. "What about you?"

"Philadelphia," Travis said. "About forty minutes away in a place called Doylestown."

"Uh-oh," Brendan said. "Eagles fan?"

"Yep," Travis responded.

"Shit," Brendan said as the young midshipmen shared a laugh. "'Skins all the way."

The die-hard Washington Redskins fan knew this Philadelphia Eagles supporter was on the wrestling team, but he couldn't remember his name, so Brendan decided to introduce himself.

"I'm Brendan Looney," he said.

"I'm Travis Manion," said Travis. "Great to meet you."

"Good to meet you, too," Brendan said. "I gotta get to practice."

"Me, too," Travis said. "Football?"

"Yep," Brendan answered. "You're wrestling, right?"

"Yeah, I had to retire from football," Travis said. "I knew I'd never be good enough to make the Eagles, and I didn't want to end up on a team like the Redskins."

After another laugh, the varsity athletes headed to separate practices. The Naval Academy freshmen (or plebes, as members of the youngest class are called) might have played different sports and rooted for different NFL teams, but each had just made a new friend.

Few wanted to line up across from Brendan at Navy football practices. As a slotback for the Midshipmen, who famously specialize in running the option, Brendan's job was to blast anyone trying to tackle the ball carrier with a crushing block. He wasn't a starter, but in practice, he was among the team's most feared players.

Before Navy and the Naval Academy Preparatory School (NAPS), Brendan played high school football at DeMatha Catholic High School. In the Washington, DC, area, "DeMatha" was synonymous with "powerhouse," as the Hyattsville, Maryland, all-men's school has been a force in high school athletics for decades. Two of its most notable football players are Brian Westbrook, who starred for many years on Travis's Eagles, and his brother, Byron Westbrook, who went on to play for Brendan's Redskins.

Ben Mathews, a Navy linebacker, became friends with Brendan after observing his almost superhuman work ethic in the weight room. After introducing himself and quickly realizing that Brendan was a warm, friendly guy, Mathews wanted to see if he could keep up with his teammate's workout regimen, which included countless squats.

The experiment ended with Mathews throwing up on the weight room floor. Brendan was an impressive physical specimen, and few could keep up with him in any setting involving athletic challenges.

On one particularly hot, stuffy day Mathews, exhausted after studying all night for an exam, was going through the motions during team drills. The first teammate to notice his lack of intensity was Brendan, who would never give anything less than 100 percent on the practice field. He reacted fiercely when he saw anyone not doing his part to prepare for the next game.

As the whistle blew, Brendan, the slotback, ran straight toward Mathews, the linebacker. While Mathews trotted toward the tailback, Brendan came seemingly out of nowhere and hammered his friend, who hit the ground almost as quickly as Brendan reached out to help him up. With blood spraying from his broken nose, the confused, disoriented linebacker took the hand of the teammate who had just embarrassed him with a bone-crushing blow.

Brendan was a man of deeds, not words, and while helping the injured player off the turf, gave him a look that Mathews interpreted as "if you want to be first team, play like it."

Mathews wasn't happy about the blood streaming down his face, but he knew it was Brendan's way of helping him become a better player. Although many jocks would have started a fight over the incident, Mathews later thanked his teammate for the wake-up call.

Like Brendan, Travis believed being the hardest worker was the key to success. On the wrestling mat, Travis was always the guy with the black-and-blue face. His ears usually looked like they'd been crumpled inside somebody's fist. But the La Salle College High School standout was strong, determined, and always one of Navy's toughest outs.

"You may never be big enough to play football or fast enough to run track," Travis once told kids at a local wrestling clinic in Doylestown, at an event covered by a local newspaper. "You work through the hardships and (you can) be successful, whether it's on the wrestling mat or in battle. (Wrestling) lays the foundation for what it takes to be a good officer."

Although some on the Navy wrestling team struggled to balance long practices and trips to away meets with academics, passing exams was never an issue for Travis, who absorbed lectures like a sponge. He attended classes, studied, and wrote his papers, but always thought wrestling would best prepare him for being a warrior and leader on the battlefield. This belief was reinforced by the qualities he saw in Captain Doug Zembiec, a two-time All-American wrestler at Navy who attended as many practices and meets as he could and frequently sparred with Travis.

"Be a battle-ax," Zembiec told him. "Hurl yourself into your opponent."

Zembiec, a 1995 Naval Academy graduate, had a big impact on Travis. In the young wrestler's eyes, the gritty, tough, seemingly invincible warrior embodied everything he wanted to become: a skilled Marine officer who used the wrestling mat to develop himself into a leader who commanded respect.

Travis was a high school and college wrestling star. After a strong junior year at Navy, which featured several epic matches against nationally ranked opponents, he was presented the Naval Academy's Weems Award for dedication and leadership.

As a preseason Top 20 wrestler going into his senior season, Travis didn't want to simply win matches and meets. He wanted to dominate and help lead the Midshipmen to a championship.

In December 2003, Travis won the Penn State Open in his 184-pound weight class. He won four straight matches that day, including a 6–4 victory in the title contest against a formidable Rider University opponent. Travis's parents, Tom and Janet Manion, never missed one of his matches and drove up to State College, Pennsylvania, for the meet. Nothing gave Travis more satisfaction than making his parents proud.

The Penn State Open was hard for Travis's mom and dad to watch. During the day's first match, Travis let out a terrible scream while grappling with his opponent. Their son's right shoulder, which he had injured during his junior year, was now a greater source of pain, especially after an unsuccessful operation left his arm practically unusable.

After he cried out in agony, Travis's right arm felt like Jell-O for the rest of the tournament. He won it anyway.

Travis knew that if he was also going to prevail in an upcoming wrestling tournament in Arlington, Texas, it would have to be with one arm, just like at Penn State.

At the January 2004 tournament, when Travis knelt on the mat before squaring off against a tough adversary from Purdue, he channeled Captain Zembiec's words and hurled himself into his opponent. On this day in Texas, however, the battle-ax had no blade.

"Come on, Trav," Tom yelled from the stands.

"Bear down!" shouted Tom's brother, Chris Manion, a former wrestling star who was almost always in Travis's corner.

The Purdue wrestler slammed his struggling opponent to the ground for a takedown, with Travis's injured shoulder thumping squarely onto the red-and-yellow mat. His right arm was already numb, and this first blow left Travis with almost no strength to attempt an escape. In a sport built on hand-to-hand combat, one hand is almost always no match for two.

"They should stop this," Janet said to Tom, who was silent as he watched his son being thoroughly dominated.

The match ended in an 11–0 shutout. It was by far the worst defeat of Travis's illustrious high school and college wrestling career and left the varsity athlete despondent as he watched the rest of the meet from the bench, clutching his injured shoulder.

Back at the Arlington Hilton after the worst meet of his life, Travis, a brawny, good-looking twenty-three-year-old with a buzz cut, sat outside the hotel talking to Navy assistant wrestling coach Joel Sharratt. Although the senior athlete and his mentor were close, this was the first time Sharratt had ever seen Travis, who insisted that he had "let everyone down," overcome by emotion. Travis knew his wrestling career was over and worried aloud that he had disappointed his parents.

"That's bullshit," Sharratt said. "Your parents support you 100 percent."

After a brief moment of silence, the assistant coach gave Travis a reason to perk up, telling the future military officer that though his senior wrestling season was over, it was now time for him to devote all his energy to becoming a Marine.

Travis understood what his coach was saying, but giving up wrestling was almost inconceivable. He loved the sport and wanted desperately to be the best at it.

He was still standing outside with Coach Sharratt when his parents got back from the match. After the coach had greeted Tom and Janet and excused himself to head upstairs, Travis hugged his mother.

"I'm sorry you guys had to come all the way down here to see that," he said.

"Travis, you tried your best," Janet replied.

Putting his hand on Travis's healthy left shoulder, Tom, the Marine Corps colonel, gave his only son some encouragement, telling him that many great things were still ahead. Regardless of how many wrestling matches Travis won, what truly mattered was that he would soon graduate from Navy and become a leader of Marines.

The fourth day of 2004 may have felt like his lowest point at the academy, but the senior midshipman had barely made it that far to begin with. Just over four years earlier, as a first-semester plebe, Travis had done something he'd never done before in his life: quit.

———•————•———

Just before Thanksgiving 1999, Travis was clearly agitated as he sat across from his Naval Academy battalion commander, Lieutenant Colonel Corky Gardner, a career Marine with many years of leadership experience. The young midshipman was fed up with the early morning classes, drills, and strict rules about always staying on campus. He had only given it four months, but to a stubborn eighteen-year-old, plebe year felt like an eternity.

If Travis had been with his sister Ryan at their dad's alma mater, Widener University, or almost any other institution of higher learning, he could have simply filled out a withdrawal form. But at the Naval Academy, where dozens of midshipmen succumb every semester to a rigorous mix of academics and military training, Travis had to complete a packet full of intentionally difficult, tedious paperwork explaining why he planned to leave Annapolis. Then he had to separately inform his squad leader, company commander, and company officer of his intention to resign, before he could even get inside the battalion commander's office.

For Travis, the final meeting presented a dual challenge. Lieutenant Colonel Gardner wasn't just his battalion commander; he was a close friend of Travis's father and had begun serving with Tom almost a decade earlier. When Travis showed up for "plebe summer," a grueling training session that results in many dropping out before the academic year even starts, Gardner was there to cut off Travis's first lock of brown hair during the ceremonial head shaving that serves as each freshman's "oh shit, high school really is over" moment.

As battalion commander, Gardner had been reluctantly accepting the resignations of plebes since summer. He wondered why Travis wanted to see him, but never imagined that this day could be one of Travis's last as a midshipman. This young man wasn't the quitting type.

Travis was disappointed about missing out on the freedom of college life. He would spend his weekends on academy grounds, which sometimes felt like a prison, and listen longingly to his sister's stories about constant parties and road trips. "It must be nice to be out there having all that fun," Travis once told Ryan, his only sibling and most trusted female confidante, during a phone call.

Chasing female midshipmen was frowned upon, and every time Travis talked to his high school buddies about their coed adventures, he was naturally envious. Of course, those same stories almost always involved alcohol, a substance that was nearly impossible for Travis and his fellow plebes to obtain.

One Friday night, a particularly desperate group, which included Travis, bet each other about how many double shots they could do of Virginia Gentleman whiskey, the only bottle of liquor they could get their hands on. In a notably futile attempt to prove his manhood and catch a buzz, Travis won the bet, but threw up violently the rest of the night and most of the next day.

Once Travis made up his mind about almost anything, there was little chance of his changing it. Given that Gardner was preparing to challenge his decision, Travis was an irresistible force about to meet an immovable object on the historic Annapolis campus.

"Sir, I've given it a lot of thought, and I've decided to leave the academy," Travis said. "I know this might surprise you, and I appreciate everything you've done for me, but I think this is the best thing for my future."

Gardner was shocked. He always tried to talk midshipmen out of resigning, even those he wasn't sure were the right fit for the academy. In this case, however, he would do everything in his power to keep Travis from leaving. As he cleared off his desk, Gardner was convinced he was sitting across from a young man who was about to make a serious mistake.

"Travis, I appreciate you being up front about this," he said. "But I have to ask why you think you'd be better off somewhere else."

"It's a bunch of things, sir . . . wrestling, schoolwork, missing my friends back home," Travis said. "But I thought about this a lot, and this is what I've decided to do."

"Have you talked about this with your parents?" Gardner inquired.

"No sir," Travis replied.

"But I thought you said you'd thought about this a lot?" the battalion commander asked.

"Well, I have, sir," Travis said, growing frustrated as he realized his decision was being contested. "I'm going to talk to them as soon as I get home."

After thumbing through Travis's withdrawal packet, which included the midshipman's excellent grades, Gardner looked directly at his friend's son.

"Well, I'm sorry, Travis, but I can't accept this," he said. "While I understand you're having a hard time, like many others do, I think you're about to do something you'll regret for a long, long time."

"But sir . . . ," Travis began.

"And either way, there's no way I could let you do this before you speak to your parents," Gardner continued. "I think you owe it to your dad, especially, to talk to him about a decision of this magnitude."

"Sir, he will never agree . . . ," Travis said as tears began to well up in his brown eyes.

"I want you to go home for the holiday, relax, talk to your folks, come back and we'll chat again," Gardner said. "Just get away from this place for a little while, enjoy yourself, and I think you might feel differently."

"I've made up my mind and don't need time to think about it," Travis responded. "I was told all I have to do is talk to you and that's it."

"Have a good Thanksgiving, Travis," Gardner said. "Please give my best to your mom and dad."

Travis jumped out of his chair, snatched his resignation packet, and hurried out of the lieutenant colonel's office. Although he had too much respect for Gardner to slam his door, he couldn't help but mutter "this is ridiculous" under his breath when he was far enough down the hallway.

While most Americans were thinking about the "Y2K" computer scare and the coming dawn of a new millennium, Travis was enduring his most difficult Thanksgiving ever. Just as he had expected, his dad was angry when Travis told him he was leaving the academy.

"Look, this is your call and your decision," Tom told his son, who he always believed could excel at the Naval Academy and beyond. "But I think you're making a big mistake."

Ever since running around his house singing the Marine Corps hymn with his sister, Ryan, when they were little kids, the academy had seemed like the most logical step to Travis. But once he actually got there, he was introduced to the daily routine: wake up at 5:30 a.m., get your room inspected, eat breakfast at 7:00 a.m., start class at 7:55, and then sit in lecture halls all day before a grueling 3:00 p.m. wrestling practice. After a full day of physical and academic challenges, Travis and other midshipmen would spend most of the evening studying and preparing for the next day's classes.

It was an exhausting routine for any college student. Travis couldn't imagine returning from vacation and starting the grind all over again.

The holiday was gloomy for Travis, who barely touched his Thanksgiving dinner. As sounds of laughter filled the living room, where his mom and dad, Ryan, and other relatives were socializing, Travis knew his time at the Naval Academy was over. A few days later, he returned to Lieutenant Colonel Gardner's office with his completed resignation packet.

"I'm really sorry to see you go, Travis," Gardner said. "I wish you the best, but I also want you to know that if you ever want to come back, I will put in a word for you."

"I appreciate that, sir," Travis replied. "But this place isn't for me."

Travis, who had made good grades at Navy, had no problem gaining admission to Drexel University in Philadelphia, where he contributed significantly as a freshman Division I-A lacrosse player while planning to join the wrestling team.

Travis didn't hate Drexel. But after spending a semester away from Annapolis, his appreciation for what Navy stood for, as well as the bonds he had forged with several academy friends, made him regret his decision to leave. There was only one place for Travis Manion, and if he could get another chance, it was time to go back.

———•———

Neil Toohey came to the Naval Academy straight out of high school without any exposure to military life prior to the fall of 2000. After getting his head shaved during "I-Day," induction day for incoming midshipmen during plebe summer, Toohey was rushing back to his room to finish unpacking his belongings before his room was to be inspected for the first time. He had already seen another plebe being berated for screwing up and didn't want that to happen to him on his first day.

Toohey arrived in his room to find a muscular, brown-haired guy going through his clothes. At first he thought it was one of the upperclassmen doing an inspection, but this guy was wearing a plebe's uniform. As Toohey was pondering the possibility that someone was going through his underwear, the young man quickly dispelled that fear by introducing himself.

"Hey, I'm Brendan Looney, your new roommate," he said. "We've got to get all your clothes folded before the inspectors get here."

Grabbing Toohey's shirts and socks from his duffle bag, Brendan quickly folded them as he heard footsteps coming down the hall.

"You've got to fold 'em like this," Brendan said. "Make the socks smile."

"Oh . . . thanks, man," Toohey said. "But just one thing. . . . You mixed up my shirts."

"Shit, that's my bad," Brendan said. "I'm colorblind."

After Toohey thanked him a second time, Brendan, an imposing figure even at age nineteen, responded with a nod and a grin.
It was already clear to Toohey that his new roommate was looking
out for him.

"Man, I just have no idea what I'm doing around here," Toohey
complained.

"Relax," Brendan said. "You're not supposed to. . . . It's our
first day."

Though Brendan was also a plebe, he was more prepared for
I-Day than most others after spending ten months attending the
Naval Academy Preparatory School in Newport, Rhode Island.
With a grueling academic, physical, and military training regimen,
NAPS had given Brendan the chance to play football against ju-
nior college and junior varsity opponents while preparing to join
Navy's Division I-A team.

About 15 percent of the incoming class came from NAPS, and
each of those 177 students, including Brendan, had a head start.
As Brendan demonstrated by helping Toohey pass inspection, the
"NAPSters" were seen as big brothers by many plebes, who felt
clueless and frightened while getting hollered at for making the
smallest of mistakes. Although Brendan still had a lot to learn
himself, he knew not making his bed in thirty seconds or forget-
ting to shine his belt buckle wouldn't get him kicked out of the
academy. His sheer physical presence gave him the appearance of
a natural leader, but it was the calming smirk he often gave the
other plebes that really demonstrated that quality.

Of the four plebes in Brendan's room, three had gone to NAPS.
After experiencing ten tough months together, the first signs of
military-style brotherhood were evident in the NAPSters, who
usually stuck together. Toohey gained inclusion by virtue of being
their roommate.

As the first-year midshipmen adjusted to the academy's grueling routine in the fall and spring of 2000, Navy's class of 2004 was

beginning to take shape. Unbeknownst to Brendan and the other plebes, however, a key member of their social circle was not yet with them.

●────────●

When Travis told his father he wanted to reapply to the Naval Academy after one semester at Drexel, Tom, still unhappy over his son's decision to drop out in the first place, was skeptical.

"That's your decision," he said. "If you want to go back, you're going to have to do it on your own."

"I will," Travis said.

A few days later, Lieutenant Colonel Gardner was sitting in his Annapolis office when a surprise visitor walked in.

"Travis?" he said. "It's good to see you again."

After asking how his good friends Tom and Janet were doing, Gardner welcomed the former midshipman into his office and asked him to have a seat. Travis explained that while he had given Drexel a try, it had only taken him a few months to realize that Gardner had been right. The Naval Academy was indeed where he belonged.

Gardner was thrilled by Travis's epiphany, but also cautious in his response. He agreed that Navy was the right place for Tom and Janet's son, but he stressed that getting into the academy a second time was very rare. Gardner told Travis that while he would do everything possible to help, it would be a challenge to convince the Naval Academy that he deserved a second chance.

Though he understood that the odds of getting back into Navy were probably against him, Travis was undeterred. For the next five months he worked exhaustively to win the hearts and minds of a skeptical Naval Academy admissions board.

Because Travis had immediately enrolled at Drexel and participated in a varsity sport during his lone semester on the Philadelphia campus, his readmission request was taken seriously. His academic record was strong, before and after leaving Navy. But what made his application stand out was a cover letter from Gardner, who wrote that he had "absolutely no doubt" that Travis would be a fine midshipman and even better military officer.

For the class of 2004, 10,296 young men and women applied to the US Naval Academy, of which only 1,224 were admitted. Travis, a second semester addition, was one of them.

Tom and Janet were watching an ABC News interview with Texas governor George W. Bush, the presumptive Republican nominee for president, when Travis walked into their Doylestown living room holding a large envelope from the Naval Academy.

"I got back in," Travis said.

"I knew it!" Janet said before jumping up to hug her son. "I knew it."

Tom was surprised and pleased, as he fully appreciated the size of the mountain his son had just climbed. After a brief pause, he shook his son's hand.

"You have a second chance," he said. "I'm proud of you, but don't forget how fortunate you are to be getting this opportunity."

Travis, who returned to Navy in the spring of 2001 as a second semester plebe, barely knew anyone on his floor, including his three roommates, who had just been through their first semester. Though he was thrilled to be back at the academy, Travis felt like a ballplayer traded in the middle of the season. There was still a pitcher's mound and ninety feet between each base, but he was surrounded by a different group of teammates, including upperclassmen who frequently reminded him how much they detested quitters. Travis was ready for the criticism, and for the most part, he took it in stride.

•————————•

The Naval Academy dorms looked more like classroom hallways than living quarters. The shiny floors, often cleaned by midshipmen who had done something to piss off a company officer or upperclassman, stretched the length of several football fields, with the open doors of aspiring sailors and Marines lining the hallways. No matter what they were doing, underclassmen always had to be ready for surprise inspections. Brendan and Travis, who carried the burden of being Division I athletes along with their academic and drilling responsibilities, rarely if ever complained.

Just after the start of the fall 2001 semester, Travis and Brendan met up for an early morning run. The wrestler and football player both had practice later that afternoon, but as two varsity athletes who wanted to be the best, they were determined to work harder than everybody else.

After talking about the start of the NFL season, their mid-jog conversation shifted to their backgrounds. They had a lot in common, including their love of sports and their country. Both midshipmen had been raised Catholic in tight-knit families, although Brendan's was a little larger.

"I have two brothers and three sisters," Brendan said as they jogged past Navy-Marine Corps Memorial Stadium and into a nearby Annapolis neighborhood.

The two younger Looney brothers, Steve and Billy, were still at DeMatha, the high school attended by Brendan and their father, Kevin. After graduation, Steve and Billy would join Brendan at the Naval Academy.

Brendan's sisters, Bridget, Erin, and Kellie, grew up wanting to hang out in "the cool room." That was their nickname for Brendan's room, where all of his younger siblings wanted to hang out. Like Steve and Billy, the Looney sisters looked up to Brendan and strove to emulate him. Not only did Brendan set an example as the ideal big brother; he was also a hardworking, stellar athlete, and all his talented younger siblings would eventually follow in his footsteps.

"It's just me and my sister, but it must be fun coming from a big family," Travis said to Brendan.

From the time Travis and his sister, Ryan, were born only fifteen months apart at North Carolina's Camp Lejeune, they were almost constantly exposed to the rigors of military life. With their father on active duty in the Marine Corps until 1988 before transitioning to the Reserves, their family always seemed to be moving around, making the bond between brother and sister even more important. Whereas making new friends at different elementary schools took time, Ryan and Travis could always depend on each other. Their mom, Janet, was the glue that kept the Manion family strong as it moved from base to base.

"How long has your dad been in the Corps?" Brendan asked.

"Twenty years," Travis replied.

For Brendan, Travis, and their fellow midshipmen, the morning of September 11, 2001, started just like any other. It was a nice, unseasonably warm day, without a single cloud littering the bright, early morning sky.

At the end of their respective classes, Travis and Brendan began hearing rumors about an awful tragedy in New York City. An airplane had crashed into one of the Twin Towers, sending smoke billowing into the skies above Manhattan.

As Brendan and Travis headed back to their rooms for a break between classes, CNN was reporting a "World Trade Center disaster," which appeared to be an accident, although nobody knew for sure. Given the bombing of the Twin Towers eight years earlier, it was clearly a terrorist target, but the 1993 attack had mostly faded from the national psyche.

When Travis, Brendan, and dozens of other midshipmen arrived back at their dorm, they found plebes who didn't have early morning Tuesday classes gathered around the lounge television, which was showing images of a gaping hole in the World Trade Center's north tower. It was 9:00 a.m., and most of the country was just realizing that something terrible was going on in New York, where a confusing, chaotic scene was quickly unfolding.

Three minutes later, a moment that would be forever etched in the memories of Brendan, Travis, and millions of Americans silenced the lounge. A second plane crashed into the World Trade Center, sending a massive fireball shooting out of the middle of the south tower.

"Oh, there's another one, another plane just hit!" Theresa Renaud, a witness speaking live to CBS News anchor Bryant Gumbel, exclaimed. "Oh my gosh, another plane has just hit. . . . It hit the other building."

"Shit!" one midshipman in the lounge said.

For the next few seconds there was silence. America was under attack.

None of the students knew what to do other than stay together, watch the news coverage, and call their families. For the next forty-five minutes, frantic students, like the rest of America, watched the surreal, horrific images of desperate victims jumping from the burning towers. At around 9:45, evacuations were ordered at the White House and Capitol after reports of an explosion at the Pentagon.

With all airspace above the United States closed, military leaders, who were scrambling fighter jets, were reportedly concerned about the nation's military academies being a potential terrorist target. "The Yard," as the Navy campus is called by midshipmen, had to be cleared as quickly as possible, with no large gatherings of students to serve as potential targets. Midshipmen still wandering around campus were told to return to their living quarters.

As a Navy battle cruiser headed toward the harbor, heavily armed Marines surrounded the academy gates. Travis and Brendan quickly went back to their respective rooms to contact their families.

Travis picked up the phone and dialed his dad.

"Tom Manion," his father answered.

"Dad, it's Trav," he said. "Are you okay?"

"Yeah, I'm fine," Tom said. "I'm up in Jersey, about an hour from New York. Are you alright? What's going on down there?"

"It's pretty crazy," Travis said. "They're locking us down inside our quarters. . . . Something happened at the Pentagon, and they think we could be a target."

"I just heard about the Pentagon," Tom replied. "Listen, buddy . . . you stay safe, and I'll let mom know you're okay."

"Talk to you later, Dad," Travis said.

He walked back to the lounge, where Brendan and several others were standing in front of the television. The south tower of the World Trade Center was collapsing. The north tower crumbled almost thirty minutes after its twin.

A few hours later, President Bush, who was crisscrossing the country in Air Force One while the Secret Service determined whether it was safe enough for the commander-in-chief to return to Washington, officially placed the US military on high alert.

"Freedom itself was attacked this morning by a faceless coward," the president said from Louisiana's Barksdale Air Force Base. "And freedom will be defended."

During the nine days after the Twin Towers collapsed, the Pentagon burned, smoke rose from a silent Pennsylvania field, and the entire Naval Academy student body realized that after graduation they would become part of a fighting force that was now at war. Exactly where American troops would be deployed was still unknown, although it was becoming increasingly clear that the most immediate security threat, Osama bin Laden's al Qaeda terrorist organization, was being harbored by the Taliban regime in Afghanistan.

Like most Americans in the aftermath of 9/11, for the students sorrow was mixed with anger, uncertainty, and fervent patriotism. But at the Naval Academy, these emotions were mixed with the burgeoning realization that this generation of midshipmen would be called upon to confront the evil that had reached America's shores.

Gathering at the same television set where they had watched the attacks unfold in real time, one group of future military leaders, including Brendan and Travis, watched President Bush address a joint session of Congress on the evening of September 20, 2001.

"Tonight, we are a country awakened to danger and called to defend freedom. Our grief has turned to anger and anger to resolution," Bush announced. "Whether we bring our enemies to justice or bring justice to our enemies, justice will be done."

"Hell yeah," one midshipman agreed.

Travis and Brendan were silent.

"And tonight, a few miles from the damaged Pentagon, I have a message for our military," the commander-in-chief said. "Be ready.

"I have called the armed forces to alert, and there is a reason," the president continued. "The hour is coming when America will act, and you will make us proud."

The "hell yeahs" around the room stopped for a moment when President Bush pulled a shiny silver badge out of his pocket and said:

And I will carry this. It is the police shield of a man named George Howard who died at the World Trade Center trying to save others.

It was given to me by his mom, Arlene, as a proud memorial to her son. It is my reminder of lives that ended and a task that does not end.

I will not forget this wound to our country or those who inflicted it. I will not yield; I will not rest; I will not relent in waging this struggle for freedom and security for the American people.

The course of this conflict is not known, yet its outcome is certain. Freedom and fear, justice and cruelty, have always been at war, and we know that God is not neutral between them.

After the murders of thousands of good Americans like George Howard, the responsibility of preventing another terrorist attack would soon fall on young military leaders like Brendan Looney and Travis Manion.

As the stirring speech concluded, many of the Naval Academy midshipmen were applauding along with the politicians on the screen. Brendan and Travis sat quietly next to each other, reflecting on the enormous challenge that they and their peers now faced.

Thirty miles from the US Capitol, where the commander-in-chief spoke into the shadows of a devastated city and country, a young generation heard its call to arms.

2

EARN IT

In October 2001, with the US military preparing to invade Afghanistan and the stakes for Travis and Brendan suddenly much higher, their frequent runs became even more intense. On their seemingly endless routes, one would always challenge the other to go further.

As they ran through the academy's heavily guarded campus, Travis asked Brendan which branch he hoped to serve in.

"I'll probably go Navy," Brendan responded. "What about you?"

"Marine Corps. . . . I hope to go that route," Travis said, knowing that becoming a Marine Corps officer like his dad was far from guaranteed.

"I hear ya," Brendan said. "With the way things are going, I can't even imagine what will be going on when we graduate."

"Who the hell knows," Travis said.

Letters laced with anthrax had just been discovered in post offices in Florida, New York, and Washington, DC. One chilling message was sent to Tom Brokaw, the eminent NBC News anchor:

09–11–01
This is next
Take Penacilin Now

Death to America
Death to Israel

Like the rest of America, which worried about everything from more hijackings and anthrax to a nuclear suitcase bomb being detonated in a major city, Annapolis was gripped by fear. Because the Navy campus was full of future military leaders, authorities believed the academy could be a prime target for terrorists planning to make another grand statement while also achieving an important wartime objective.

Travis and Brendan's class of 2004 still had time to prepare, but the graduating class of 2002 was only months away from going to war, which had changed the entire campus mind-set.

On the first Saturday of December 2001, with American bombs pummeling the mountainous region of Tora Bora near Afghanistan's border with Pakistan, where Osama bin Laden was believed to be hiding, President Bush entered the Navy football locker room at Veterans Stadium in Philadelphia. In just a few minutes, the Midshipmen would square off against their West Point counterparts. Even though Navy was winless and Army had prevailed in just two contests going into the season's final game, the 2001 matchup, held as Ground Zero still smoldered less than three months after 9/11, was one of the most significant Army-Navy games ever played.

Standing a few feet from Brendan, the president thanked Navy's coach after being presented with a football autographed by all members of the team. After a few words of encouragement and a handshake with his former GOP presidential primary rival, Senator John McCain of Arizona, President Bush headed over to the Army locker room, where Operation Desert Storm hero and West Point graduate General Norman Schwarzkopf was meeting with the Army squad.

The president, who had taken office less than a year earlier after one of the closest elections in American history, was in his first weeks as a wartime commander-in-chief. But in his address to the Army players, he left no doubt that the war on terrorism, as his administration called the new conflict, would be part of America's fabric for many years to come. President Bush told the Army Black Knights that though Navy's players were their rivals on the field today, they would be their brothers in arms on the battlefield tomorrow.

Back in the Navy locker room, Senator McCain, one of the academy's most famous graduates, delivered an impassioned speech to the players representing his beloved alma mater. While McCain's words were potent, Brendan and his Navy teammates only needed to look into the eyes of the sixty-five-year-old senator, who had endured years of brutal torture and solitary confinement while being held captive in a North Vietnamese prison, to know that this landmark game was one step on a long journey toward becoming warriors.

Travis was in State College, Pennsylvania, to compete in the annual Penn State Open wrestling tournament. He would have to rely on accounts from friends, including Brendan, to truly understand the atmosphere that day at "the Vet."

Army and Navy roared onto the field led by huge American flags. Navy SEAL and Army paratroopers, also with US flags in tow, glided onto the field's artificial turf with Army and Navy parachutes. The Navy and Army team captains then stood at midfield with President Bush for the coin toss, as chants of "U-S-A!" filled the stadium.

With visibly cold air billowing from his mouth, Brendan, who wore number 37, soaked in the atmosphere from the sideline while looking up at the stands. Standing next to J. P. Blecksmith, a wide receiver and backup quarterback, Brendan listened to a stirring rendition of the national anthem while looking up at the massive group of uniformed midshipmen, which included many of his friends.

Army won the game, 26–17. But for one day, a stadium full of more than sixty-five thousand screaming fans was united, as was much of the country.

"There's never been a game, ever—including the eight Super Bowls that I've called—there's never been a game more important than calling that Army-Navy game," legendary broadcaster Dick Enberg, who handled play-by-play announcing for CBS Sports that day, later said.

In 2002, as the war in Afghanistan continued and talk of another war in Iraq intensified, Travis and Brendan, who were now roommates, understood the significance of the times they were living in. They also knew how to have fun.

Andrew Hemminger was one of Travis's wrestling teammates. He had known Brendan since their plebe year. When his two buddies became roommates, goofing off in their room became one of Hemminger's favorite activities. He was entertained not only by Brendan and Travis's shared sense of humor, but also by their epic video game showdowns in Madden football and Tiger Woods golf.

When Travis beat Brendan, Brendan would sit quietly and steam for the next few hours until Travis wanted to play again. When Brendan beat Travis, Travis would bother him incessantly until Brendan finally granted his request for a rematch. What impressed Hemminger the most, however, was how quickly the roommates could refocus when it was time to be serious.

During a summer fishing trip to North Carolina's Outer Banks, Hemminger and his brother, Dan, were with Brendan and several friends when the booze began to flow on the eve of their boat excursion. As more and more drinks were consumed, several of the guys began arguing over who would catch the biggest fish when they went out on the water the next morning.

Numerous friends offered Brendan drinks as he sat quietly amid the increasingly boisterous festivities. Brendan, sporting his customary smirk, politely declined.

"Are you sure you guys want to keep drinking?" Brendan cautioned the group, who carried on for several more hours despite his warning.

The next morning, in the boat out on choppy waters, Brendan shook his head as the Hemminger brothers and everyone else draped themselves over the sides of the vessel. Hung over and seasick, they were throwing up while Brendan adjusted his fishing rod.

"Remind me again who's going to catch the biggest fish?" Brendan asked with a grin.

Though Brendan was in the best condition that morning, he wasn't really concerned about catching the biggest fish. Instead, he sat in the boat and shared laughs with his nauseated friends, making sure they rehydrated after vomiting for most of the morning.

During a subsequent trip to Colorado Springs, the Hemminger brothers were with Travis when their wrestling coach challenged them to a grueling 12½-mile trail hike to the top of Pikes Peak. Naturally the athletes turned the climb into a fierce competition that Travis was determined to win.

After the Hemmingers, Travis, and their teammates separated into respective groups of three, they didn't encounter each other again until they were just steps from the mountain's summit. Travis had indeed beaten the Hemmingers there, but the biggest member of his group, heavyweight wrestler Steve Kovach, was struggling to breathe after several hours of climbing through the thin Rocky Mountain air.

Travis wanted to reach the gigantic mountain's soaring peak first. But upon seeing his teammate's condition, he set the competition aside.

"I'm going to head back down with Stevie," Travis said.

By the time Travis had helped Kovach almost twelve miles down the Pikes Peak trail, it was clear to everyone what he was all about. Travis wanted to win, but like Brendan, his friends came first.

During most of their time in Annapolis, Travis and Brendan shared another trait. As red-blooded American college kids, they wanted to meet as many beautiful women as possible. Travis was often popular with the ladies and would usually return from a night

at the bars with at least one new phone number. In one memorable case, his charm extended into the classroom, when Travis
managed to put a female professor in a better mood during a disas-
trous presentation by one of his friends.

As his buddy Myles McAllister stumbled through the assignment, Travis sat in the back of the classroom, laughing hysterically
and smirking at the instructor. While smiling back at Travis and
chuckling at his antics, her attention was diverted from McAllister's cringe-inducing performance.

"You really saved my ass in there," McAllister said as they
laughed about the presentation after class.

"I have to admit, that was the worst presentation I've ever
seen," a smiling Travis said while reassuring McAllister that he
would probably receive a passing grade. "You'll be fine. . . . I think
that teacher's got a crush on me."

Travis's friend did in fact receive a passing grade from the
teacher.

Though Brendan had a similar effect on the women of Annapolis, he was usually more reserved in classroom and social settings.
That all changed on Memorial Day weekend in 2003.

With the country now at war in Iraq, on that Sunday Brendan,
a Naval Academy junior, was driving back from the Jersey Shore,
where he had met up with some high school buddies. He was heading to Baltimore to hang out with a large group of DeMatha friends
at Fell's Point, a quaint, popular area of waterfront shops, restau-
rants, and bars that bore a striking resemblance to Annapolis.

As Brendan walked into The Greene Turtle sports bar to greet
his buddies, his gaze wandered to a large table, where a gorgeous
blonde was sitting with mutual friends near a wall covered with
Baltimore Orioles and Ravens memorabilia. She was sipping a mar-
garita, nodding and smiling as one of her friends told a funny story.

Brendan couldn't get over her big brown eyes. She was the
most beautiful woman he had ever seen.

"Go talk to her," said Ryan Gillis, who had noticed Brendan staring.

"No way," Brendan said. "She's way too hot. . . . I'd have no chance."

"Fine," Gillis, now a football player at Notre Dame, remarked as several at the table, including the young woman Brendan was admiring, got up and moved to the dance floor. "I'll go dance with her then."

Gillis, who openly admitted to being a terrible dancer, headed out to the dance floor in order to motivate his reluctant friend, much as Brendan had once inspired him to keep busting his tail during long "two-a-day" high school football practices.

"Dude, seriously, she's still looking over here," another friend said to Brendan as Gillis made the woman's friends laugh with some truly terrible dance moves.

Brendan quickly changed the subject and started talking about the recent return of Hall of Fame coach Joe Gibbs to his beloved Washington Redskins. But after a few minutes of guy talk, about five friends gave the imposing, nearly six-foot-tall midshipman an ultimatum.

"Go talk to that girl, or we're all going to kick your ass," one friend said.

Gillis returned from the dance floor just in time to hear the challenge.

"Are we still talking about this?" asked Gillis, out of breath from dancing. "Looney, I mean it this time, if you don't go over there I really will dance with her." He smiled. "So it looks like you have two choices. One, you go talk to her; two, I go dance with her and on top of it, we all punch you in the face."

Responding with his customary smirk, Brendan took a deep breath as he walked toward the radiant blonde and her group of friends, who were dancing in an open area near the bar. As the setting sun reflected off the Baltimore Harbor outside the front

window, Brendan took a gulp of beer and walked over to introduce himself.

Just as he was about to say hello, one of his friends, who was already drunk, pushed him right into the middle of the group, causing him to bump into the young woman he had been admiring
since walking in the door.

"I'm really sorry," Brendan said.

"That's okay," she said with a laugh. "I'm Amy."

"Brendan," he said, extending his hand.

After spending the next minute or two dancing, Amy Hastings, who could tell this good-looking guy liked her but was hesi-
tant, finally broke the ice.

"Do you play football?" she said.

Brendan, who was two hundred pounds of pure muscle with a
white "Navy Athletics" hat on top, certainly looked the part of a
college football star.

"I actually just started playing lacrosse," he said. "I was on the
football team my freshman and sophomore year. I only started
playing lacrosse a year ago, but I love it. My brothers have been
playing for years."

What instantly struck Amy was not which sport Brendan
played, but his commanding presence and the sincerity with which
he spoke. She was attracted to him.

Brendan and Amy went over to the bar, where he bought her
another drink and asked where she was from. Amy told him about
growing up in Delaware before moving south to Maryland, where
she was currently attending Johns Hopkins University in Baltimore. Both Brendan and Amy smiled when they realized that
their respective high schools, Archbishop Spalding in Severn and
DeMatha in Hyattsville, were less than thirty miles apart.

Amy had grown up watching her mother juggle a full-time job
and a single-parent home, whereas Brendan came from a family of
two happily married parents and five siblings. But even after the
minor contrast surfaced, Amy and Brendan quickly realized they

had much in common. They both loved their families and friends; they had attended local high schools; and they shared many of the same values, goals, and dreams. With Brendan at Navy and Amy at Johns Hopkins, they knew they both possessed the strong work ethic required to succeed at academically rigorous institutions.

While continuing to talk, Brendan and Amy decided to play the popular "Golden Tee" video game. Brendan may have been one of the most competitive people on the planet, but if there was ever a time to let someone else win, this was it.

Before the game was over, Brendan glanced over toward his buddies, who were psyched to see him hitting it off with such a beautiful girl.

"Gentlemen, I propose a toast," Gillis said to some of Brendan's closest high school friends. "I think we just did a good thing."

Brendan smiled in their direction before turning back to the young lady he could already tell was special. After exchanging more pleasantries, Amy said that she should probably get back to her friends. If Brendan didn't speak up, he would probably never see her again.

As Amy picked up her purse and headed back over to the dance floor, Brendan channeled all his willpower to say five words.

"Can I get your number?" he asked.

"Sure," Amy replied, relieved that he had asked.

Amy and Brendan flipped their respective cell phones open and saved each other's numbers. She then gave him a quick hug and said good-bye.

Afraid of appearing overly anxious, and perhaps inspired by the dating advice Vince Vaughn gave Jon Favreau in the 1996 cult movie *Swingers*, Brendan waited three days before calling Amy, who lived about a half hour away in Columbia, Maryland. Despite being surprised and slightly annoyed by the seventy-two-hour wait, Amy gave Brendan a chance to redeem himself on their first date. He succeeded, and after a few short months, the young couple were inseparable.

On November 26, 2003, Amy got a Hallmark card in the mail, postmarked from Annapolis:

> Amy,
>   Hard to believe that 6 months ago we met. Time has really flown by. I guess the saying is right, the last 6 months have been the best I have ever had. I would not trade a single day for anything in the universe. You truly have made me a better person and given me a lot. I am excited for the next 6 months, a lot will be changing, but with you there it will not be as bad. I love you with all my heart sweet heart and can't wait to see what is in our future.
> Love ya!
> Brendan

Amy had already met Travis, Brendan's funny, likable roommate, who always seemed to be wearing an Eagles hat and telling her new boyfriend that the Redskins were lousy. She also went along with Brendan and Travis for what was supposed to be a three-mile jog, until the roommates started challenging each other to keep going.

After jogging more than twelve miles—nearly a half-marathon—Amy convinced them to turn around. Whether it was NFL football, video games, or running, everything was a competition for Brendan and Travis.

Although she enjoyed Travis's company, Amy wasn't expecting to see him one late April Friday night in 2004, which was supposed to be a dinner and movie date with Brendan, whom she was meeting at the Arundel Mills Mall in Hanover, Maryland.

Inside Arundel Mills, Amy walked around a crowded bar and restaurant, weaving through the crowd while seeking Brendan. After looking around for about ninety seconds, she saw Travis sitting in the rear section of the bar area, almost exactly where Brendan had said to meet him.

Brendan's roommate's gaze was transfixed on CNN, which was showing searing images from the Battle of Fallujah. One of the Iraq war's most intense, violent clashes erupted after terrorists murdered four American contractors, mutilated their corpses, and hung their bodies from a bridge. Thousands of Americans, including US Marine Captain Doug Zembiec, the former Navy wrestler whom Travis looked up to, were going street by street, battling insurgents inside the decimated western Iraqi city.

Travis was so focused on the television that he almost didn't hear Amy speak.

"Hey, Travis," Amy said, looking surprised. "What are you doing here?"

"Oh, hey, Amy," Travis said. "Yeah, I'm actually meeting you and Brendan."

"Oh really?" Amy asked. "Are you going to the movies with us, too?"

"Yeah, didn't Brendan tell you?" Travis asked with a grin.

As Amy and Travis shared a laugh, Brendan showed up a few minutes late after an extra long workout.

"So, Brendan, did you plan on telling me Travis was coming along tonight?" Amy asked with a smile. "I thought this was supposed to be a date."

"It is," Brendan replied. "But this loser Eagles fan is going to be our honorary chaperone."

Brendan, Amy, and Travis ate dinner and then went to the movie theater to see *Mean Girls*, starring Lindsay Lohan and Rachel McAdams.

Inside the theater, Amy enjoyed Travis and Brendan's reactions even more than the movie itself. They were laughing so loudly that Amy couldn't help but join in. Though she may have preferred to be on a romantic date with Brendan, it was impossible not to have a good time when Travis was around.

Later that night Travis, Brendan, and Amy stopped at a bar for a quick beer.

"Brendan, I'm not sure if you saw some of the shit that went down in Fallujah today," Travis said.

"I was watching one of the news channels at the gym earlier," Brendan replied. "Brutal stuff, man."

"It's terrible," Amy said.

"Well, you know what?" Travis said. "I want to propose a toast to our men and women fighting over there. . . . Only God knows what they're going through right now."

"I'll drink to that," Brendan said.

"So will I," Amy said as their three glasses clinked.

The Iraq war and upcoming presidential election were dividing the country in the spring of 2004. The conflict had dragged on longer than many Americans had expected after US troops routed Baghdad and watched as Iraqis tore down statues of Saddam Hussein just weeks after the initial invasion.

In Iraq in 2003, 486 US service members died; 849 American families lost loved ones in Iraq in 2004. Senator John Kerry, the Democratic presidential nominee, was running on a platform opposing America's involvement in the Iraq war. President Bush, who had lost much of the record-high popularity he enjoyed after 9/11, insisted his strategy was working and that America would ultimately prevail in Iraq.

Unlike the general public, of which only a fraction of 1 percent had fought overseas since 9/11, the sacrifices being made by brave US troops and their families were touching Annapolis on an almost daily basis. Naval Academy graduates like Captain Zembiec and Second Lieutenant J. P. Blecksmith, a teammate of Brendan's in the 2001 Army-Navy football game, were fighting on Iraq's war-torn streets at that very moment. Places like Fallujah and Ramadi were under siege by al Qaeda terrorists and Iraqi insurgents bent on destroying the country rather than letting it be reshaped. Every single day, American blood was being spilled.

In May 2004, Brendan and Travis graduated with their Naval Academy classmates and were commissioned as US military officers. Brendan would go on to serve in the Naval intelligence community, while Travis would head to The Basic School for Marine Corps officers in Quantico, Virginia.

"I can say with certainty that you will have a role in fighting this war on terrorism," Air Force General Richard Myers, chairman of the Joint Chiefs of Staff, told Travis, Brendan, and 988 fellow Naval Academy graduates on May 28, 2004. "You will face many enormous challenges. You will go into harm's way. The sacrifice that you have learned by now is part of the job description."

Three days after graduation, Navy was seeking its first men's lacrosse national championship in thirty-five years. Though the Midshipmen were underdogs against Syracuse, one of the most storied programs in the sport's history, the ongoing wars in Iraq and Afghanistan made Navy the overwhelming sentimental favorite. That the 2004 NCAA men's lacrosse national championship game was played on Memorial Day only added to its significance.

Names of other Navy lacrosse players, including Brendan's brothers Steve and Billy, may have shown up more often in the box score, but Brendan, who wore number 40, was the team's heart and soul. It didn't matter that he had only been playing lacrosse for less than three years, whereas everyone else on the team had been playing for at least a decade. His athletic prowess and work ethic were so fierce that the oldest Looney brother immediately became a force as a defenseman.

In practice, Brendan had performed almost exactly as he had in football, with raw determination and zero tolerance for anyone giving less than 100 percent. He had eventually earned significant playing time on the lacrosse team, which often forced opponents to alter their strategies.

Earlier that season, in a game against Georgetown, the Hoyas' best player—one of the nation's top midfielders—had run over to the referee in the middle of a game and pleaded for him to blow the whistle. He wanted protection from Brendan, who was playing such tenacious defense that the player could barely breathe, let alone think about scoring. Navy's starting goalie, Matt Russell, a sophomore who lived on the same floor as Brendan and Travis, referred to his teammate as the most "violent" lacrosse player he had ever seen. In a sport built around a combination of skill and toughness, being an aggressive player was a good thing.

Yet as soon as the final whistle blew, Brendan was a gentleman. When the teams shook hands after the games, Brendan was one of the first in line.

Navy men's lacrosse captain Thomas "Bucky" Morris had met Brendan while they were preparing for academy life at NAPS, but got to know him better after Brendan went out for lacrosse. Though Brendan initially made the lacrosse team as a "rider," with the specific role of recovering loose balls, his rapid improvement led Navy coach Richie Meade to give him a central role as a defensive midfielder. Playing the position for the first time in his young lacrosse career, Brendan worked closely with Morris, one of the nation's top defensemen.

Morris was impressed with Brendan's intensity and wanted to help him learn the sport even more quickly. He knew Brendan had played football and was obviously well versed in team sports, but what inspired him most was the way Brendan watched over and protected his younger brothers, who were both rising stars on the Navy squad.

In the middle of a game that ended in a Navy blowout victory against Holy Cross in 2004, Billy had made a freshman mistake, getting burned on a face-off, which allowed an opposing player to score; he celebrated wildly with his teammates. Shortly after watching his brother get chewed out by Navy coaches on the sidelines, Brendan, a senior, took the field with his sights set squarely on the Holy Cross player who had embarrassed Billy. As the player fought for a grounder, Brendan hammered him with a pulverizing, yet clean, hit.

"Oh my God, Brendan just crushed that kid," a Navy player on the sidelines said to his teammates.

The Holy Cross player was fine, but everyone on the Navy team, including Morris, had seen how closely the Looney brothers stuck together. When Steve or Billy made a rookie mistake, Brendan was the first person in their faces. But if someone else dared to show them up, Brendan would roll through that opponent like a freight train.

Early afternoon rain fell in Baltimore on Memorial Day 2004, yet 43,898 fans still showed up at M & T Bank Stadium, home of the NFL's Baltimore Ravens. At the time, it was the largest crowd to attend a nonbasketball championship game in NCAA history.

In the parking lot was Second Lieutenant Travis Manion, a newly commissioned US Marine officer who had just graduated in front of his proud mom, dad, sister, and someone who had been instrumental in making his second chance at the Naval Academy possible: Lieutenant Colonel Corky Gardner. Travis was standing on top of a car leading a "Let's go Navy" chant by hundreds of frenzied fans. After his shoulder injury had caused him to miss the entire second half of his senior wrestling season, this was a championship game for Travis, too.

In the stadium, Travis sat with the midshipmen, while Tom and Janet Manion joined Brendan's parents, Kevin and Maureen Looney. Exactly one year earlier, Brendan had met Amy just a few blocks from the stadium where he was about to play the biggest game of his life. Now Amy was stuck at work and couldn't attend the game, but she was planning to meet the Looney brothers and Travis almost immediately afterward.

As newly commissioned US Navy Ensign Brendan Looney sat in the Ravens locker room, he was reminded of the 2001 Army-Navy football game, especially when his coach pointed out that Naval Academy graduates were currently fighting overseas. Ever since Navy had started its NCAA tournament run, and especially since the Midshipmen had beaten Princeton in Saturday's national semifinal, messages of support had poured in from military bases all over the world, including Iraq and Afghanistan.

Syracuse head coach John Desko admitted that some of his own players were struggling with the idea of seemingly playing against their country. "One of our guys just read an article in the Baltimore paper about Navy and Memorial Day and wartime and said, 'I almost want Navy to win,'" Desko said. "They'll have a lot of people rooting for them."

Indeed, there was no such thing as a "neutral" fan at the 2004 NCAA Men's Lacrosse National Championship Game. You were a Syracuse student, parent, or graduate, or you were a Navy fan. Some Syracuse alumni even bought Navy hats to wear with their Orange T-shirts and ponchos. They wanted to show that despite rooting for Syracuse, they appreciated the sacrifices being made by the Navy athletes and their classmates.

The final seconds before the Navy players ran out on the field felt like the countdown to a Super Bowl or a Rolling Stones concert. The atmosphere, created in part by rowdy midshipmen like Travis, who was chanting "U-S-A!" and crowd surfing, made the Syracuse players and coaches feel like they were playing a road game instead of a neutral-site contest.

Each Navy sports team had a Marine as its official liaison, and Gunnery Sergeant John Kob, who had spent time with Travis and the wrestling team, took his duty with the men's lacrosse team very seriously. Kob had joined the Army in 1983 and served seven years as a soldier before joining the Marine Corps. The hard-nosed warrior had already deployed to Somalia before being assigned to the Naval Academy in 2001 and was now just months away from deploying to Iraq's Babil province with 1st Battalion, 1st Marine Division, based out of California's Camp Pendleton.

Before each game Kob would lead the Midshipmen out onto the field carrying a massive American flag, which always excited the supportive home lacrosse crowds in Annapolis. But this day's opening ceremony was even more special.

As Brendan, his brothers, and their teammates stood in the tunnel leading out to the M & T Bank Stadium field listening to the thunderous applause above them, Kob, a bald, imposing figure whose face could easily appear in the dictionary next to the definition of "Marine," dashed out onto the field with the gigantic American flag, waving it so vigorously that the pole nearly broke. From the lower bowl to the upper deck, a crescendo of patriotism swept the stadium, with Travis cheering as his roommate tore onto the field with his hands raised proudly toward the cloud-filled sky.

Rain pelted down on the grassy turf as the game went back and forth. Brendan and other Navy defensemen were focused on Syracuse's Michael Powell, one of the greatest attack men in NCAA lacrosse history and the only player to ever win the Tewaaraton Trophy—similar to college football's Heisman Trophy—twice. For Navy to have any chance of defeating the Orange, its defensemen, including Morris, Brendan, and other midshipmen, would have to contain Powell.

The crowd was in a frenzy as a goal by Navy's Ben Bailey gave the Midshipmen the early lead, with more "U-S-A" refrains replacing the stadium's usual chant of "Let's Go Ravens." Travis, who had played lacrosse in high school and later at Drexel, had closely followed his roommate's team all season.

Brendan was playing his heart out, as always, but there was a reason Syracuse had won two out of the past four national championships. After tying the score with five minutes to play, the Orange took the lead ninety seconds later, resulting in a nervous hush throughout most of the stadium. It didn't help that Russell, Navy's starting goalie, was forced to leave the game because of a collarbone injury.

Syracuse had a 13–12 lead with 1:05 left when its most dangerous player, Powell, darted like a missile toward Navy's backup goalie. Brendan closed his eyes as the ball hit the back of the net, giving Syracuse a two-goal lead with a minute to play.

"Shit," Travis said to a fellow midshipman in the stands.

Though Navy followed with a goal, Syracuse won its third championship in five years and eighth overall title.

Brendan was absolutely crushed by the 14–13 defeat. This was supposed to be Navy's day. It would take some time for the loss to sink in, but Brendan, who had just played his final collegiate game, and everyone associated with the Navy program knew deep down that the team's improbable Final Four run had been a truly amazing feat.

"What a game and what a crowd," Tom Manion said after the game, as Janet nodded in agreement. "That's the kind of thing that really makes you proud to be an American."

Travis, Amy, Brendan, and Steve were supposed to be having a victory celebration that night at the second home the Manions owned in Annapolis, where they would often hang out on weekends, before heading out to McGarvey's, O'Brien's, and their other favorite downtown bars. But even after a devastating defeat, there was still something to be happy about. The US Naval Academy class of 2004 had just graduated.

With a light mist falling, music blared through the Manion house as a cooler full of Bud Light chilled on the back porch. While Amy and Brendan's brother joked around inside, Brendan went outside to talk to Travis.

"I don't think I've ever felt this low, man," Brendan grumbled. "We should have won that fucking game."

"I know," Travis replied. "But don't do what I did to myself in wrestling."

"What do you mean?" Brendan asked.

"When I lost that match in Texas, I thought my whole life was over," Travis said. "I hadn't been that miserable since I quit the academy. But there are bigger things out there. Think of what we're probably going to be doing a year or two from now."

Without saying anything, Brendan held out his plastic cup, as if to say "cheers." After graduating as officers in the US Navy and Marine Corps, respectively, Brendan and Travis quietly commemorated their achievement before heading inside to laugh, drink more beer, and get their minds off the game's disappointing outcome.

A few minutes later, as the music got even louder, Amy laughed as Travis and Steve made an awful attempt at break dancing on the floor. Temporarily snapping out of his dejected mood, Brendan managed to crack his customary grin as he walked up to his girlfriend and put his right arm around her. Though he wished he could have changed the result of the championship game, Brendan knew he was blessed to have found a great girl and such good friends during his Naval Academy years.

———•——•———

While waiting for their duty assignments, Travis and Brendan worked at the academy for part of the summer after graduation. Travis was living in his parents' house, while Brendan lived with some former lacrosse teammates in Annapolis's Eastport neighborhood.

On one particularly hot and humid day, Brendan asked Bucky Morris, the lacrosse star who had helped him become such a solid defenseman, if he wanted to go mountain biking on a nearby trail.

"Sure, man," Morris said.

"Cool," Brendan said. "We just need to ride downtown first and meet Trav at his place."

When they arrived at the Annapolis house, Travis was sitting on the back porch enjoying a glass of water. A cooler full of ice cold beer was beside him, which would surely serve as a reward when the three young officers returned from their afternoon ride.

The bike ride started normally, as Travis, Brendan, and their buddy rode out of the city and headed into the woods. They had traveled ten or fifteen miles when Morris suggested turning back.

Travis and Brendan, both realizing the usual afternoon thunderstorm was probably on the horizon, agreed to head home, with one catch.

"We'll ride back single file, and whoever's last has to try to make his way up front," Brendan said.

"Yeah, let's do that the whole way back," Travis said.

Morris may have been the most talented athlete of the three, and he had no reason to doubt he could keep up with Brendan or Travis. He just didn't understand why they couldn't casually ride back to Travis's house without engaging in what was sure to be an exhausting competition.

When their contest started in a wooded, downhill stretch of the trail, Travis was in the back and Brendan was in the front. They hadn't been riding for more than five minutes when Travis cranked his way past his former roommate.

"See ya later, assholes!" Travis called, laughing.

As Morris had seen at countless lacrosse practices, Brendan wore an intense frown as he roared toward his challenger. Though he and Travis were the best of friends, there was no way he was about to be defeated.

Brendan pedaled harder and harder, getting so close to Travis's bike that the contest began to look like the famous chariot race in *Ben Hur*. Morris was keeping up so far, but knew he couldn't last another two miles at this ridiculous pace. As he tried to catch his breath, Morris pleaded with his friends to ease up.

Travis and Brendan were already gone, racing one another down the mountain, through the woods, and toward the city where they had grown from young plebes into military officers. As dark clouds filled the sky before the inevitable storm, Morris, who would later become a Navy fighter pilot, pedaled alone. He was slightly pissed at his friends for leaving him, but also amused at how Brendan and Travis turned everything, even a routine bike ride, into a contest.

When Morris finally made it back, he locked his bike to the Manions' front gate. As he walked toward the door, he heard the unmistakable sound of Travis and Brendan laughing on the back porch. They were drinking beer and joking about leaving their unsuspecting buddy in the dust, leading Morris to think the stunt may have been planned.

"Really, guys?" Morris asked as he stepped onto the porch. "We couldn't just go on a relaxing bike ride?"

"Nice of you to join us," Travis said, throwing a Bud Light to Morris.

"You guys are something," Morris said with a grin. "So who the hell won?"

"Me," Brendan said.

"Bullshit," Travis yelled. "I was ahead until he cheated."

As the Foo Fighters song "Times Like These" played and cold beer flowed, the laughter of three young military officers filled the air until it was finally overtaken by thunder. Though their Naval Academy days were over, it was times like these that Travis and Brendan would always remember.

A few days later, Travis packed up his car to leave Annapolis. He would soon head to The Basic School in Quantico, where all newly commissioned Marine officers must train, to learn how to lead Marines in battle. Brendan was commissioned as a Navy intelligence officer, and before heading to Virginia Beach he would mentor and coach young lacrosse players at NAPS in Rhode Island.

As Travis drove out of Annapolis with the radio tuned to Baltimore's rock station, the music added to his relaxed, reflective mood. Pulling onto King George Street, Travis looked at the Naval Academy gates, which were once closed to him after he decided to quit. He saw the historic buildings where he had attended classes, wrestled, and learned how to lead. He also looked out toward the harbor, where ships had been stationed to protect the Naval Academy during the 9/11 attacks.

The car's brakes screeched as Travis, whose attention had momentarily drifted, narrowly avoided rear-ending the car in front of him. The sudden stop sent several items packed in the backseat flying, including a small box he had kept on his desk throughout his four-plus years as a midshipman.

The brown plastic box, which hit the dashboard when Travis pumped the brakes, was filled with index cards, which scattered all over the front seat. On each card was a different movie quote that had inspired Travis during many nights of watching videos and DVDs with Brendan and other Naval Academy friends.

As he pulled over to clean up the car, picking up the cards one by one and putting them back in the box, one in particular caught his eye. It contained the dying words spoken by Captain John Miller, played by Tom Hanks, to Private James Ryan, played by Matt Damon, in Steven Spielberg's *Saving Private Ryan.*

"Earn this" was written on the index card in Travis's handwriting. "Earn it."

In the years to come, Travis, Brendan, and thousands of fellow US military academy graduates would lead courageous troops into battle. As officers, these brave young Americans weren't being given the responsibility of making crucial life and death decisions by accident. After years of hard work, sacrifice, and adversity, they had earned it.

3

TAKING A STAND

Now that he was a young second lieutenant training at The Basic School (TBS) in Quantico, Virginia, it was difficult for Travis to imagine that the months after graduation could be even more challenging. But in the fall of 2004, the harsh reality of war became more personal for Travis, Brendan, and their fellow Naval Academy graduates.

On September 2, 2004, Marine First Lieutenant Lt. Ronald Winchester, a driven, popular former Navy football player, became the first combat death in the Naval Academy's 2001 class when he was killed in a roadside bomb attack in Iraq's Al Anbar province. Less than forty-eight hours later, Travis and his fellow Navy wrestling alums were hit by another freight train upon learning that Marine Second Lieutenant Brett Harman, a friend and teammate who had graduated in 2003, was murdered during a melee at a North Carolina State University football tailgate.

Joel Sharratt, the Navy assistant wrestling coach who once consoled Travis after the worst loss of his career, was sitting behind the anguished young Marine on the flight to Chicago for Harman's funeral. Sitting next to Travis was Marine Second Lieutenant Brian Stann, a 2003 graduate who had played football at Navy and had become friends with Travis after watching the Tom Cruise movie *Vanilla Sky* in Travis and Brendan's room one night with a large group of fellow midshipmen. The film's dream sequences were offbeat and strange, but Stann and Travis both liked the movie's theme of confronting one's worst fears. Their friendship grew stronger while Stann was stationed at Quantico, especially after Travis moved there to start TBS training. Stann also knew Brett Harman and was on the football team along with another young player, J. P. Blecksmith, when Ronnie Winchester was a senior offensive tackle.

Sharratt, who had stayed in touch with both Stann and Travis after they graduated a year apart, was also mourning the death of Harman, whom he had mentored and coached. So when Sharratt put his head around the edge of Travis's seat and started to speak, both Marines listened.

"Let's do an exercise. . . . I'd like you both to close your eyes and picture that you're leaving a building," Sharratt said. "A friend picks you up and takes you to a place where people are somber, crying, and there seems to be an audience. Then you realize that you're at your own funeral. Write down a few words about what you'd want a family member or person of faith to say when reflecting on the lives of Travis Manion or Brian Stann."

Stann nodded, and after a few minutes of pondering what to write, started jotting down a sentence about one day being remembered as a good husband, a loving father, and a US Marine.

Travis went through several pieces of paper before settling on one sentence: "Travis Manion was a man unafraid to stand for what was right."

•———————•

By November 2004, the Second Battle of Fallujah was exploding in the heart of Iraq's Al Anbar province. Seven months after a clash ignited by insurgents who had strung the bodies of four

American civilian contractors from a bridge, the First Battle of Fallujah, which had produced some of the most jarring images of the Iraq war, had ended after a cease-fire was imposed. Soon after the United States announced its withdrawal from Fallujah, al Qaeda terrorists like Abu Musab al-Zarqawi declared victory against the "infidels."

Even after the bloody battle's frustrating conclusion, the heroism of US forces in the First Battle of Fallujah was lauded throughout the military community. Captain Doug Zembiec, the former Navy All-American who had once told Travis to "be a battle-ax" on the wrestling mat, became known as "the Lion of Fallujah" after courageously leading his Marines into numerous firefights.

Like the 1st Reconnaissance Battalion that Travis would join after completing officer training at TBS, Zembiec's Echo Company was part of the 1st Marine Division, which had helped define modern military courage in legendary battles like Belleau Wood, Guadalcanal, Okinawa, and Chosin Reservoir. Even before the US military won the historic second battle, "Fallujah" was already part of the Marine Corps' proud lexicon. The brave Marines who tore through enemy fighters on the Sunni stronghold's narrow streets were real-life American heroes who were featured in news coverage across the nation.

One of the Marines who distinguished himself during the Second Battle of Fallujah was Second Lieutenant J. P. Blecksmith, the former Navy football team member who had played with Brendan, Winchester, and Stann.

Stann, an aspiring mixed martial arts (MMA) fighter, often asked Travis to be in his corner for big fights. In addition to his passion for the sport, Travis had collegiate wrestling experience, which helped Stann tremendously as he transitioned from the football field to the MMA cages and rings.

As Stann sat in his Virginia Beach hotel room listening to Travis give an impassioned prefight speech on November 12, 2004, they were suddenly interrupted. Stann later recounted the moment in his book *Heart for the Fight*:

> Travis' cell phone rang. He stepped out of the room and into the hallway. As the door closed behind him, I heard the tone of his voice go flat but couldn't catch his words. When he returned a few minutes later, his pre-fight energy had evaporated. I looked up to see him staring morosely out the window, his face betraying a mix of shock and rage.
>
> "What's up, Trav?"
>
> "Nothing."
>
> I stood up and walked over to him. "What was that phone call, Travis?"
>
> He looked at me with pain-filled eyes. A flutter of dread coursed through me.
>
> "Nothing," he repeated, his voice devoid of strength.
>
> "Don't bullshit me, Trav. What the fuck is going on?" I said, trying to control the panic I felt.
>
> "I'll tell you later," he evaded.
>
> "You'll tell me now," I demanded.
>
> He looked away. "After the fight."
>
> "No, give it to me straight," I demanded. "What is going on?"
>
> "J. P. Blecksmith was killed in Fallujah last night."
>
> The mention of his name brought back memories of the tall, blue-eyed athlete whose competitive fires evoked so much admiration in me.
>
> Then it dawned on me what Travis had just said.
>
> "What?" I asked weakly.
>
> *Three of us in one fall?*
>
> "He was shot on a rooftop. That's all I know," Travis said. (Travis) looked absolutely miserable.

It was another dreadful moment for Stann, Travis, Brendan, and everyone associated with the Naval Academy. On November

11, 2004, twenty-four-year-old Blecksmith, of San Marino, California, was killed by enemy small arms fire alongside twenty-year-old Marine Lance Corporal Kyle Burns, of Laramie, Wyoming. Blecksmith was the first US military officer killed during the Second Battle of Fallujah.

After Stann subsequently lost his fight in the aftermath of the shocking news, Travis called Brendan, who was coaching NAPS lacrosse in Rhode Island before moving to Virginia Beach, where he would be stationed as a Navy intelligence officer. Brendan, who had stood beside Blecksmith on the sidelines during the unforgettable 2001 Army-Navy game, was also devastated.

"I don't even know what to say," Brendan said.

"I know," Travis said. "I don't think I should have told Brian before the fight, but he kind of forced it out of me."

"What were you supposed to do?" Brendan interrupted. "He would have been upset either way."

"Yeah, I guess," Travis replied. "These past few months have just been brutal, man."

"I know, but we have to keep pushing forward," Brendan said. "I think that's what all these guys would have wanted."

In August 2005, less than a year after graduating from TBS, all of Travis's hard work culminated in one key moment. Finally, after more than four years at the Naval Academy and six months at TBS, Second Lieutenant Travis Manion was dodging improvised explosive devices (IEDs) in searing desert heat.

Surrounded by tall mountains and hot sand, Travis was coordinating the movement of a helicopter providing air support to the dozens of Marines and vehicles in his unit. It was the middle of the afternoon, and Travis had been outside since about 5:30 a.m. in heat that now measured well over 100 degrees. Despite his neck being so sunburned that it felt like a boiling teapot, Travis was keeping hydrated and focused on his job. After all, fellow Marines were depending on him.

Travis knew there were IEDs around the patch of desert the Marines were slated to patrol, so he was navigating them in a safer direction while checking with the helicopter to make sure there were no signs of enemy fighters preparing to ambush the platoons. The helicopter would also check adjacent mountains for snipers using large rocks and the midafternoon sunlight's glare as cover.

After a few minutes, the chopper pilot indicated everything was clear. Travis would radio his command, which would then give the final go-ahead for the patrol. It's this kind of vigilance that often saved American lives on the battlefield.

As Travis pressed the button on his radio to relay the final order, a loud, familiar voice suddenly overtook the frequency.

"Uh, Lieutenant, this is Coyote 6," the voice said. "I'm not really sure what you're trying to do out here, but you're not following proper radio procedure."

"Sir?" Travis asked, puzzled.

"You need to figure out what you're trying to do, because I sure as hell can't tell by listening to your orders over this radio," the rising voice said. "Do things right or do us all a favor and just go home."

Travis wasn't in a battle in Iraq or Afghanistan. He was in the miserable frying pan of Southern California's Mojave Desert. The Marine Corps Air Ground Combat Center at Twentynine Palms—the world's largest Marine base—is where thousands train every year for twenty-first-century desert warfare. In August 2005, Operation Mojave Viper involved several mock Iraqi and Afghan villages and enough sand to fill most of Rhode Island. Upon his arrival at a base that housed well over ten thousand Marines, Travis had been astonished by its size and scope.

The Marine yelling at Travis over the radio was a "coyote," tasked with making sure units headed for Iraq and Afghanistan were learning the proper techniques, tactics, and procedures developed during nearly four years of war. Though they could be a thorn in a Marine's side during long, grueling training exercises, their close attention to detail helped make the Marine Corps a well-oiled battlefield machine. Still, Coyote 6 was particularly antagonistic and had just embarrassed Travis in front of dozens of Marines listening on the radio.

Clicking his handheld radio, Travis said the two safest words in the Marine Corps: "Yes, sir."

Everyone hurried back to work after the coyote-induced stoppage, continuing the desert patrol while following what they thought was proper communication procedure. The sooner they got it right, the sooner every Marine could take a cold shower.

Travis was once again talking to the helicopter, making sure that no enemy fighters, who were usually played by contractors or fellow Marines, were lurking on the faux battlefield. Though their guns shot blanks and IED explosions were simulated using Hollywood-style special effects, even a fake battle could be loud and jarring.

After about five minutes of going back and forth with the helicopter pilot, the Marines were surprised when Coyote 6 retook the airwaves. Aside from a misplaced word here and there while relaying orders, Travis was doing nothing wrong, and it was clear by this point that the coyote was singling out "the new guy."

"Lieutenant Manion, this is Coyote 6," he said as dozens of eyes rolled. "I have to ask you a question, son. Do you have any idea what the hell you're doing?"

The radio was dead silent for almost thirty uncomfortable seconds as everyone, from coyotes to Marines out in the desert, waited for the young second lieutenant's response.

"No, sir," Travis said. "But I did stay at a Holiday Inn Express last night."

A crescendo of hooting, hollering, and laughter ensued as Marines, young and old, exorcised a long day of stress in the desert. While Marines closest to Coyote 6 did their best to contain their amusement, others, including the helicopter pilot, laughed the hardest they had in days. The audacity displayed by this young Marine officer was downright astonishing. What would the overbearing instructor do to him in response?

Silence filled the airwaves as the combat simulation continued. Coyote 6 never responded, because after all, what could he say? Without defying authority, Travis had disarmed the coyote with his dry sense of humor. Confronting Travis would have been an unpopular move, and the instructor knew it.

When Travis returned to battalion headquarters, fellow Marine officers patted him on the back as they replayed what had already become a classic moment.

Less than a month later Travis was once again "the new guy," but this time in Iraq's Al Anbar province, where so much American and Iraqi blood had already been spilled. As the 1st Reconnaissance Battalion's maintenance management officer at Camp Fallujah, his responsibilities, which were focused on making sure vehicles were correctly allocated, fueled, and repaired, were undoubtedly important. But sitting on the sidelines while others went "outside the wire" to fight was definitely not what the Marine had envisioned at Twentynine Palms.

Throughout the predeployment exercises, Travis thought he was about to spend the next eight months fighting for his country on the streets of Al Anbar province. Soon after arriving at Camp Fallujah, however, Travis worried that he was going to spend the next nine months stacking supplies and pushing pencils.

His yearning to leave the base and confront the enemy was visible, and the older, more seasoned officers serving with Travis thought the new guy from the Naval Academy needed to chill out. Being the unit's only second lieutenant—the most junior of officer ranks—made life even more difficult for Travis, as second lieutenants were almost always subject to an "initiation" phase in which they would be put in their place by the officers in charge. It was all harmless, but for someone with ambitions as high as Travis had, it wasn't always easy.

Travis didn't want to leave Iraq feeling that he had not had a chance to use the skills he spent so many years developing. He discussed his concerns with First Lieutenants Carlo Pecori and Croft Young, two Marines he had met in training who were also part of the 1st Marine Reconnaissance Battalion. The two Marines, who had already seen action in Fallujah, urged Travis to keep his chin up and look for opportunities to make a difference. He appreciated their advice, but remained frustrated.

Then Travis got an e-mail from one of his mentors, Coach Joel Sharratt.

"Do not let your guard down or become complacent with your job," his former wrestling coach wrote. Sharratt, who had consoled Travis after his worst wrestling defeat and on the flight to Brett Harman's funeral, told Travis to focus on the honor and privilege of having the chance to have an impact where he could.

"Learn everything you can every second you can," he wrote. "Study the tactics, study the people, study the culture [and] know them. More importantly, know yourself and be vigilant not to let up on yourself preparing for the unexpected."

The first major bright spot for Travis was playing a big role in preparations for Iraq's historic constitutional referendum on October 15, 2005. In order for millions of Iraqis to exercise their newfound right to vote, security had to be heavy, especially in violent Sunni strongholds like Al Anbar province. With al Qaeda vowing to attack polling stations and a deep Sunni-Shiite divide over whether the draft constitution should be adopted, the potential for mass casualties was high.

Before the vote, Travis wrote an e-mail to Navy Captain John McGurty. Travis had dated McGurty's daughter, Jess, and John was a close family friend who happened to be serving in Iraq as well.

Sir,
    Thanks for writing, it's good to hear from you. I'm sorry that we couldn't hook up before you left. We've been pretty

busy getting ready for these elections. It's definitely been an
eye opener for me so far but I'm excited to play a role in the
event. Hopefully it goes well for these people's sake.
Semper Fi,
Travis

As October 15 dawned in war-torn Iraq, Travis and thousands
of fellow Marines were protecting polling stations, which al Qaeda
leader Abu Musab al-Zarqawi and other terrorists had vowed to
attack. In Atlanta, where Travis's father was stationed during the
aftermath of Hurricane Katrina while awaiting his Reserve unit's
move back to New Orleans, Tom and Janet were nervous. Tom
was using every Marine Corps resource at his disposal to check for
updates on referendum-related violence, while Janet was holding
her rosary beads and asking the Lord to protect her son.

"Hope all goes well and your operation is a success," Tom wrote
to his son in an e-mail sent just a few days before the referendum.
"Love, Dad."

Indeed, Travis was risking his life as he and other members of
his unit, like Marine Staff Sergeant Paul Petty of Texas, set up
sandbags, wiring, and concrete barriers. They were working hard
to make sure citizens of Al Farris, a western Iraqi municipality
nicknamed "Tower Town" because it was in the shadow of a huge,
futuristic-looking water tower, could have their say in Iraq's new
constitution.

Like most of the areas Travis passed through during convoys, Al
Farris was made up of narrow streets sandwiched between multistory apartments, although it was more modern and less violent
than cities like Fallujah, which was quieter than in 2004 but still
a very dangerous place. Though Al Farris wasn't exactly Center
City Philadelphia, Travis enjoyed seeing different parts of the unfamiliar land and knew the nationwide referendum was a crucial
moment for the country's future.

"It's nice to finally get the chance to do something like this," Travis said to Petty, the Marine who was handing him sandbags to stack around polling stations.

"Yes, sir," Petty said. "It's great to get outside the wire once in a while."

"I hear that, Staff Sergeant Petty," Travis said. "Where'd you say you're from again?"

"Texas, sir," Petty said.

"That's right," Travis said. "We went to Texas a few times for wrestling tournaments. I liked it a lot down there."

Though everything was going according to plan, Travis, like almost any US service member out on patrol in Iraq that day, was on edge. He was keenly aware that an explosion or firefight could erupt at any moment, and he reminded his Marines to stay alert.

For the most part, the violence never occurred. American news outlets reported isolated attacks in Baghdad, but the voting on October 15, 2005, was mostly peaceful. Almost ten million Iraqis cast ballots, with just under 80 percent voting to adopt the Constitution. In Al Anbar province, the Sunni stronghold where Travis was deployed, an incredible 97 percent voted against the constitution, which underscored the huge challenges American forces still faced in western Iraq. The overall vote, however, paved way for Iraq's historic national election on December 15, 2005, which Travis and his fellow Marines also played a big role in protecting.

●————————●

During one late evening convoy through Fallujah, the deafening thunder of an IED shattered the relative tranquility of the 1st Reconnaissance Battalion patrol. The group of Marines had been attacked before, but this was the first time that Travis was with them during a hostile incident. Keeping his composure while following the orders of the more experienced officers, Travis, his heart pumping and his ears ringing, helped evacuate a Marine who was wounded in the attack.

It was Travis's first encounter with IEDs, which were killing and maiming troops and civilians all over Iraq and Afghanistan. Despite the seriousness of the threat, the budding battlefield leader was in his element while helping ensure that a brother in arms survived.

Later that night Travis, looking to burn off some tension from his first experience with a roadside bomb, went over to a make-shift gym he had been instrumental in helping build for Marines on Camp Fallujah. While financial constraints made the project a tough sell, Travis, with extra time on his hands after finishing his duties each day, kept pushing his superiors about the importance of staying in shape, especially since an exercise regimen centered on running was sometimes difficult to maintain in Iraq's scorch-ing heat. Without Brendan there to challenge him during gru-eling workouts, Travis pressured himself to stay in good physical condition.

As he changed out of his fatigues and walked into the tiny weight room wearing a politically incorrect "Infidel" T-shirt, which had been mailed to him by Brendan, he saw a familiar face under the bench press bar. It was the 1st Reconnaissance Battal-ion surgeon, Reagan Anderson, a US Navy physician attached to the battalion.

"Lieutenant Manion, how are you?" Anderson inquired.

"Hey, sir, I'm doing alright," Travis replied. "Just gonna lift and get rid of some of the day's stress, you know?"

"I hear that," Anderson said.

Travis was about to start his bench press workout, then turned back to Anderson.

"Hey, sir," Travis asked. "How are you holding up?"

Anderson stopped his reps to answer the Marine's question. Despite having a tough day, Travis genuinely cared about how Anderson was doing.

"You know what, that's the first time anyone's asked me that in a really long time," Anderson said. "I'm doing well, Lieutenant, and thanks for asking."

"Do you want a spotter?" said Travis, who moved behind the doctor to support the bar he was lifting in case it became too heavy to control.

"That would be great," Anderson said.

While out on a convoy mission a few nights later, Travis spotted First Lieutenant Croft Young. Surrounded by palm trees under the bright desert moon, the deployed Marines were far from enjoying cold glasses of beer while watching television, as they often had done at Twentynine Palms after the day's training concluded. Instead, they were fueling up Humvees under cover of night in an ancient, mysterious place.

Even though Young's job was often filthy, exhausting, and dangerous, Travis would have given almost anything to join him.

"It must be great to be outside the wire so much," Travis remarked to Young.

"I'm not sure 'great' is the word I would use," Young said. "I haven't taken a shower in two weeks."

Travis realized the inconveniences that came with the territory, but still wanted to be part of the main combat effort in Al Anbar province.

During the deployment, Travis sent an e-mail to Marine Captain Ryan Gilchrist, who had taught and mentored Travis at TBS:

As far as the deployment, we've been really busy with the referendum lately. There were a lot of moving parts associated with the whole operation as I'm sure you'd understand. It's also been tough on the Bn [Battalion] as we are usually assigned tasks that would suit an infantry Bn, and don't really fit our task organization.

In terms of my role, I'm really excited to be out here affecting change where I can, but I'd be lying if I said I was pleased with my situation.

Other than that, I also wanted to thank you again for the guidance you gave in Quantico, I think about the things you taught us every day I've been out here (and not just what you told, but by your actions too).

In his reply, Gilchrist offered encouragement and probably the highest praise that could be bestowed upon a junior Marine Corps officer.

"Keep after it," Gilchrist wrote. "I see stars on your collar in twenty-five years."

Travis helped make history as proud Iraqis waved their ink-soaked fingers after voting in two democratic elections to help determine their country's future. In between the momentous votes, Travis celebrated his twenty-fifth birthday.

4

"IF NOT ME, THEN WHO . . ."

Iraq changed newly promoted First Lieutenant Travis Manion for the better. As the Marine's mom, dad, sister, and several Naval Academy buddies all noticed, he was still the same Travis who had willingly traded Doylestown for one of the world's most dangerous places. But after returning to the United States, Travis carried with him an aura of seriousness and quiet self-confidence that was unfamiliar to some of his closest friends and loved ones.

When Travis talked about life, he acknowledged its fragility, having felt the pulse of an IED blast and seen dead bodies in the streets. When he dated, he was cautious, knowing that he would probably deploy to Iraq again soon. When he had fun, he knew when to call it quits, even more so than in his Naval Academy days.

For a young Marine who had just spent eight months in Fallujah, it was almost impossible not to mature. No matter what Travis was doing, he was acutely aware that every single day Americans, Iraqis, and Afghans were fighting and often dying. He had already lost too many fellow midshipmen and Marines to violence and could still picture their flag-draped coffins.

As Travis wrapped up his first combat tour in the spring of 2006, Brendan was deployed to Chinhae (now Jinhae), South Korea, where he worked as a Navy intelligence officer. He was proud of Travis and his many classmates serving in harm's way, but as the former roommates corresponded, Brendan was also frustrated that he couldn't be part of America's efforts in Iraq or Afghanistan.

He also missed his girlfriend, Amy, and would often send her postcards from the Korean peninsula:

> These last couple months have been tough, not much fun w/ out you. I get very bored here and miss you like crazy. I don't like not having you around. Life is better with you in it. One day though, right?
> Love, Brendan

Despite his desire to shield his girlfriend from the realities of serving during wartime, Brendan would frequently tell Amy how much he wanted to transfer from Navy intelligence to Special Operations, which would almost certainly give him the chance to deploy to Iraq or Afghanistan.

"Amy, I've got to do more," Brendan said during a late-night phone conversation. "Travis is there, my other buddies are there, and I want to be there with them."

When Amy reminded him of the dangers his friends, like Travis, were facing, Brendan was undeterred.

"I should be in the fight," he insisted.

Brendan wanted to be a Navy SEAL. But every time he couldn't distinguish the colors of two shirts in his drawer, he was reminded that the SEALs did not accept colorblind candidates. Though anything was possible, the odds of Brendan ever risking his life in top secret SEAL missions were extremely low.

Still, the concept Brendan's father had instilled in him and his brothers since childhood—being selfless and always doing the right thing—was firmly planted in the back of Brendan's mind. If there was any chance of serving in combat or becoming a SEAL, Brendan was going to do everything in his power to find a way.

While Brendan finished his first overseas deployment, Travis was often surfing near his West Coast base or playing pool and drinking beer on the lower level of his parents' new house during visits back east. He was also anxious to lead Marines into battle the next time he was called upon to serve in combat. Just before he had left Iraq, the February 2006 shrine bombing in Samarra, north of Baghdad, had ignited a firestorm of sectarian violence that few had envisioned before the war.

Despite the sacrifices made by some of America's bravest men and women, Fallujah was still a top destination for terrorists yearning to kill Americans. To the dismay of Travis and many other Marines he had served alongside in Al Anbar province, conditions in the heavily Sunni city seemed to be worsening.

One indisputably positive development in the ongoing war effort was the death of Abu Musab al-Zarqawi, the Jordanian-born al Qaeda terrorist who had spent years murdering US troops and civilians. His victims included American contractor Nick Berg, who the CIA said al-Zarqawi had beheaded in a horrifying videotaped execution. After a massive manhunt, the terrorist leader was finally killed in a June 2006 bombing raid near the northern Iraqi city of Baqubah.

Later that summer, an extraordinary terror alert originating from Britain rocked the Western world. Authorities announced that al Qaeda was once again targeting commercial air travel, this time through the use of liquid explosives. From Europe to the United States, putting toothpaste or perfume through X-ray machines in clear plastic bags, along with throwing out water and soda bottles, became the norm while trying to navigate the post-9/11 airport security albatross. Five years after the terrorist attacks, Americans were still living in a new, evolving world.

By fall 2006, the image of Saddam Hussein as a uniform-donning dictator was replaced by his fiery rants as a defendant standing trial for crimes against humanity. Saddam was hanged shortly after Christmas, and the video of his execution was subsequently leaked on the Internet. While political divisions over the Iraq war were still deepening at home and around the world, few mourned the demise of a brutal despot who had used chemical weapons on his own people.

In the United States, President Bush, nearing the midpoint of his second term, was steadfast in his commitment to the war effort, although the resignation of Defense Secretary Donald Rumsfeld in November signaled the commander-in-chief's apparent willingness to consider tactical adjustments. Public opinion polls on the Iraq war fluctuated throughout 2006, often depending on the latest developments on the ground. But the 2006 midterm elections, in which the GOP lost thirty-one House and five Senate seats, were a clear sign of the American public's growing frustration with the three-and-a-half-year-long conflict.

Although ignoring the political debate over the war was virtually impossible, Travis, Brendan, and thousands of their fellow US troops had an uncanny ability to focus on the big picture. Where terrorists wreaked havoc, with Fallujah serving as a prime example, warriors like Travis and Brendan wanted to bring them to justice. Travis's previous encounters with the enemy's cruel tactics, coupled with the fact that his fellow Marines were being killed and wounded in Iraq and Afghanistan, made his desire to hunt down those responsible even more urgent. Nearly a thousand American families lost their loved ones to war in 2006, a fact that was not lost on Travis or his former Naval Academy roommate.

Brendan, who was back in Virginia Beach after returning from Korea, called his girlfriend in Maryland to have what initially seemed like a casual conversation. Amy was at work and fairly busy, but would always make time to take a call from her boyfriend. As the conversation progressed, though, Amy sensed that Brendan was about to share something she probably didn't want to hear.

"So I should probably tell you something," Brendan finally said, then paused. "Somebody talked to me today about going to Iraq. I'd be leaving really soon, but I think this is something I need to do."

Brendan then told Amy that he would be heading to Camp Fallujah for a few months.

"Do you promise to be careful?" Amy asked.

"Of course," Brendan replied.

"That's all I can ask," Amy said.

After exchanging "I love yous," Brendan and Amy ended their phone call as they always did. Since Brendan's Korean deployment, the word "good-bye" had been banned from the young couple's vocabulary.

"See you later," Amy said.

"See you later," said Brendan.

Soon after hanging up, Brendan called Travis, who was making a short trip back east to unwind from his first deployment before heading back to California to await his next assignment. First he would drive down to Annapolis to meet up with Brendan, Amy, and other college friends. While his former roommate considered waiting until the weekend to share his big news, he couldn't keep something this significant from Travis.

"Dude, get this," Brendan said. "I'm going to Iraq."

"No way," Travis said, knowing how much Brendan wanted to get in the fight. "Congrats man. Where are you headed?"

"Doing intel at Camp Fallujah," Brendan replied. "Your old stomping grounds."

"That's wild," Travis said. "Well, Fallujah can be a crazy place, but just keep your eyes open and you'll be fine."

"I won't be outside the wire very much," Brendan said. "I'm just glad to finally be doing my part."

"You have been doing your part," Travis said. "But believe me, I know what you mean."

Travis, Amy, Brendan, and Steve met up that weekend at the Dock Street Bar & Grill, which was close to the water and about two football fields away from the Manions' Annapolis home.

Naturally the bar was packed on Saturday night, with hundreds of mids (as midshipmen are nicknamed), graduates, and thirsty locals packing the relatively small restaurant well beyond capacity. After showing the bouncer their IDs and walking inside, Brendan headed to the restroom, while Travis took Amy and Steve to the bar to order four drinks.

As he tried to get the busy bartender's attention, a particularly intoxicated patron bumped into Amy so hard that she almost fell over.

"Um, excuse me . . . ," Amy said as Steve made sure she was okay.

Travis yelled "hey" as the guy walked away, completely oblivious, and sat down at the crowded bar, where he had left a light spring jacket to hold his spot.

After checking with Steve to make sure Amy was alright, Travis went straight up to the drunk guy.

"You just bumped into my friend's girlfriend right there," Travis said, pointing in Amy's direction. "You need to apologize."

"I didn't bump into nobody," the guy said. "Go back over to your woman."

"That's not my girlfriend," Travis said. "I already told you that's my friend's girl and you need to apologize to her."

"Fuck off," the guy said.

Shaking his head in incredulity, the Marine, who wasn't the least bit intimidated, cracked a wry smile.

"Look man, this is up to you," Travis said. "This is your chance to do the right thing."

Just as Brendan walked out of the bathroom, the drunk jumped up and slammed his beer bottle on the bar, startling many patrons, who could immediately tell that a brawl was about to erupt. Before Travis, Brendan, or Steve could do anything, however, a bouncer grabbed the guy from behind and dragged him out the front door. The unruly customer's hand, cut by the broken glass, was bleeding profusely.

When Travis told Brendan what had happened, the concerned boyfriend immediately went over to Amy, who said she was fine.

At the same moment the guy who had bumped into her was being kicked out of the loud, busy bar.

"Get the hell off me, man!" he yelled as security pulled him outside.

"You're lucky we're throwing you out," the bouncer, who remembered Travis and Brendan from their academy days, said to the bleeding patron. "I know those guys, and you would have been in big trouble if you tried to mess with either of them. They would have torn you apart." He then pushed the ejected patron toward the street.

When things calmed down, the three friends raised their glasses, much as they had done a couple of years earlier during the Battle of Fallujah, and said a toast with Steve to the men and women fighting overseas. After taking their respective sips, Brendan looked over at Travis with a nod and his famous grin.

"Thanks," Brendan said.

In August 2006, Brendan deployed to Fallujah, where he gathered and analyzed intelligence for combat missions, including operations carried out by Navy SEALs. While working out after his shift ended was a foregone conclusion, Brendan also went to the gym before breakfast and even on most lunch breaks. With his application for a lateral transfer to the SEALs being processed, Brendan was not going to be caught off guard if he was accepted into the next training class. Sure, there was only one "restricted" candidate placed in each incoming group, and the likelihood of Brendan being the first formally colorblind Navy SEAL in American history was at best remote. But just in case, Brendan maintained a ferocious workout routine.

Meanwhile, Travis was making another visit to the East Coast, for the christening of his niece, Maggie Rose Borek, in Avalon, New Jersey. Travis had first met Maggie shortly after her June 16, 2006, birth, but getting the chance to hold his sister's daughter was always special.

Adding to the August trip's significance was Travis's recent discovery that he would be returning to Iraq with the 3rd Battalion,

2nd Brigade, 1st Iraqi Army Division Military Transition Team (3-2-1 MiTT). Not only would Travis finally get the chance to spend almost every day leading Marines into battle, but he would also be tasked with training Iraqi Army soldiers to protect their country from insurgents and terrorists.

A crescendo of "Travis!" filled the house as the smiling Marine walked into the bright, bustling living room. After hugging his parents, who were excited to see their son for the first time in months, Travis walked straight toward Maggie, who was in her mother's arms.

"Hey, Ryan," Travis said to his blonde-haired sister. "Are you gonna give me that baby or what?"

"Hey, Trav," Ryan said. "She's all yours."

Travis took Maggie and sat down on the couch, looking straight into her eyes and smiling while quietly whispering into her little left ear. For the rest of the day Travis treated Maggie like she was a bag of gold, holding her for hours at a time and rarely agreeing to let her go. After all, during Travis's last visit Ryan had told him he was Maggie's godfather, which reaffirmed his obligation to always protect her.

When looking at Maggie, perhaps Travis saw the generation he was shielding from fighting in future wars. Perhaps he saw the Iraqi children who wandered around Fallujah's unforgiving streets, some of whom were killed and maimed by enemy roadside bombs or tragically caught in the crossfire of firefights with insurgents.

Not long after Travis returned to California after his niece's baptism, he got a call from his former Naval Academy roommate, who was still deployed in Iraq. Brendan was at Camp Fallujah, where Travis had spent so much time from the summer of 2005 to the spring of 2006.

"Guess what, Travis?" Brendan said. "My lat transfer to the SEALs was approved."

"Wow, that is awesome, man!" Travis said. "What did they say about you being colorblind? Didn't you say they've never accepted a colorblind candidate before?"

"I guess they decided to give me a shot," Brendan said. "I was lucky enough to get some good recommendations."

"Man, that's just great," Travis said. "So when do you start training?"

"I'll probably head out to San Diego next spring," Brendan said. "BUD/S is going to be hard as hell, but it's great to at least get a chance at it."

Travis knew most candidates wound up quitting Basic Underwater Demolition/SEAL (BUD/S) training, but he also knew that his former roommate never quit anything. If anyone could handle the world's most unrelenting audition, it was Brendan Looney.

"You're going to kick ass," Travis said. "The next time we hang out, I'll take you on a run and whip you back into shape."

When Brendan told Travis he would be home around November 2006—the same time Travis was scheduled to take a trip back east—the two friends planned a visit.

"I'll have to check the schedule and see when the 'Skins and Eagles play each other this year," Travis said.

"Sounds good," Brendan said. "Eagles are going down!"

"We'll see about that," Travis said with a laugh. "Well look, man, congratulations and make sure to stay safe over there."

"Thanks, Trav," Brendan replied. "Oh, and don't say anything to Amy about when I'm coming home. . . . I'm going to try to surprise her and my mom."

Shortly after their phone call, Travis called his dad to tell him he had just heard from Brendan.

"Dad, Brendan got picked up to try out for the Navy SEALs," he said.

"That's great, Travis," Tom said. "The SEALs made the right call."

"Yep, Brendan's as tough as they come," Travis said.

Knowing that Brendan would probably become a Navy SEAL motivated Travis even more, just as hearing Travis's stories from Fallujah helped push Brendan to continue pursuing special operations.

Now that they were military officers, everything had a much bigger purpose than during their days at the Naval Academy. By driving each other to succeed, they were making each other better leaders.

Just prior to Thanksgiving 2006, Travis flew to Philadelphia to spend a few weeks with family and friends. He had been home in June and again in August and was planning to take a trip to Australia with friends before his mom pleaded with him to visit again before deploying to Iraq. Like most sons, Travis occasionally rolled his eyes at his mom's protective nature, but at the same time, he knew how important it was to spend time with her before going back to war.

One of the first things Travis did was meet up with Marine Major Steve Cantrell, an assistant Navy wrestling coach and economics professor whom Travis looked up to and respected. Cantrell had both coached and taught Travis in Annapolis and subsequently developed friendships with Tom and Janet after he moved to Pennsylvania.

Even after Travis had left the academy and come back, Cantrell had admired the young man's strength of character. He saw Travis's will to succeed over and over again in the wrestling room and also noticed how his hunger for success carried over into the classroom. Cantrell, who had served on a selection board that ultimately determined the path Naval Academy graduates would take inside the military, was thrilled when Travis had made the Marine Corps his goal.

Cantrell was subsequently assigned as the future first lieutenant's mentor. Aside from guiding Travis's physical training, including a rehabilitation program after a second surgery on his badly injured shoulder, Cantrell had also helped Travis prepare mentally for TBS and the rigors of becoming a Marine officer.

"You were a leader on the wrestling team," Cantrell often told Travis. "Now you're going to be a leader on the battlefield."

Even though Travis was a much younger, less seasoned Marine, he managed to inspire his mentor. Not only did Cantrell, who had graded Travis's essays and exams, know this young man was bright enough to do anything he wanted in life, he always marveled over how Travis strove for tough assignments. Because he had excelled so greatly at TBS, Travis had been permitted to pick his unit, and he chose the 1st Reconnaissance Battalion with full knowledge that at least one combat deployment was on the horizon. Cantrell admired Travis's courage and determination.

Travis and Cantrell decided to spend a few days in New York City, where Cantrell had arranged a visit to the New York Fire Department's Rescue 1 headquarters. Located in Hell's Kitchen, Rescue 1 had become a revered place over the past five years. The small Manhattan building, which was still fully functioning, had been the home base for eleven firefighters—almost half the unit—killed in the September 11, 2001, terrorist attacks.

When Travis walked through Rescue 1's open red garage door, he saw men who had sacrificed and endured. It reminded him of the brave Marines he had seen on the front lines during his first deployment. The firefighters were welcoming, especially when they learned that Travis would soon be heading to Iraq for a second time.

The firefighters assembled several tables of mementos for Travis to look at, including patches from the uniforms of several firefighters killed on 9/11. The names of every fallen Rescue 1 firefighter were carved into one of the tables, and Travis did his best to remember all eleven names after he left the firehouse.

"Steve, I still can't believe what these guys were willing to do," Travis said to his friend and mentor. "I don't know if I could run into a burning building."

"You've already done it, Travis," Cantrell said. "There's nobody more prepared to get the job done than you are."

As they were leaving the firehouse, one firefighter and former Marine thanked Travis for coming to visit.

"Lieutenant Manion, I want you to have these hats and shirts," the Marine Corps veteran said. "No matter how crazy things get over there, you can always put one of these on and remember what you're fighting for."

Upon returning to his parents' house, Travis headed down to the lower level, where his dad was working in his home office. When Tom asked his son about his trip, Travis said that though he and Cantrell had had some fun, the Rescue 1 visit was clearly the highlight.

"I've never seen anything like it," Travis said. "The truly awesome thing is how much they support us."

After talking more about the day's events, Travis pulled a blue hat out of his bag. With the Rescue 1 FDNY logo on the front and "9–11–01 Never Forget" on the back, it was a symbol of the war that had begun when al Qaeda attacked the United States.

"Dad, I want you to have this, and please wear it while I'm gone," Travis said. "No matter what happens, always remember that this is what we're fighting for."

As Tom took a long look at the hat before putting it down carefully on his desk, he felt an immense sense of pride. As a Marine himself, Tom knew the sacrifice Travis was making for his country. But as a father, Tom also recognized the danger on the horizon, and he was worried about his only son.

"Now remember, you're an advisor, so that means you tell the Iraqis what to do and then step back and watch them execute," the Marine colonel said.

Suddenly Travis went silent. When his dad asked if he understood, the younger Marine finally spoke up. "Yeah, dad, I've got it."

But Tom knew his son had no plans to "step back." As a warrior and US Marine Corps officer, Travis would always lead from the front.

•———————•

On December 4, 2006, a few weeks before Travis was scheduled to leave for California to embark on his second Iraq deployment, he attended a Philadelphia Eagles–Carolina Panthers game with his sister Ryan's husband, Dave Borek, at Lincoln Financial Field. Travis had been going to Eagles games with his dad since he was a little boy, and Dave, who grew up in the Jersey Shore community of Avalon, where Ryan first met him during a summer trip, was also a big fan.

This was an important Monday night football game for the Eagles, and Travis and Dave approached it as they always did, with a first-rate tailgate party, cold beer, and hearty laughs. But as the sounds of rabid football fans filled the dark, foggy sky, Travis and his sister's husband were well aware of the night's significance, even if they shied away from discussing it. In less than a month Travis would be involved in bloody urban battles in one of the world's most dangerous places.

By any measure, Travis was ready for the streets of Fallujah, especially after his previous combat tour and two rounds of pre-deployment training. He was well prepared, focused, and except for maybe his junior year as a Navy wrestler, in the best physical condition of his young life.

Even so close to going back to Iraq, Travis's demeanor was calm. He was doing exactly what he wanted with his life, and instead of complaining about spending the next twelve months in a war-ravaged city that could justifiably be labeled a hell hole, he felt fortunate for the chance to put all the hard work of the last eight years to good use.

As they listened to one of Travis's favorite iPod playlists, which consisted of everything from Johnny Cash and Elton John to Ben Harper and The Roots, Dave took a sip of his beer and leaned against his car in silence as his visible breath blended with smoke from a small grill to fill the chilly air near the two-man tailgate. Dave knew young Americans were dying in Iraq almost every day, including a soldier named Private First Class Ross McGinnis, who had died the previous weekend in Baghdad. The nineteen-year-old Knox, Pennsylvania, native, who dove on top of a grenade to save the lives of fellow Army soldiers, would later become the fourth US service member to be awarded the Medal of Honor for heroism displayed in Iraq.

Dave was an avid reader, particularly of military-themed books and magazines, and was following the war closely. He knew Travis faced severe risks in Fallujah, particularly in a unit that guided Iraqi soldiers around the city's hostile streets. Though he never mentioned the full scope of his fears to Ryan, or for that matter Travis, he was worried about whether he would see his brother-in-law again. In fact, part of him wished he could talk Travis out of leaving, even though he knew it would be an exercise in futility.

"Hey, Dave, are you alright?" Travis asked.

"Yeah, buddy, just thinking about the big game," Dave said with a nervous grin. "Let's head inside."

The Eagles came from behind in the fourth quarter to defeat the Panthers, 27–24, in a game that would spark a five-game winning streak and an NFC East division title. But as the crowd hooted and hollered while filing out of the stadium after the big win, Dave couldn't get out of his mind the images from Iraq he had been seeing on television: burning cars, crumbling buildings, and huge explosions.

As they reached a flight of stairs near the Lincoln Financial Field exit, Dave, with a clear hint of humor, finally conveyed his concerns to Travis.

"Hey, Trav, if I tripped you right now and you fell and broke your ankle, do you think they'd let you sit this deployment out?" he asked.

Travis chuckled at Dave's joke, but didn't say much in response. A brief moment of slightly awkward silence followed, while drunken Eagles fans shouted and chanted all around them. Suddenly Travis spoke up.

"You know what though, Dave?" Travis said with an unmistakably serious look on his face. "If I don't go, they're going to send another Marine in my place who doesn't have my training."

"If not me, then who . . . you know what I mean?" he continued. "It's either me or that other guy who isn't ready, so I'm the
one who has to get the job done."

Dave was worried that he had offended Travis, but he also fully
understood his point. His brother-in-law would spend the next
year fighting insurgents and terrorists in Fallujah, and there simply
wasn't any guarantee he was coming home safely. It was a tough
pill to swallow, but this was the nature of warriors like Travis and
Brendan.

Travis wasn't angry with his sister's husband. Just like Ryan
and her parents, Dave simply wanted him to come home safely.
But tonight wasn't about the heavy stuff. Travis just wanted to listen to some music by the car, watch the postgame traffic dissipate,
and enjoy the Eagles' victory.

"Don't worry," he said to Dave, patting him on the back.
"Everything's going to be alright."

Nearly seventy thousand green-and-white-clad Philadelphia
Eagles fans packed Lincoln Financial Field that night, but only
a handful had fought for their country in Iraq or Afghanistan.
Travis was one of them, and probably the only fan who would
spend Super Bowl Sunday patrolling the streets of Fallujah. Even
after a prior Iraq deployment, it was impossible for the seasoned
Marine officer to predict what would happen after leaving the
City of Brotherly Love. Travis was only sure of one thing: he was
willing to die for every single person in that stadium.

After Dave got home from the game and gave his wife a hug,
Ryan asked him how the night went. Dave said it was fun, but at
the same time, he couldn't stop thinking about the exchange he'd
had with Travis as they left the stadium.

"I hope I didn't offend Trav by joking around about tripping
him and breaking his ankle," Dave said to his wife.

"Oh come on, Dave, I'm sure he knows you're just worried
about him," Ryan said. "We all are."

"Yeah, but one thing he said afterward really stuck with me," Dave said. "He talked about the Marines who'd have to go over there instead if he didn't go back."

After a pause, Dave repeated Travis's words.

"If not me, then who . . . "

———————•————————•———————

A few days later, Amy was at work in Arnold, Maryland, when a surprise visitor walked in. She gasped.

It was Brendan, who smiled and opened his huge arms to give her a hug. The Navy officer had just come from nearby Silver Spring, where he had surprised his mom, and couldn't wait to embrace Amy after three months in Iraq. He was finally home.

Later in the week, Brendan was calling friends to let them know he was back in the States. During one call, Amy wasn't sure who was on the other end of the line.

"It's your favorite," Brendan said with a smile.

Amy knew instantly that it was Travis. He and Brendan were coordinating hanging out during Travis's planned visit to Annapolis, where he would serve as a groomsman in the wedding of his friend Ben Mathews, whom Brendan had once given the friendliest of bloody noses at football practice.

"I can't believe Brendan surprised me like that," Amy said to Travis. "Did you know?"

"Guilty as charged," he said with a laugh.

"Well listen, Trav, I'm thrilled to have him home, but I want you to stay safe over there, too," Amy said. "I'll probably be at work when you come down to Maryland, so if I don't see you, good luck over there."

"Thanks, Amy," Travis said. "Take care of the big guy for me."

A few days later Travis and Brendan met up for the weekend in Annapolis before attending the Sunday Washington Redskins–Philadelphia Eagles game at FedEx Field in nearby Landover.

When they had gone to previous Redskins-Eagles games together in Philadelphia, Brendan had boldly entered a notoriously hostile environment to cheer on his hometown team. But sporting their sense of humor and mature realization that the winner of a football game didn't have a huge impact on the world, Brendan and Travis would occasionally trade jerseys and pretend to root for the opposing team. One time when Travis was being yelled at by a fellow Eagles fan, Brendan collapsed into his seat with laughter.

As always, the afternoon was filled with cold beer, great stories, and some friendly trash talk after the Eagles pulled out a 21–19 victory. The former roommates had once again switched jerseys to fool the fans around them.

"It's not going to be easy over there," Travis told his good friend as they walked out of the Redskins' stadium. "But I guess doing something important never is."

"Well, if there's one motto I try to live by, it's this," Brendan said. "If you make the most of what you are doing, there is no way to regret what you are doing."

"Thanks," said Travis. "I'll remember that one."

More than a hundred American troops were killed in Iraq in December 2006, including Major Megan McClung, the highest-ranking female Marine officer to die in the Iraq war and the first female Naval Academy graduate to be killed in combat. McClung was a thirty-four-year-old former classmate of now Major Doug Zembiec, the Naval Academy wrestler-turned-warrior whom Travis admired. She was killed along with two US Army soldiers by an enemy roadside bomb in Al Anbar province on December 6, less than three weeks before Travis was scheduled to arrive.

"It'll be tough for both of us," Travis now said. "But just think, the next time we hang out . . . you'll be a SEAL."

"Yeah, if I can make it through BUD/S," Brendan replied.

"You will," Travis assured him. "Just pretend I'm there trying to finish first."

"That might work," Brendan said with a grin. "And the next time I see you, you'll have made it out of Fallujah twice and probably be a captain."

Brendan, in a rare display of emotion, reached out to pat his friend on the back.

"You stay safe over there," Brendan said.

"I'll try," Travis said. "I'll definitely try."

After a few days that felt like old times, the onetime roommates were once again going their separate ways, like thousands of friends and family members separated by war. While predicting the future was impossible for any warrior deploying to Iraq or Afghanistan, the close friends couldn't have known that particular day's significance. It was the last time Brendan and Travis would see each other alive.

5

NO GREATER HONOR

All First Lieutenant Travis Manion could taste was chlorine as he vomited on the bombed-out rooftop of a Fallujah government building on the morning of March 28, 2007. Surrounded by explosions, vapor, gunfire, and debris as he looked down at a chaotic scene resembling the aftermath of the Oklahoma City bombing, the twenty-six-year-old Marine Corps officer for 3-2-1 MiTT felt as though he'd just swallowed a gallon of water from a filthy pool. This was the hellish reality of the Iraq war, in which Travis was embroiled in an al Qaeda chemical attack using two one-thousand-pound chlorine bombs.

Earlier, just after sunrise, American and Iraqi forces were scrambling to evacuate wounded personnel and secure the Fallujah Government Center's vulnerable perimeter when Travis and two fellow Marines appeared on the roof to relieve US Navy Lieutenant (SEAL) Eric Greitens and a young Marine, who were providing cover for troops below. Greitens had first awakened to deafening blasts and strange burning sensations at around 5:00 a.m., when terrorists unleashed chemical warfare on American troops, Iraqi soldiers, and bystanders.

"In the barracks, I heard men coughing around me, the air thick with dust. Then the burning started," Greitens later wrote in his book, *The Heart and the Fist*. "It felt as if someone had shoved an open-flame lighter inside my mouth, the flames scorching my throat and lungs."

Greitens was in the western barracks when gunfire and the massive first explosion rocked the entire compound. Travis, meanwhile, was asleep at the nearby civilian military operations center. He jumped out of his bunk when he heard the first explosion. It didn't sound like the usual mortar fire from al Qaeda and groups of Iraqi insurgents. This had to be something even more serious.

Before several of his fellow Marines, including First Lieutenant Chris Kim and Staff Sergeant Paul Petty, had the chance to blink, Travis was already dashing toward the command operations center (COC), which he helped operate, to radio Iraqi soldiers at the building to his west, where Greitens, other Americans, and their Iraqi partners were under attack.

"What the fuck is going on?" a bleary-eyed Petty shouted.

"I don't know, but I'm going over to the COC to find Manion," said Kim, quickly putting on his fatigues. "Meet us over there."

Travis was already on the radio to the Iraqis.

"This is the COC," he said. "We need to know if you have suffered any casualties."

The chaos of the attack, along with the already difficult language barrier, rendered Travis's efforts all but useless. Then an equally deafening second explosion shook the entire Fallujah Government Center, which put the Marines of 3-2-1 MiTT squarely in the middle of a coordinated, all-out terrorist assault.

As gunfire echoed through the compound and lights flickered all around the Marines, Petty came darting down the hall to find Travis putting together a plan.

"Shit, I think we lost radio contact in that last explosion," Travis said. "We need to get the hell over there and help those guys."

"What we need is a four-man team," he continued, looking at Kim. "Chris, grab two men and come with me."

"What do you want me to do, Lieutenant?" Petty, still confused after waking up to the alarming jolt, asked Travis.

"We need airpower and tanks," Travis said. "You're the communications guy, so get up on the roof and get us some communications."

"Yes, sir," said Petty, who had trusted and admired Travis since they trained at Twentynine Palms together before their first deployment. Whether it was having a few beers after a long day of training, stacking sandbags during the historic October 2005 Iraqi constitutional referendum, or conducting raids on high-value targets, Petty, who enlisted out of love for God and country, always felt safe around Lieutenants Manion and Kim. If they asked him to follow them to the gates of hell, Petty wouldn't hesitate.

As bursts of enemy gunfire and blasts from rocket-propelled grenades (RPGs) rattled out from the west, Petty carried a large antenna and other radio equipment to the south building's roof. By that time Travis had already loaded his M-4 rifle, which had an M-203 grenade launcher attached. Travis was already known for using the grenade launcher, which many of the Marines referred to as his "badass M-203," effectively on the battlefield.

With bullets flying everywhere, presumably from insurgents outside the gates and Iraqi Army soldiers firing back, Travis, Kim, and two fellow Marines ran a distance of about two football fields to the western building, which was covered with powder and residue from the chemical bombs. The white-walled barracks building, which looked like it was being pummeled during the frigid World War II battle of Stalingrad, was riddled with bullet holes and all but gutted on one side.

Although gunfire was sporadic and vigilant guards had just stopped two more terrorists at the gate, who had detonated their suicide vests, the situation remained perilous for Travis and everyone else inside the blood- and chlorine-soaked compound. If the outside looked like Stalingrad, the inside of the barracks felt like a Russian bathhouse. It was hot, uncomfortable, and smelled like a collection of large pools.

Travis, coughing and trying to cover his nose and mouth, asked Iraqi soldiers if they were alright as they ran past him trying to escape the dispersing chlorine. He didn't see any dead bodies, but assumed there were many in need of help. In order to evacuate the wounded, however, Travis knew someone had to guard against another attack. He again looked toward First Lieutenant Kim.

"Chris, you stay down here and help these people," Travis said. "I'm taking these two [Marines] and heading up to the roof."

Travis didn't need an engineering background to know that the building could easily collapse. With an entire side of the barracks cut open by a massive bomb blast, ascending to the roof could have been a death sentence. But much like the brave firefighters he had recently visited in lower Manhattan, Travis put the safety of others ahead of his own.

Taking one last deep breath before plunging into the chlorine vapor and heading up the stairs, the young Marine ran straight into a precarious situation.

Greitens, the Navy SEAL, later wrote in his book that he was in desperate condition just before Travis arrived: "The sun rose. We felt the heat of the day begin to sink into the roof. We waited. We watched. My breathing was still shallow, and I felt as if someone had tightened a belt around my lungs and was pulling hard to kill me."

As the weakening SEAL's skin and lungs burned from the desert sun and weaponized chlorine, the arrival of an already queasy, slightly disoriented Travis was a welcome sight.

"You got it?" Greitens, who had been on prior patrols with Travis, asked.

"Yeah, I got your back, sir," Travis told the SEAL.

Greitens would never forget him.

Fortunately, Petty had established communications from the other building, and US tanks were arriving. It was time for Greitens and the young Marine to get to the hospital before breathing became impossible.

Shortly after Greitens left for the hospital, Travis threw up. With the sun bearing down from above, the ground below him was still littered with wounded Iraqis and Americans. As Travis pointed his rifle toward the chaos, it was incredibly difficult to distinguish good guys from bad amid so much confusion, yelling, and gunfire. To make matters worse, there were still body parts from the two al Qaeda suicide bombers littered near the front entrance. A stray cat was dragging around a dead terrorist's severed hand.

After throwing up a few more times, Travis rallied to push his physical symptoms aside, knowing from the hellish sights below that many could be killed in a subsequent explosion or firefight. Every time his stomach churned or his eyes started to burn, Travis would block out the discomfort and focus on his responsibility to save lives. After identifying the area from which insurgents were still shooting, Travis pointed his rifle and began to fire.

Major Joel Poudrier, a Marine officer whose head had been wrapped by MiTT team Navy Hospital Corpsman Edwin Albino after it was nearly crushed by falling debris, was subsequently flown to Baghdad for urgent medical care. In addition to Poudrier and Greitens, fifteen US troops were wounded and experiencing severe complications from the explosion and chlorine vapor, while seventy Iraqi troops were injured. Thanks to the rescue effort, which was protected by Travis and his rooftop security team, all were evacuated from the blast zone safely. Every American survived.

Later, when Greitens told the wounded major that Travis was the first Marine from the other building to run through more than two hundred yards of bullet-filled chaos to relieve him of his post and secure the battle zone, Poudrier wasn't surprised. Travis had been running toward danger during the entire deployment, and the major had once been moved to try to calm him down.

"Hey, man, you don't have to get shot at every single time," the higher-ranking officer told Travis after about a month in Fallujah.

"Take it easy. . . . It's a long deployment, and we need you to stick around."

Travis appreciated the advice, but tried to explain that he was just doing his best to get the Iraqis ready.

"I understand that, Travis," Poudrier said. "But you can try to let other people lead from the front once in a while."

Poudrier knew it was almost impossible for a warrior like Travis to let anyone step in front of him. But when the major was later wounded during the chemical bomb attack, Travis rushing toward the chaos played a large part in Poudrier being safely evacuated.

As the story of the chemical attack was subsequently told, Travis and his Marines—the guardian angels—were applauded for risking their lives to take the rooftop and shield the Americans and Iraqis below from more danger.

It is no wonder that shortly following the March 9, 2007, release of the movie *300*, which was playing to full movie theaters back in Doylestown and all over the United States, Travis was among the first US service members in Iraq to get his hands on a bootlegged copy. The intense action film, full of triumphant rhetoric and bloody battle scenes from Greece's epic conflict with the Persians in the Battle of Thermopylae in 480 BC, inspired Travis as he fought a ruthless enemy in one of the world's most dangerous places.

"Spartans never retreat," the film's narrator proclaims. "Spartans never surrender."

Although Travis arrived in Iraq in late December 2006 and didn't see the movie until mid-March, the film, like the Steven Pressfield book *Gates of Fire*, which all Marine officers read at TBS in Quantico, had a huge influence on the rest of Travis's deployment. Just as King Leonidas (played by Gerard Butler) repeatedly tells the 299 fellow Spartans he leads into battle, Travis believed there was nothing more honorable than sacrificing everything for the country he loved. He didn't want to die, but if that was the result of his second deployment to Iraq, so be it.

"Freedom isn't free at all," Queen Gorgo, played by Lena Headey, says in the film. "It comes with the highest of costs: the cost of blood."

———————●————————

Travis had seen his share of blood, but had never needed to wash any from his hands. That all changed in January, less than a month after he returned to Fallujah for his second deployment.

Although the city had been violent during his first deployment, when Travis's role was split between administrative duties and running supply convoys to units on the front lines, early 2007 was an even more dangerous time. Skepticism over whether the strengthening insurgency in western Iraq could ever be defeated was growing in Beltway circles, and less than three months before Travis returned to Fallujah, some inside the military were questioning whether an area where so much American blood and treasure had been spilled could ever be turned around.

"The chief of intelligence for the Marine Corps in Iraq recently filed an unusual secret report concluding that the prospects for securing that country's western Anbar province are dim and there is almost nothing the U.S. military can do to improve the political and social situation there, said several military officers and intelligence officials familiar with its contents," Thomas E. Ricks wrote on the fifth anniversary of the 9/11 attacks.

With the troop surge that President Bush would eventually order in January 2007 being hotly debated, most press reports about the Iraq war, along with public opinion polls, were decidedly negative.

"(Colonel Pete) Devlin reports that there are no functioning Iraqi government institutions in Anbar, leaving a vacuum that has been filled by the insurgent group al Qaeda in Iraq, which has become the province's most significant political force, said the Army officer, who has read the report," Ricks wrote. "Another person familiar with the report said it describes Anbar as beyond repair; a third said it concludes that the United States has lost in Anbar."

Travis, who called home as often as he could from the war zone, had a much different view. He was in Fallujah when the troop surge started, and he believed more Marines would help the US and Iraqi militaries turn the tide against al Qaeda once and for all.

"We're close to getting the job done, dad," Travis said in one phone call. "The extra support is really going to help the Marines on the ground over here."

Travis and his fellow MiTT members went on combat patrols virtually every day, sometimes running as many as three missions over a punishing eighteen-hour span. In Fallujah and throughout Iraq, Marines, soldiers, sailors, airmen, and Iraqi troops did everything from hunting insurgents and enemy weapons caches to disposing of dead bodies. Using his operational expertise and prior experience with Fallujah's jagged urban terrain, Travis planned many missions and would often use PowerPoint slides to prepare his team for the day's operations. The Marine's planning was so meticulous that Petty, who had served with Travis in Fallujah a year earlier, would sometimes needle him about the detail of his presentations.

"Hey, sir, how about you keep the next one to five slides instead of twenty," Petty once joked.

Travis laughed and took the teasing in stride. In the first lieutenant's mind, there was no substitute for thorough preparation, and he would leave no stone unturned before leading Marines into one of the most dangerous cities on the planet.

Adding to 3-2-1 MiTT's challenges were joint patrols with the Iraqis through some of Fallujah's most dangerous sectors. The Iraqi soldiers would sometimes respond to the slightest sign of violence with what some US team members nicknamed the "Iraqi death blossom." When a shot was fired in their direction, the Iraqis would sometimes form a circle and fire in every direction, with little regard for the consequences, including tragically catching innocent civilians in the crossfire. Civilian casualties were a sometimes unavoidable reality of war, but Travis and his fellow Marines were determined to use every means at their disposal to prevent them.

While some MiTT team members understandably became frustrated with the often untrained, underpaid Iraqi soldiers, Travis positioned himself as a mentor. During lunch, he would bring his chow to their mess hall and sit with Nick, an Iraqi translator who helped bridge the gap between the US and Iraqi armies. They talked not only about combat strategy, but about simple things like soccer. That July, Iraq's national soccer team was scheduled to compete for the Asian Football Cup, and the sport seemed to be the only thing that truly united the war-torn country's Sunni and Shiite populations. Travis used his appreciation of soccer to forge an initial connection with the Iraqi troops, who he knew were essential to the overall US mission in Anbar province.

The senior officer of 3-2-1 MiTT was Major Adam Kubicki, a thirty-five-year-old Marine from Kenosha, Wisconsin, on his first deployment to Fallujah. Travis, Kim, and Jonathan Marang were the first lieutenants, along with Navy Lieutenant JG Jared Tracy, while Second Lieutenant Scott Alexander was the MiTT team's junior officer. The rest of the team was made up of enlisted personnel, including Petty and several other young men from cities and towns across America. They had different backgrounds, beliefs, and stories, but all had joined the Navy and Marine Corps to serve their country. Fallujah was about as close as it got to hell, but serving there in 2007 also represented a chance for these twenty- and thirtysomethings to make history.

Travis, raised Roman Catholic and in possession of a strong moral compass instilled by Tom, Janet, and his grandparents, hated the idea of killing another human being. He read about death, watched movies about death, and talked to other Marines about death, but had never actually had to kill anyone during his first deployment. Yet when a sniper fired at him on one January morning in Fallujah, Travis did what he was trained to do, without hesitation.

While walking on foot with enlisted US Marines and Iraqi soldiers on a patrol through one of the city's notoriously narrow streets, with low-hanging power lines blocking the view from the high-rises and towers above, crackles of gunfire began echoing through the alley. Travis and the other Marines instantly took cover as Travis shouted to the Iraqi troops in Arabic, a language that he was gradually learning, to hold their fire.

After ensuring that Iraqi Army bullets would not start flying into surrounding houses and apartments full of civilians, Travis scanned the area and saw a figure and flashes of light from the top of a tower. It was an enemy sniper, and though his aim was poor, he was a threat to Travis's entire patrol.

With his M-203 grenade launcher loaded and attached to his M-4 rifle, Travis, with the same look in his eyes that had once intimidated wrestling opponents, took aim and fired at the tower. The sound of the grenade launch was initially merely a pop—louder than opening a can of Pringles but not much more dramatic—but when it struck the tower it was as loud as any explosion the MiTT team members had heard during almost nightly enemy mortar attacks.

When Travis's grenade hit the tower, the explosion and crumbling stone left no doubt that the target had been eliminated. The gunshots immediately stopped, and other than some hooting from the Marines, the alley was quiet. It was then that Travis knew for sure that he had just killed a man.

Later that night on the outskirts of Fallujah, where he often slept, a somber Travis placed a call to Major Steve Cantrell, the friend and mentor who had taken him on the momentous visit to the Rescue One firehouse in lower Manhattan just before he left for his second deployment.

After exchanging greetings and catching up on how things were going back in Pennsylvania, Travis told Cantrell about his unit's violent encounter with an enemy sniper.

"I killed him," Travis said. "I had no choice."

After a brief pause, the Marine asked Cantrell for help.

"I'm not sure how to deal with this," Travis said. "I've never killed anyone before, and even though I know this was one of the bad guys, I can't stop thinking about it."

"I understand, Travis," Cantrell said. "But you said this guy was trying to kill you and your Marines, right?"

"Right," Travis said.

"You did exactly what you were supposed to do," Cantrell said. "You did exactly what you were trained to do, and if you didn't, your mom or another Marine's mom might be getting a knock on the door right now."

Just like seeing the uniform patches of firefighters killed in the 9/11 attacks, Cantrell's words helped the first lieutenant put his mission into perspective. Nothing mattered more to Travis than the safety of his fellow Marines, and if his actions helped ensure that no MiTT team members were killed, he would have no regrets. Travis thanked Cantrell for his advice.

On January 25, 2007, Travis sent an e-mail to his friends and family members as the first month of his second deployment came to a close:

> All,
>
> It's been great to hear from all of you. I've gotten a lot of e-mails and I really appreciate them. We've been really busy doing good things, which makes the time go by fast.
>
> As far as the job is going, the area is not good right now— but it's getting better, and to be honest I'm amazed at the ability and dedication of some of these Iraqi soldiers. There is definitely a good amount of deficiencies with the IA's (Iraqi Army members), but overall I feel we have a strong and aggressive battalion. Our team is settling in and we are awaiting our additional augments. These additional Marines will greatly increase our size and they are arriving very soon. This will take a good deal of the workload off the existing

members, and will allow us to concentrate more on advising and training these guys; getting them to the point where they are self-reliant.

After a month on the job I can definitely say the experience here with the IA's so far has been very interesting and educational. I have a couple of jobs right now (working with the battalion logistics section and advising one of the line companies). These have both posed an equally worthy challenge, but honestly the company advising has been much easier than dealing with their lack of logistic support. The IA's in this battalion are very eager to fight and to take control of this city. This makes my company advisor job easy (for the Marines on this list it's almost like being an SPC at The Basic School, albeit in a very different setting). Contrary to reports in other IA battalions the company I work with is pretty competent operationally.

That's pretty much it, I hope this e-mail finds you all well and gives a little insight into what I've been up to. It's been a very challenging Relief-In-Place during a very difficult time in this area of operations, but there is nothing more inspiring on a daily basis than seeing the dedication, warrior ethos, and sacrifice of the men and women out here fighting this fight. It was at times frustrating the first time I was here and it will and has been this time, but as in anything in life, true success does not come from battles won easy.

Semper Fi,

Travis

Indeed, 3-2-1 MiTT's mission would not be easy, especially as some proclaimed the battle in Anbar province already lost. But as US Army General David Petraeus, the new commander of Multinational Force-Iraq, began implementing a troop surge and innovative counterinsurgency strategy aimed at winning the hearts and minds of Iraqis, it was the blood, sweat, and measured restraint of ground warriors like Travis who gave the new Iraq war plan, which faced enormous opposition at home and abroad, a chance to succeed.

Although almost every American agreed that Saddam Hussein was an evil dictator, the failure to find weapons of mass destruction in Iraq had significantly damaged trust in the Bush administration, which argued that Iraq was central to its post-9/11 strategy to defeat terrorism. By early 2007 the American public was split over the Iraq war, but also confused. What was the mission in Iraq? Why were so many US troops still dying after Saddam had been deposed and executed? Shouldn't the focus of our military be in Afghanistan, where Osama bin Laden was still at large? What did Iraq have to do with the global war on terrorism?

At dinner tables across the country, varying answers to these questions were proposed and refuted by supporters and opponents of the Iraq war. Every member of the MiTT team knew both sides of the debate and had his own opinion about the mission in Iraq, how it should be accomplished, and whether it was a war worth fighting in the first place. The irony was that in Fallujah, one of Iraq's most lethal places, the answers to the war's many questions could be answered rather easily.

Of everyone on the MiTT team, Travis may have understood that the most, as a January 22, 2007, e-mail from his mom to concerned family and friends highlighted:

> Travis is now in Fallujah or nearby embedded with an Iraqi unit. He is one of 11 or so Marines attached with that unit to help their mission along.
>
> He told Tom a story last week about the Iraqi Colonel briefing them upon their arrival. The Colonel addressed them by saying he appreciated all that they are doing for the Iraqi people and their help is much needed. Travis said he expressed that they want to succeed. He also asked them to remember, whenever you think of Iraq and the situation here, think of us and our desire to win.

Though the Iraqi colonel's words were moving, Travis knew any missteps or perceived disrespect toward the Iraqis by the US Marines could quickly render their shared mission meaningless. The MiTT team could help capture or kill hundreds of insurgents and terrorists during the deployment, but it wouldn't matter unless Iraqi troops and civilians in Fallujah finally stepped up to prevent more bad guys from using the battered city as a launching pad.

"We need to do more than just fight," Travis told Kim, a fellow officer who was quickly becoming a trusted friend. "We need to show these Iraqis that we care."

In February 2007, Fallujah was full of terrorists who wanted to kill as many Americans as possible. Though the enemy was often portrayed in news reports as "Iraqi insurgents," al Qaeda loyalists of almost every nationality under the brutal desert sun were using western Iraq as the launching pad for attacks against US troops, Iraqi soldiers, men, women, and children. If there was one place in the world serving as a vacuum for fanatical Islamic extremists, Al Anbar province was at the very top of the list.

The only way to defeat such a ruthless enemy, General Petraeus and others believed, was not only to confront al Qaeda militarily in cities like Fallujah, but to get enough Iraqi soldiers and civilians to buy into history's oldest concept: good and evil. While controversy over the invasion, worldwide scandals like Abu Ghraib, and thousands of years of history made the new strategy seem impossible to some, it was clear that Travis and his team members were not in Iraq to shoot innocent people or blow up hospitals, schools, or places of worship. They were young and hardened, but also decent and noble. Because they communicated with Iraqi troops mostly through interpreters and broken English and Arabic, their actions had to speak louder than words. The Iraqi people had to see the difference between US troops and foreign terrorists.

That same month, Travis sat down at his forward operating base in Fallujah to check his e-mail. The deployed Marine smiled when he saw one from Brendan, who was getting ready to leave for BUD/S training in Coronado, California:

Travis,

I am the worst friend ever. . . . I am sorry I have not written you and that you have not gotten my care package yet. On the plus side, the longer I wait the more magazines you get, so I guess it could be worse.

Well I have my orders. . . . I'll check out of Virginia Beach in two weeks, go home for a few days and then Steve-O and I are going to hit the open road. We have not decided on a route yet, but are leaning towards driving to New Orleans and then through Austin or San Antonio, but who knows, there is also Nashville. TBD though.

I am working out . . . not too hard but not too soft. . . . Everyone I talk to tells me not to over train so I am trying to keep that in mind.

Well that's about it, I hope all is well and I will talk to you soon.

—Brendan

Before packing up for that night's combat patrol, Travis sent a reply:

Brendan,

Good to hear from you, brother. Don't worry about it; I'm sure you're really busy, as am I.

Things are going well over here. I'm not sure how to read the current situation here; it's definitely different than when I was here last year. I'm just trying to focus on my piece and affect positive change where I can. We're getting close to the two-month mark so the time here is definitely going fast—there have been some pretty intense days. Working with my team has been somewhat frustrating. Since the mission is somewhat gray, there are a lot of different views on how it should be accomplished. I'm sure we'll talk about it later over some beers, so I won't bore you too much.

Looks like you're ready to head off to SoCal. Get the place ready for me. . . . I know you'll be somewhat indisposed, but I may be in Coronado before you know it. What is the actual start date? I think you got the right advice about not training too hard. None of that crap is actually a physically hard event on its own; it's just designed to break you down time after time. They told us when I was training for BRC [Basic Recon Course] that you need to be in good enough shape to get through it and recover without any issues, but too much workload will just break you down before you even get there. The thing I concentrated on a lot was swimming/finning because it was low impact, a good workout, and I just wasn't that good at it at the time.

That's pretty much it. I hope the last weeks of prep go well (remember to take some time to relax before you go). It sounds like you'll have some fun going (cross)-country with Steve. Tell him and Billy I said what's up, as well as the rest of the family. I've gotten some e-mails from your parents, so please tell them I really appreciate it. Keep me updated when you can, it's good to hear from you. Alright bro, take care. Talk to you soon,
Travis

Most 3-2-1 MiTT raids were at night. Morning or afternoon patrols through the heart of the city were often suicide missions, as American Humvees might as well have had the words "attack us" painted on their front doors. As an essential part of mission planning, Travis would often interact with Iraqi lieutenants and staff sergeants who were initially skeptical of a partnership with the Americans.

Just as some US Marines became frustrated by the raw battlefield tactics of the Iraqis, which could put all their lives at risk, some Iraqi soldiers rolled their eyes when Americans gave them orders. Whereas previous Marine lieutenants had barked instructions at the Iraqi Army leadership, Travis took a different approach, starting with a knock on the door of the Iraqi lieutenant, Jalal.

"Good day, Lieutenant, I was wondering if I could please speak with you about the upcoming raid on the high value target in the industrial sector," Travis said through the interpreter, Nick. "I was wondering what time you would like to execute our mission."

"I think 5 p.m. would be a good time to leave," Jalal replied. "My men had a long day and I don't want to keep them up too late."

"Okay," Travis said. "But I am wondering if you might consider leaving a bit later, possibly after sunset? My concern is that our presence during daylight could endanger neighbors who live near the house we're going to strike, not to mention little children who could be playing in the street. Respectfully, Lieutenant, I wouldn't want to be the one to tell their parents that their son or daughter might still be alive if we [had] waited a couple more hours."

After a pause and a sip of water, the Iraqi officer nodded. The raid would not start until 8:00 p.m.

The high-value-target raid on that evening in February 2007 was aimed at capturing or killing a terrorist who had come to Fallujah all the way from Sudan. The suspect and the weapons he was smuggling into the city were almost certainly responsible for the deaths of several Iraqis and US troops, and taking him out was essential.

"Let's go get this bag of trash," Petty said before slamming the door of his Humvee. "We own the night."

The Marines and Iraqis, equipped with thermal night vision, turned off their vehicle lights as their patrol descended on the suspected terrorist safe house. The Marines pulled up front, while the Iraqis parked just around the corner to keep watch. Above them, an F/A-18 provided reconnaissance from the night sky.

Travis, who had kicked in plenty of doors since his first days
of Mojave Viper training in faux Iraqi villages, led the way inside
the tiny, decaying house. But soon after they entered and got into
position, it became apparent nobody was home.

"Your squeaker's getting away," the F/A-18 pilot said over the
radio. "He's headed for the mosque."

"Motherfucker," Petty said from the Humvee. "These bastards
never cease to amaze me."

As Travis and a fellow Marine, Sergeant Rich Olsen, walked
out of the house, conversation outside shifted toward storming the
mosque. Surely, some on the team believed, the end would justify
the means, as the consequences of a bunch of Americans entering
a holy site couldn't be any worse than allowing a Sudanese terrorist to continue killing kids with his guns and bombs.

"Negative," said Travis, interrupting one of the Marines who
was talking about storming the mosque. "This is what we have the
Iraqis here for."

Not only could Muslim soldiers enter the mosque, but Travis,
Kubicki, and fellow MiTT team officers had spent valuable time
fostering a relationship with the local cleric. While the "bag of
trash" probably thought he had found his night's refuge, Travis
smiled as American and Iraqi troops cordoned off the mosque's
exterior. This guy had no idea what was about to hit him.

Minutes after a phone call to the cleric, Iraqi soldiers were
dragging the foreign suspect out of the mosque, where many of
their families prayed to Allah. All the American forces could initially do was watch as some Iraqi soldiers muttered expletives and
pushed around the defeated suspect.

While Travis and his fellow Marines wouldn't tolerate violence against any defenseless prisoner, they also understood the
line between abuse and justice. The Iraqi soldiers regarded the
Sudanese terrorist as the NYPD would 9/11 mastermind Khalid
Sheikh Mohammed if he were captured in lower Manhattan. To
the Iraqi troops, this was a murderer who had no business inside

their country, and until the Americans intervened and took possession of the prisoner, they were going to get some payback. As was the case on any battlefield, emotions were running at levels that civilians who had never experienced them could not possibly comprehend. It certainly wasn't the first time in history that an enemy combatant had been greeted with anger by his captors.

When the Iraqis handed over the prisoner to the Americans, Travis and Olsen took him to a makeshift interrogation room on a nearby forward operating base (FOB). Because of the Sudanese terrorist's capture, one or more innocent Iraqi teenagers who would have been blown up as children are probably walking the streets of Fallujah today. The raid was a small but significant victory for both the MiTT team and the people of Iraq, and it went a long way toward building trust with the Iraqi soldiers, who appreciated the help of Travis and his patrol in making it happen.

On February 25, 2007, a tired but upbeat Travis sent another update to the e-mail list that included Tom, Janet, Ryan, Brendan, and many other close friends and relatives:

> All,
>
> My job is definitely going well. After all the horror stories we heard about the Iraqi Army and their unwillingness to work with the MiTTs (us), they have been very open and willing to listen to advice. Creating an initial relationship with my counterparts was the right move and it has allowed me to really help them start shaping operations. There are many dedicated men in this Army and it's been an eye-opening experience so far. The best IA's are definitely dedicated to their cause and have a warrior mentality that rivals some Americans. However, there are still those enemies out there that wish us to fail.
>
> There is a lot of work left to do, but the city is definitely at a different place than it was last year. I really feel that it is at a critical point where if the situation continues to

progress it could have a huge positive impact in the area. Also, I have found a good balance between my logistics job and my company advisor role. Although going on operations definitely requires a good amount of time, I am able to work with the battalion logistics officer on a fairly regular basis.

I also appreciate all the good food and gear that has been sent. Workouts and your support have definitely helped keep me going. As I said before, we're pretty busy, but I wanted to take a minute to thank you guys for everything and keep you updated.

Please continue to write-I enjoy your updates as well. Take care and I'll talk to you soon.

Semper Fi,

Travis

In Fallujah, where Travis had spent the majority of the previous eighteen months, the Marine could feel the tide beginning to turn. He was a part of history, not only because he was one of the few Americans there to see it, but because he was helping make it happen.

As Travis patrolled some of the most volatile sections of Fallujah's eight square miles, in which every house represented a possible IED factory or sniper hideout, it was obvious to everyone on the MiTT team that he had been to the city before. The calm, composed Marine exhibited the exact blend of experience and toughness the team needed to weather almost daily threats and what seemed like constant explosions and firefights. Travis was also eager to respond when someone needed help.

Eleven days before the massive chlorine attack, on March 17, 2007, Sergeant Justin Bales, a US Marine reservist and New York City firefighter, found himself pinned down behind a bulldozer. He was holding a bleeding Iraqi soldier who had been wounded by artillery shrapnel and a sniper's bullet. After Bales and Lieutenant

JG Jared Tracy pulled the Iraqi out of the street, only a bulldozer bucket separated them from a hail of enemy fire.

As a firefighter and Marine, Bales was accustomed to dicey situations. But with insurgents bearing down, it was only a matter of time before Bales, Tracy, and the wounded Iraqi would be killed. Bales had already tried radioing for help, but to his knowledge, nobody was volunteering for the risky rescue assignment.

Suddenly the direction of the enemy machine gun fire changed. A few seconds later, it was clear that the insurgents were firing at someone else.

Sure enough, their target was Travis and Kubicki. If anyone was bold enough to volunteer for what some might have considered a suicide mission, it was Travis and 3-2-1 MiTT. Knowing that a quick reaction force had finally arrived, Bales and Tracy could redirect their attention to caring for the wounded Iraqi soldier.

As the American force strengthened, the enemy began to retreat. The insurgents were simply no match for the increased US firepower, and after a few minutes the battle was over.

"Hey, Lieutenant," Bales later told Travis. "I appreciate you coming out here, sir."

"Anytime, Sarge," Travis said. "That's what we're here for."

The next morning Travis and his teammates awoke around 5:30 a.m. to a huge explosion. A few minutes later, they learned that Observation Post Baghdad—a new makeshift base they had been working to set up in Fallujah—was a pile of rubble.

"We were scheduled to be there today at 0800," Petty said upon hearing the news. "I guess that makes us all pretty fucking lucky."

"Let's get over there now," Travis said. "We need to cordon off the area and see if anyone is still alive."

The Marines took two Humvees to the explosion site, having no idea what they would encounter. Travis, Kubicki, Kim, Petty, Alexander, Sergeant Matthew Hill, Navy Hospital Corpsman Second Class Edwin "Doc" Albino, and others arrived to find a scary scene, which resembled Oklahoma City or even 9/11. A building had been partially destroyed after barrels full of explosives were placed inside a shop at the lowest level of the multistory complex. Iraqis inside the chaotic blast zone were fleeing to escape being crushed by rubble or caught in another attack. To make matters even worse, insurgents were peppering a then-shaky perimeter with small arms fire.

"Let's get this area secure!" Kubicki shouted, pointing toward the rubble, where people were almost certainly trapped.

"Roger that, I'm already on it," Travis said as Kim, Petty, and others tackled security. "Doc, let's go."

With gunfire initially surrounding them before a secure perimeter was established, Travis, Albino, and others spent the next eight hours entering and reentering the rubble while their team members controlled the crowd outside. For all they knew, the rest of the bombed-out complex could have crumbled, or there could have been another bomb timed to go off when the quick reaction force team arrived. They went into the ruins anyway.

Carrying a large flashlight, Travis crawled into the rubble. Sweating profusely due to the heat, which was exacerbated by small fires burning throughout the compound, Travis dug through dirt, sand, and remnants of brick, searching for trapped Iraqis.

"I think I see someone down there," Travis told Albino after eyeballing some movement in a dark area under the first floor's collapsed ceiling.

"I'll check it out," said Albino, who had barely taken a sip of water in four hours. "Keep looking for others."

"Doc, Travis, anyone else, do you need a break?" Petty asked over the radio from his Humvee. It was about 90 degrees outside, which wasn't as hot as usual, but still daunting considering the amount of gear Travis and Albino were carrying.

"Negative," Travis and Albino answered virtually simultaneously.

About twenty minutes later, Albino and a US Army reservist helped carry an Iraqi soldier out of the debris. The crowd, which would normally have been hostile to the Americans, was mostly supportive as the Navy corpsman and Army reservist carried their injured Iraqi partner out of the devastated structure's ruins. Cut and bleeding, the Iraqi soldier's leg had been all but shattered by falling concrete.

"I think this might need to be amputated," said Albino, the MiTT team's medic.

"I've got an ambulance right over there," Travis told him. "Do you think there's time to get him to a hospital?"

"Yes, sir," Albino replied.

Soldiers from the 1st Iraqi Army Division, which 3-2-1 MiTT was training, watched as Travis, covered in dust, dirt, and blood, helped the badly wounded Iraqi to the ambulance and continued coordinating with Petty, Albino, and others. After several hours of being on the scene with Travis, Lieutenant Jalal turned to a fellow Iraqi officer.

"Here is an American who really cares," he said.

Travis stopped to wipe his face with a towel and take a quick sip of water before returning to the ruins. After a few minutes of crawling, he found another Iraqi soldier pinned down, by twisted metal piping that Superman would have struggled to lift.

"I am going to help you," Travis said to the Iraqi. "You're going to be okay."

Mixing in some broken Arabic, Travis tried to comfort the scared, thirsty Iraqi, who could barely understand what the US Marine was saying but could tell he was there to help. After giving him the water that was left in his canteen, Travis got on the radio and began asking someone to bring an industrial saw to cut through the metal piping and free the trapped Iraqi.

"Umm . . . we don't have one of those here, Lieutenant," a Marine told Travis.

"Well then, we need to find out who does," Travis responded. "This guy is being crushed."

With simultaneous insurgent attacks all around them, finding the necessary equipment, even to save lives, was difficult. But after many more radio calls from the persistent Marine officer, who wouldn't take no for an answer, a unit found the saw and rushed to the scene to free the wounded Iraqi. He survived.

Travis, Albino, and their teammates recovered two injured Iraqis and two dead bodies from the attack site. Their selfless actions had an enduring impact on many of the Iraqis who bore witness.

Less than twenty-four hours later, Travis's ears were ringing after an IED blew up beneath his vehicle. The blast's jarring, pounding force loudly and abruptly halted his vehicle's patrol through the city's volatile eastern industrial sector.

Travis had encountered IEDs during his first deployment and as recently as nine days earlier. After ensuring that fellow Americans and Iraqis were uninjured, Travis looked down at the sandy street, where the crude explosive device was buried.

"See that wire?" Travis said to another Iraqi lieutenant. "That's a command wire, and it's stretching toward that building."

"Gather your men and follow me," he said to the Iraqi before turning to his Marines. "You and the other guys cover us in case there are snipers."

"Lieutenant, why don't we just leave?" the Iraqi said to Travis.

"Because they'll keep planting bombs around here and kill more of my men, more of your men, and probably some kids," Travis said. "So respectfully, Lieutenant, I'm going over there to find who's responsible, with or without you."

After a brief pause, the Iraqi lieutenant got three of his men and followed Travis as he traced the command wire's origin.

Rounding a corner, Travis saw a man in civilian clothes kneeling over what appeared to be a pile of grenades, which along with the attached wires, appeared to be some sort of booby trap. Without hesitation, Travis squared up to confront the threat.

The Marines out on the street heard the pop of Travis's M-203 grenade launcher and the subsequent explosion. Several ran toward the sound, while others stayed to keep watch over the exterior.

The tall, sweaty insurgent took off running, now being chased by a fearless, determined Marine. Travis had a bad guy in his sights, and he wasn't going to let him get away.

"Stop," Travis shouted in Arabic while pursuing the suspect.

By the time the US and Iraqi reinforcements arrived, Travis was dragging the frightened suspect down off a wall he had tried to scale in an unsuccessful attempt to escape. After body-slamming him to the ground, Travis put the insurgent's hands behind his back, then made sure he was taken in for questioning.

The suspect eventually led the MiTT team to a room not far from the booby trap, which contained grenades and many more bomb-making materials. Without losing any lives or ruffling more feathers in the Sunni enclave, Travis had helped remove deadly weapons and another terrorist from Fallujah's streets.

———•———

Half a world away in California, about three hours from the desert where Travis had trained for his two Iraq deployments, Brendan was about to embark on his most difficult challenge since 9/11: BUD/S training. While his cross-country drive and Travis's daily combat missions made it difficult for the close friends to communicate, the focused Navy SEAL candidate put his feelings on paper in a March 22, 2007, journal entry:

> So tomorrow is the big day. Checking into BUD/S. Kind of crazy to think I was in South Korea this time last year. I feel like I should be more nervous than I am. This is kind of like a big game, but I have played in plenty of those situations before so maybe my body is used to it. (My brother) Steve and I drove out here almost two weeks ago with stops in Nashville and Austin. Austin was by far the best and we were able to see [a good friend]. Good times. Nashville was not too bad either though.

I am living in IB (Imperial Beach), pretty low key. It is no Coronado, but it will work. I am living with Rob Sarver also. Together he and I will crush BUD/S. Up first is the big inspection. We will see what it has to bring. Other than that, it is just some other check in stuff. I am looking forward to the challenge and plan to excel.

———•————————•———

Back in Fallujah, the MiTT team's morale was surprisingly high as April began, especially considering that they had already been in a miserable, violent place for three months.

"We're fucking invincible right now," one Marine said.

Travis didn't respond. He felt fortunate not to have lost any MiTT team members so far in the deployment, yet he knew the cruel randomness of war could leave several Marines—or even him—dead in a split second. Still, 3-2-1 MiTT seemed to be defying the Iraq war's steep odds.

He took things one day at a time, waking up every morning with another quote from *300* in the back of his mind: "Today, no Spartan dies."

After speaking with Lieutenant Jalal one morning about the coming day's mission, Travis turned to Nick, the interpreter who helped him communicate with Iraqi troops.

"What do you think of all the crazy things we're seeing here?" Travis asked the Iraqi.

"I don't know," Nick said. "But thanks to you, I know what Saddam used to say about all Americans being bad isn't true."

After nodding to acknowledge his kind words, Travis asked Nick where he hoped to end up after the war was over.

"I want to go to your country," Nick said. "I want to go to school and start a new life."

"That's good," Travis said. "America would be lucky to have you.

"Listen," he continued. "If there is anything I can do to help you, like a recommendation or getting your paperwork to the right people, make sure to let me know."

"Thank you, Lieutenant," Nick said.

After his conversation with the interpreter, Travis briefed his team on what would be another full day of danger in Fallujah's narrow, treacherous alleys.

"Spartans, prepare for glory," Travis announced, to laughter from Petty and others. The Marines had already heard him quote enough *300* lines to feel like they'd seen the entire movie.

While helping turn the tide in Fallujah, First Lieutenant Travis Manion wrote a letter to *The Intelligencer*, one of his hometown newspapers in Bucks County, Pennsylvania:

> There are many views on our mission here; however, all I can
> say with certainty is that there are thousands of Americans
> over here working hard towards a positive outcome in Iraq.
> Every day I am here I see great things being accomplished
> under harsh circumstances from young Americans. I am truly
> honored to serve beside these Marines, Sailors, Soldiers,
> and Airmen. I am not sure the average American sees the
> positives these servicemen and women accomplish or even
> understands the sacrifices of their efforts, however, whatever
> course of action our leadership decides upon, there are those
> in waiting ready to carry out the mission in support of our
> country and in defense of its people and their freedoms.
> Respectfully,
> Travis Manion
> 1stLt USMC

On April 22, 2007, Travis's dad was enjoying a sunny Sunday afternoon on his porch when his cell phone rang. A special code appeared on the screen, which indicated that his son was calling from Iraq. Though their connection was marred by more static than usual, Tom was thrilled to be hearing from Travis for the first time in over a week.

After they greeted each other, Travis told Tom that he had been following updates on the April 16, 2007, mass shooting at Virginia Tech. The Marine said he was heartbroken for the thirty-two victims and their families, and he discussed the shocking tragedy with his dad. The images being beamed around the world from the Blacksburg, Virginia, campus were horrifying, even to someone experiencing the hell of war.

Travis then spoke about the terror he had seen on the faces of countless civilians, including children, in Fallujah. He explained that like the Spartan warriors portrayed in *300*, his Marines and the Iraqi soldiers were protecting those who could not protect themselves.

"Dad, for the Spartans, there was no greater honor than to fight and defend your country and its freedoms," Travis said.

As their conversation wrapped up, Tom, who was deeply moved by his son's resolve, told Travis he was proud of him.

"I love you, buddy," he said.

The poor cell phone connection cut out before Travis heard his father's words. Though Tom was disappointed, he didn't fret. He knew he would talk to his son again soon.

On the next day, April 23, 2007, Travis was involved in a chaotic firefight, during which he braved enemy gunfire and helped save the lives of two Marines. During daily street fights in Fallujah, Travis wasn't imitating a Spartan warrior. He was one.

6

THE PIZZA SLICE

The morning of April 29, 2007, in Doylestown, Pennsylvania, couldn't have been more glorious. Spring was finally upon the Philadelphia suburb, and the start of this particular Sunday, with its bright sunshine and barely noticeable chill, may have been the most beautiful morning yet.

Tom and Janet Manion were engaged in their normal Sunday morning routine: having coffee on stools in their large second-floor kitchen, which opens up onto a deck overlooking a big, green backyard and tall trees. They had sat out on the patio earlier that morning, but now they were back inside reading sections of the Sunday *Philadelphia Inquirer*.

On the living room television, visible from the island in the center of the kitchen where the couple were sitting, Tim Russert was interviewing Senator Joe Biden—a Democratic candidate for the upcoming 2008 presidential election—on NBC's *Meet the Press*. Both parents looked up when Russert asked a particularly pointed question about the Iraq war.

"Do you believe the war is lost?" the host inquired, paraphrasing Senate Majority Leader Harry Reid, who had made the controversial proclamation a little over a week earlier on the Senate floor.

"This is not a game show, where you know . . . a football game. What this is about is we have lost 3,300 dead, we have 24,000 wounded . . . and we still have an opportunity to deal with the possibility of not trading a dictator for chaos . . . but it will not happen unless we have a serious change in our operating strategic premise," the future vice president said.

In the spring of 2007, everyone in Washington had strong opinions and/or talking points about Iraq, especially after President Bush's recent troop surge and the dawn of the 2008 campaign. But almost no politician had the insight of Tom's son, who was in his second combat tour in the volatile Al Anbar province, where thousands of Marines were executing the new surge strategy. As Senator Biden spoke to Russert, all Tom heard was Travis's impassioned words during that recent satellite phone call.

"We're close to getting the job done, Dad," Travis had said.

Janet was also thinking about her son, but in different terms. As Biden spoke, she put her elbows on the kitchen island, bowed her head, and thought about what Travis might be doing in Fallujah at that very moment.

"Lord, please keep him safe," she prayed while looking at her watch, which was set to Baghdad time.

With their son in combat, every day was a struggle. But fortunately for the Manions, they were surrounded by family and friends throughout the Delaware Valley.

"Let's have some people over today," Janet said, turning to Tom, who knew that having family around would comfort his wife.

At the front of the house, just a few steps from the kitchen, an American flag waved ever so slightly in the gentle spring breeze. In a few hours the Manion house would be filled with familiar faces for a Sunday afternoon barbeque.

About six thousand miles away, the Marines of 3-2-1 MiTT had an early afternoon barbeque of their own on a small FOB in eastern Fallujah. As smoke—for once from something other than an explosion—filled the tiny, makeshift base, the Marines smiled and joked despite the depressing, predictable landscape around them. The sand beneath their boots was almost the same color as the wooden panels that surrounded the FOB, and the sky seemed to always look the same: hazy and unforgiving.

Still, the MiTT team, including Travis, who was quickly becoming its heart and soul, tried to make the most of this relaxing barbeque, which was an extremely rare occurrence and also a welcome change from their usual diet of MREs (meals ready to eat). Four months into a deployment marked by bloody street fights with a relentless, ruthless enemy, moments of levity were the antidote to insanity.

"One day we're out and someone thought they heard a gunshot, and the Iraqi soldiers start shooting in every direction," said Marine Lance Corporal Chuck Segel. His listeners laughed. "It's like they're shooting in a giant circle instead of at a target."

Travis hadn't known Segel very long, but he liked him, especially since he, like Travis, had served in Fallujah about a year earlier.

"I totally get what you're saying," Travis said. "And remember, that's why we're here . . . to train the Iraqis."

"Roger that," Segel said with a nod.

As the Marines talked about their girlfriends back home and argued about the still-young baseball season, there was an unusual sense of calm. Except for the 113 degree heat and pungent stench of trash and raw sewage nearly overwhelming the smell of their hot dogs and hamburgers, it almost felt like home.

Then, amid a temporarily jovial atmosphere, one Marine remembered he was still in Fallujah.

"Today is going to be fucking terrible," First Lieutenant Chris Kim, the brawny Asian American officer from California, said to a fellow MiTT team member. He had had a bad feeling about that Sunday ever since waking up and smelling the awful stench of garbage on the streets of Fallujah.

The MiTT team, still more confident than ever while leading and advising the Iraqis, had been preparing for a huge mission in the city that day, called Operation Steel Resolve. But as was often the case in such a volatile, unpredictable area, the mission had been delayed until later that week, which meant Marines on the MiTT team weren't sure how they would spend the rest of this hot, wretched day.

As the MiTT team mulled around the tiny wooden base, eating their lunches before the outside odor turned their stomachs, Major Adam Kubicki, the senior officer, was discussing alternative missions with First Lieutenant Jon Marang.

For weeks an enemy sniper had been stalking an area of western Fallujah known as the "Pizza Slice," a distinctively shaped section of narrow, crowded alleyways between two main arteries that fed off two bridges crossing the Euphrates River. The northern, much older bridge—the "Blackwater Bridge," which drivers crossed while driving west on "Route Elizabeth," as the Marines had nicknamed it—was already infamous as the site where terrorists had strung up the bodies of murdered American civilian contractors working for Blackwater in March 2004, when Travis and Brendan were still at the Naval Academy. The atrocity had ignited the US-led Operation Vigilant Resolve, otherwise known as the bloody First Battle of Fallujah. There had already been a great deal of bloodshed—American and Iraqi—inside the pizza-shaped enclave formed by the two main roads.

Using armor-piercing bullets, the sniper had wounded several Americans and Iraqis, and every Marine on the MiTT team wanted to bring him down. Armed with intelligence about a neighborhood in which he might be hiding, this particular Sunday afternoon seemed to the Marines like a perfect time to end the threat.

The problem Marine officers were wrestling with was that in the spring of 2007, US troops almost never ran daytime missions inside the Pizza Slice. The marketplaces were overwhelmingly crowded, which made it extremely difficult to maneuver and nearly impossible to distinguish civilians from insurgents. With the Blackwater

Bridge as an ominous backdrop, it was a volatile sector in which Americans were obviously not welcome.

Travis was far from reckless, but he also had a reputation for being the first to run toward the chaos of a Fallujah firefight. In fact, he had recently told "Doc" Albino, the Navy hospital corpsman who was eating a hot dog while getting mustard stuck in his thick mustache, exactly how he felt about serving in a war zone.

"Someday, I want to be able to look back on these years and know I did my part," Travis told Albino.

After discussing the idea with several fellow officers, including Travis, Major Kubicki announced that a team would head into the Pizza Slice to follow up on new intelligence about the sniper's whereabouts. Hopefully they could finally find the terrorist who was shooting at US Marines, Iraqi soldiers, and civilians. Two American Humvees would accompany two vehicles full of Iraqi Army troops. In one Humvee would be Kubicki, Albino, and Kim. They would be joined by the driver, Staff Sergeant Paul Petty, and the turret gunner, Staff Sergeant Josh Wilson.

Marang and Segel would ride in the second Humvee. The driver would be Staff Sergeant Chad Marquette, turret gunner Corporal Zebulin Bryner, and Mohammed, an Iraqi interpreter.

Travis and Second Lieutenant Scott Alexander, a friend and fellow MiTT team member, were supposed to go to a nearby school with Iraqi soldiers and hand out candy, crayons, and coloring books to local kids. Travis was excited about the mission because he cared about the Iraqis and loved to see the smiles of their children.

As the MiTT team members finished their lunches, packed up their gear, and prepared to head their separate ways, Travis was approached by First Lieutenant Kim, another close buddy. Manion, Kim, and Alexander, who often hung out together, had been nicknamed the "three amigos" by Major Joel Poudrier, the battalion-level Marine officer who was wounded in the chlorine bomb attack.

Kim, who had smelled ugliness in the air when he woke up that morning and had reiterated his uneasiness just minutes earlier, told Travis that the smiles of Iraqi schoolchildren would be a welcome sight. Kim was a brave Marine who repeatedly distinguished himself on the battlefield, but on this day he felt worn down. Fortunately he and Travis were close enough that he felt confident asking his friend to take his place on Major Kubicki's Pizza Slice patrol team.

"Is it cool if I head over to the school instead?" Kim asked.

"No problem," Travis replied, his eyes lighting up because he knew this meant he could go help find the sniper.

"Are you sure?" Kim insisted.

"Go ahead with Scott to the school," Travis said. "We're all good."

"Thanks, Travis," Kim said. "I'll see you in a bit."

"See you back here," Travis said with a nod.

Off the battlefield, Travis was a true friend. On it, he had already earned from the Iraqis the nickname "asad," one of many Arabic words for "lion."

Travis knew Kim, who would certainly return the favor later in the deployment, needed a break. In addition, Travis wanted to confront the sniper. Just as in his wrestling days at Navy, he was eager to fight against the opposition's most skilled, intimidating opponent. Yet as Travis packed up his gear, including his M-4 rifle and its attached M-203 grenade launcher, it was impossible not to remember a recent conversation with his mother, which had left him so shaken that he had discussed it with Kim one night when they both couldn't sleep.

Like any loving, caring military mom, Janet was in anguish knowing that her son was in combat on the volatile streets of Fallujah.

"I understand you have to do your duty," Janet had said emotionally to Travis via satellite phone a few nights earlier. "But please make sure to be careful."

Brendan Looney and Travis Manion met as midshipmen at the United States Naval Academy in Annapolis, Maryland.

After starting his collegiate sports career as a Navy football player, Brendan played three seasons of lacrosse. Travis attended several of Brendan's games, after which Brendan would often join the postgame tailgate celebration.

Travis had an illustrious collegiate wrestling career at Navy, where he defeated many of the nation's top wrestlers in tournaments around the country. After being nationally ranked during his junior year, Travis's senior season was derailed by a shoulder injury.

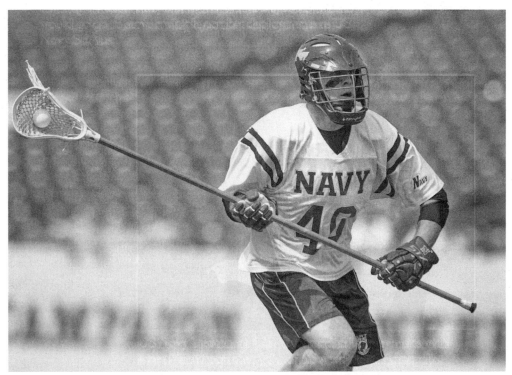

Brendan, a defensive midfielder, was a crucial part of the Navy Midshipmen men's lacrosse team that made an improbable run to the 2004 NCAA Final Four and National Championship game at M & T Bank Stadium in Baltimore. *Courtesy of the US Naval Academy*

Brendan Looney and Amy Hastings met on Memorial Day weekend 2003 and quickly fell in love. While dating, the couple would endure Brendan's two overseas deployments as a US Navy intelligence officer.

Brendan, Amy, Travis, and Enza Cestone—future wife of Andrew Hemminger, a Naval Academy classmate of Brendan and Travis—enjoy a fun evening on the town in Annapolis.

Travis's father, Colonel Tom Manion, and mother, Janet Manion, pin the bars signifying their son's commissioning as a Second Lieutenant in the United States Marine Corps.

US Marine Second Lieutenant Travis Manion and US Navy Ensign Brendan Looney stand shoulder to shoulder at their Naval Academy graduation on May 28, 2004, in Annapolis. At the ceremony, US Air Force General Richard Myers, chairman of the Joint Chiefs of Staff, told the 990 graduates that they would play a key role in fighting the nation's post-9/11 conflicts.

Amy, Brendan, and Travis enjoy a friend's wedding shortly after graduating college.

Tom, Ryan, Travis, and Janet Manion join family and friends to celebrate Travis's graduation from the Naval Academy.

Travis opens his arms to the world during his 2005–06 deployment to Iraq.

As the 1st Reconnaissance Battalion's maintenance management officer at Camp Fallujah, Travis went on numerous patrols in and around the city to uncover weapons caches and provide operational security.

Travis and his fellow Marines played a key role in overseeing security for Iraq's October 15, 2005, constitutional referendum and December 15, 2005, national election.

Travis holds his niece and godchild, Maggie Rose Borek, shortly before his second deployment to Iraq.

Travis was a Philadelphia Eagles fan, while Brendan rooted for his hometown Washington Redskins. But when they attended NFL games together, one friend would often wear the other's jersey as an inside joke.

Travis receives a kiss from his mom at a Pennsylvania restaurant on the night before heading to the West Coast to leave for his second deployment to Iraq. The December 2006 dinner with Janet, Tom, Ryan, and Dave, along with friends Ben and Sarah Mathews, would mark the last time Travis saw his family.

US Marine Sergeant Justin Bales, a reservist and New York City firefighter, discusses a 2007 mission with US Marine First Lieutenant Travis Manion in Fallujah, who he often joined on combat patrols. During Travis's second Iraq deployment, he and a fellow Marine helped Bales and two others escape an enemy ambush.

After exchanging gunfire with enemy forces, Travis—an officer for 3rd Battalion, 2nd Brigade, 1st Iraqi Army Division Military Transition Team (3-2-1 MiTT)—leads the response to a March 18, 2007, terrorist attack in Fallujah. The heroic actions of Travis and his teammates resulted in the recovery of Iraqis killed in the blast, as well as the rescue of two injured Iraqis from the rubble.

"I know what I'm doing, mom," Travis had replied. "I have an obligation to help these Marines and Iraqi soldiers."

Janet was enormously proud of her son, but that didn't make knowing he was in danger any easier. Similarly, Travis knew his mom fully supported him, yet it was still extremely difficult to hear her anguish from thousands of miles away.

As the MiTT Marines got into two Humvees and began their journey to a another FOB in the western part of the city, where they would pick up supplies and meet up with the Iraqi soldiers before heading into the heart of the Pizza Slice, Travis put on his headphones to help drown out the haunting memory of his mom's aching voice.

Fallujah in 2007, and particularly the Pizza Slice, was similar to the streets of Mogadishu, Somalia, portrayed in Ridley Scott's film *Black Hawk Down* and the book by Mark Bowden that it was based on. Everything was narrow, crowded, run down, and inherently suspect. For American troops, picking out an Iraqi insurgent in Fallujah was akin to police searching Yankee Stadium for a suspect wearing a dark blue hat with an interlocking "NY."

As the two Humvees headed west toward the FOB, with horns blaring and lights flashing, Iraqi civilians parted like the Red Sea and reluctantly let the Americans through. Anyone in the crowd could have had a gun or bomb strapped to his chest, but this was standard operating procedure for Travis and his fellow Marines in Fallujah. The only difference was that some of Travis's teammates had never been inside the Pizza Slice during the day.

As Staff Sergeant Petty drove the Humvee, with Major Kubicki in the passenger seat, Staff Sergeant Wilson up in the turret, and both Travis and "Doc" Albino in the back, Kubicki was conversing by radio with battalion leadership at Camp Fallujah. Though two helicopters would be provided for their mission to find the sniper, they only had another ninety minutes before the choppers would have to refuel and leave for a previously scheduled operation in a different part of the city.

"We better hurry," Kubicki said to Petty as the Humvee hit one of many huge potholes. "We lose air cover at 1500 [3:00 p.m.]."

It was already 1:15 p.m., and the two American Humvees were just arriving at the second FOB. Fortunately the two Iraqi Army vehicles were already there, and the Americans rushed inside to grab some gear before heading into the Pizza Slice. They had also planned to take some extra water, until Marang realized that there wasn't nearly as much water at the FOB as the Marines needed. Segel had asked him for another bottle, but there simply wasn't enough to go around.

The four-vehicle combat patrol started out with the two Iraqi vehicles in the front and back, the American Humvees sandwiched in between. Travis and Kubicki's Humvee followed Marang and Segel's. Every American on the patrol knew this was the most dangerous part of their day, and they sat quietly in the vehicle, scanning the huge crowds surrounding their vehicles on Route Elizabeth, the marketplace-filled artery that feeds off the infamous Blackwater Bridge.

It was getting hotter and hotter, and knowing the enemy was almost certainly lurking amid the unfriendly Fallujah civilian population caused extra sweat to form on several foreheads. Yet the Humvees continued to make their way through the crowds, with some Iraqis pounding on the sides of the vehicles as the Americans passed. The Marines and their Iraqi counterparts pressed westward, determined to pinpoint the sniper and complete their mission.

The Marines were headed to a building where they believed the sniper could be hiding. Travis was familiar with the suspected safe house, but from experience he was also concerned about false intelligence.

In the backseat of the other Humvee, Segel looked out the window at a large cemetery as the patrol took a circular route to the target building. Taking the shortest way would have been too predictable, in case an enemy ambush was being planned. Segel hated coming to this area just as much as he had last year, and having to look at a huge cemetery didn't make things any easier while struggling with the emotions of war.

"Let's go get this fucking guy, sir," Segel said to Marang, who was riding up front.

"Roger that, Lance Corporal," Marang responded.

As both Humvees pulled up at the intersection of two narrow side streets, the Marines and their Iraqi counterparts jumped out to set up a perimeter and quickly perform a search of the building in question. There were a few civilians in the area, but it seemed less crowded than normal.

Travis dismounted and took charge on the ground, with Kubicki, who was standing with the interpreter, chiming in when he felt it was necessary. Petty and Marquette stayed in their respective vehicles along with the turret gunners, while Segel and Albino kept watch over the area and the officers, including Marang, established a perimeter. As Travis led a few Iraqi soldiers into the building, it became clear to everyone that something was off.

Right then Travis got a call over the radio. It was from one of the helicopters watching over them.

"You've got large groups of civilians moving away from your AO [area of operations]," the pilot shouted, with the thundering sound of the rotating helicopter blade nearly drowning out his voice.

"Roger," Travis replied.

Several other Marines also heard the transmission, which sounded strange, but at the same time, the heavily Sunni population in Fallujah was known to avoid Americans, especially after the bloody battles three years earlier. And since most soldiers in the Iraqi Army division being trained by the MiTT team were Shiite, the animosity was even more palpable.

Although it was possible this was nothing to worry about, Segel was particularly concerned.

"How much do you want to bet something happens in the next twenty minutes?" Segel asked the Navy corpsman. "This smells bad."

"Everything smells bad here," Albino quipped, with mustard still stuck in his mustache.

Segel forced a laugh while reaching for his canteen for a drink of water to wet his mouth, which was parched by thirst and nervousness. After taking a few sips, the lance corporal realized he had just drunk the last of his limited supply.

As Travis and the Iraqis came out of the building empty-handed, Segel approached the officers to make sure they knew about the crowds moving away. It seemed a little weird, they all agreed, but the patrol was leaving this intersection now and heading to another house a few blocks to the northeast. They had additional intelligence indicating that the sniper might be hiding in a safe house near the location of a previous shooting. Despite coming up empty on the mission so far and the potential signs of danger, the Marines weren't about to stop hunting the sniper.

Instead of going the most obvious way, the joint patrol circled back up north to Route Elizabeth. They would avoid predictability while also getting a better handle on what the dispersing crowds might be up to.

When the four Humvees reached Elizabeth, just two blocks east of the Blackwater Bridge, things seemed to be mostly in order. The marketplace was still jammed with people, some of whom glared and once again pounded on the passing Humvees. The Marines' watches all read 1450 (2:50 p.m.), and their patrol was about ten minutes from losing air cover.

As the vehicles slowly turned down the narrowest of alleys, far thinner than any road they had encountered so far during the patrol, Kubicki ordered everyone to stop about a quarter mile from what they thought was the safe house zone. While the American vehicles were facing south, in between the two Iraqi vehicles and pointed away from Route Elizabeth, the Iraqi vehicle closest to the marketplace artery was pointing west, and the southernmost Iraqi vehicle, which was parked near a tight intersection, was pointing west as well.

Not far behind the southernmost Iraqi vehicle, which was leading the patrol, Segel, Marang, and Mohammed dismounted, walking a few steps north to meet Travis, Kubicki, and Albino. The two drivers and turret gunners stayed inside their Humvees, which were packed like sardines in the minuscule alleyway.

"If anything happens, they'll tear us up," Staff Sergeant Petty, the hard-nosed Texan driving Travis's Humvee, said to Staff Sergeant Wilson, the turret gunner. "There's no fucking way I can turn around and get us back to Elizabeth."

Just after Petty's remark, the patrol lost its eye in the sky.

"I see more people moving away from you, so be careful down there," the pilot said. "Over and out."

"Well that's just fucking great," Petty said to Wilson.

In part to make up for the lost air cover, Travis ordered Segel and Albino up to a rooftop to keep an eye out while he and fellow officers questioned neighborhood residents about encountering the sniper or any other insurgents. Travis, Kubicki, and Marang, along with the interpreter, were speaking with a heavyset Sunni local when one of the more competent Iraqi soldiers, Lieutenant Jalal, motioned for his American counterparts to come over. He was standing with a young boy who couldn't have been more than eight years old.

"I think he knows something," Jalal said in broken English.

Through the interpreter, Travis asked the child if he had seen a bad man shooting at people in this neighborhood. The boy, looking up at the tall, imposing Marine, stepped backward without answering.

While another Marine standing in a dangerous intersection in searing heat may have grown frustrated, Travis, who had just recently become an uncle, knelt down and smiled before running his gloved hand through the boy's hair. He had the interpreter ask the question again.

"There," the boy said in Arabic, pointing at a yellow, two-story house just south of the rooftop Segel and Albino were guarding. "That one."

"Thank you," Travis called as the boy ran away.

Getting on his walkie-talkie, Travis informed the team that he, Marang, and some Iraqi troops were going to check out the building, which was almost directly to the right of where Travis's Humvee—the northernmost of the two American Humvees—was still facing south. Clutching their weapons in heat that was well over 100 degrees, the three officers headed toward the building's entrance.

Watching from the roof, Segel saw no obvious threats but continued to see people vanishing from the area, including Route Elizabeth just to the north.

"I still think something weird is going on," Segel said to Albino.

The officers and their Iraqi counterparts searched the bottom floor of the building, which was almost completely empty except for an old, burned-out couch. They then headed for a stairway, only to find it blocked off by a large stack of cinderblocks. This was a common enemy tactic to prevent combat teams from entering buildings, but it was another in a series of strange signs.

"I haven't seen that in this sector," Marang said about the cinderblock pile.

Travis would normally have wanted to kick the cinderblocks down and head up the stairs, but the desolate building's dark silence left almost no doubt that it was empty. Any further searches would in all likelihood be a waste of time. But it could still be some kind of setup, as al Qaeda and Iraqi insurgents had been known to intimidate innocent children into fooling Americans in the past.

"I don't know about that kid anymore, Jon," Travis said to Marang.

"Let's get out of here," Marang said.

As the officers suddenly appeared from the building, Lieutenant Jalal, his finger circling in the air, signaled that an ambush could be brewing. In an alley that felt like a trash compactor, staying any longer could make the patrol sitting ducks.

"Ambush," Jalal shouted in Arabic to the rooftop, motioning to Segel and Albino to come down.

While the Marines hurried toward their respective vehicles, Travis, clutching his lethal M-4/M-203 combo weapon, waited at the bottom of the stairs for the lance corporal and Navy hospital corpsman to descend from the other building's roof. While he was sweating from the ungodly heat and his heart still pounded from the suspicion that they could be moments from a firefight, Travis wasn't comfortable leaving until he knew everyone in the patrol was safe.

Just across Route Elizabeth, a turbaned, possibly Chechen marksman set his sights squarely on the former wrestling star from Doylestown, Pennsylvania. With his finger on the high-powered rifle's trigger, the sniper planned on cutting down the most imposing Marine in the group with an armor-piercing bullet. As in previous attacks, he would then slip away while a ragtag group of Iraqi insurgents provided AK-47 cover fire from other buildings.

With sweat dripping off his chin, the sniper was about to squeeze the trigger when Segel and Albino suddenly stepped in front of Travis. The two Marines and Navy corpsman almost instantly dispersed, with Travis moving quickly toward his Humvee, which was still facing south. The sniper, to his frustration, could no longer see the muscular American he had been only a split-second from shooting.

With Segel rapidly moving south, his back unknowingly turned to the gunman, the sniper suddenly had a lousy shot at this Marine as well. It was then that the shooter set his sights squarely on Doc Albino.

Because of Albino's slightly different uniform, darker complexion, and large mustache, the trained killer may have wondered if he was an Iraqi soldier. Never mind that he was actually a US Navy hospital corpsman, on patrol with US Marines to provide emergency medical care. To this terrorist, Albino was just another infidel and enemy of Allah.

"Let's go," Travis said upon arriving at the Humvee.

"This felt like a fucking setup," Segel said at almost the same moment while approaching the other American vehicle. "Where's the Doc?"

The sniper pulled the trigger, blasting what felt like a metal pipe through Albino's lower left abdomen. The bullet, which ricocheted off the corpsman's radio, then tore through his left lung. Albino fell to his knees, dropping his weapon and landing flat on his face in the sordid, trash-filled street.

"Motherfucker," yelled Petty, who had gotten a thumbs-up from the Doc a split-second before. In an instant Travis and Kubicki started running toward the wounded corpsman.

"CASUALTY!!!" screamed the turret gunner of the other American Humvee. He was the only one in that vehicle to see Albino go down.

Everyone in the Humvee froze.

"Iraqi?" a stunned Marang yelled in response.

Despite the sudden jolt of adrenaline, their hearts sank when they heard the gunner's response.

"It's the Doc!" he yelled, opening fire. "Ambush!"

Travis had reacted as soon as the first shot rang out. He took off running toward his wounded comrade as the thunderous sound of American turret gunfire rang out in the once-quiet alleyway. Even with the enemy shooting from above, Travis didn't care about his own safety. He knew this could be his only chance to save the Doc.

At the other American Humvee, Marang and Segel also took off in Albino's direction. Though they were trained to never run toward a sniper's victim, the warrior ethos of never leaving a fallen comrade behind had overridden their sensibilities.

Travis, who reached the Doc first, grabbed him by the left shoulder, and Kubicki, who was running close behind, clutched Albino's right arm a few seconds later.

"Come on, Doc!" Travis yelled as he and the major pulled Albino closer to the Humvee.

Bullets were now raining down from multiple rooftops, which meant that more insurgents had been waiting with the sniper to ambush the American and Iraqi troops. The MiTT team was encircled by insurgents, and without a fierce counterattack, the entire patrol was almost certainly doomed.

As bedlam ensued, the Marines realized that both Iraqi vehicles in their patrol were gone. After the Iraqi soldiers heard the gunfire, the front vehicle subsequently hit an IED while trying to loop around toward a better fighting position. The Iraqis were stranded, which meant nine Americans and their interpreter were left outnumbered in a confined, chaotic space.

Travis and Kubicki dragged Albino out of the kill zone and closer to the vehicle's front side, where the sniper couldn't deliver a fatal blow to their bleeding, gasping corpsman. As they tended Albino's wounds, Travis saw Marang and Segel running toward him at full speed.

Another piercing crack of gunfire abruptly echoed through the alley. In an instant Segel was somersaulting in midair, feeling like Mike Tyson had just punched him in the stomach, and landing in the middle of the bullet-riddled street. All around Segel, who broke his rifle while collapsing to the ground, a hectic battle was unfolding in an eerie, slow-motion silence.

Segel's wrist convulsed with tremendous pain. The sniper was firing at the wounded Marine as he lay in the street, and the young lance corporal, who had just been shot in the wrist—and still unbeknownst to him, in the stomach—would soon be dead if he didn't get in front of that Humvee.

As Segel lay powerless, unable to do anything but wait for the crushing blow of another sniper bullet, Travis pulled him out of the sniper's crosshairs. Moments later Segel lay next to Albino, who was still being worked on by Kubicki.

By the time the confused lance corporal looked up into the dust, Travis was gone. He had already run back into a cloud of bullets.

Travis dashed into the street, not far from where Segel had been hit twice and Marang had barely escaped death. Without blinking, he blasted a grenade onto one of the buildings' rooftops, sending chunks of concrete tumbling to the ground. When Travis switched to M-4 rounds, his suppressing fire was equally relentless, which gave Kubicki and Marang enough time to help the wounded.

With one rooftop silent after stunned insurgents had experienced the crushing power of Travis's grenades and countless M-4 rounds, the battle's tide began to turn. Segel and Albino couldn't see Travis firing, but they could hear the welcome sounds of the American counterattack, which only paused when Travis needed to reload.

"Go!" Travis screamed to his fellow officers, who moved into new positions so they could join him in firing at the enemy. Travis, moving east in the alleyway from the Humvee's passenger side to the driver's side as he blasted away at another rooftop, was now causing the same kind of pandemonium among the enemy that the sniper had initially wrought among the Americans.

Just in front of Segel, the corpsman initially pulled to safety by Travis and Kubicki had dragged himself almost completely under the vehicle, with only his legs sticking out. Trying desperately to breathe while tasting a mixture of sand and his own blood, Albino was almost certain he was going to die.

Amid dizziness, extreme thirst, and the crashing sounds of concrete, the wounded corpsman pictured his mother, whom he didn't want to suffer in the wake of his death. But at the same time, Albino could see Travis's boots firmly planted in the sand while he fired on enemy positions. The situation was bleak, but maybe there was still a chance to survive.

Although the sniper would usually have been long gone by now, the AK-47 fire from the other buildings caused so much initial confusion that the MiTT team still wasn't sure which building he had fired from. Like a vulture circling its prey, the enemy marksman continued scanning the alley before again spotting Travis, who was firing away at the other rooftop.

The sniper had wanted to kill Travis from the moment he first saw him. Given that the muscular twenty-six-year-old Marine had jumped into the line of fire to wreak havoc on insurgents, Travis—now fully exposed to the sniper's position—was the gunman's prime target.

With Kubicki and Marang firing from the west and both turret gunners blasting away at the rooftops, Travis started to smell victory as he led the counterattack from the east and drew fire away from his teammates. With his watch reading 1525 and the clock ticking down toward the end of the bloody bout, the heart and soul of 3-2-1 MiTT once again reached down for more ammunition.

Across the city, First Lieutenant Kim was handing crayons to smiling Iraqi kids with Second Lieutenant Alexander. Though Kim wondered how Travis and the guys were faring inside the Pizza Slice, they had been through so many battles in the last five months without a casualty that the MiTT team seemed indestructible.

As Kim knelt with a happy child, he suddenly heard unintelligible screaming from the radio inside his vehicle.

"Contact," yelled a voice, possibly Staff Sergeant Petty, the driver of the Humvee Kim was originally supposed to be in.

Kim looked straight at Alexander, who had heard the same frantic sounds, and both men motioned to their Iraqi counterparts to sit with the kids while they checked things out.

The transmissions were broken, but now the sound of Petty's voice screaming "contact" came through crystal clear. Without saying a single word about what to do next, Kim and Alexander jumped into separate vehicles with their respective drivers, told the Iraqis to handle the rest of the school supply drop, and sped toward the Pizza Slice's unknown turmoil.

As they listened to broken radio transmissions and tried to communicate with Petty, who was frantically trying to contact

Camp Fallujah and request a quick reaction force (QRF), the Marines silently navigated through the Pizza Slice's narrow, confusing streets, not completely sure where their MiTT team brothers were pinned down. They knew a battle was raging, but neither Marine had any idea how serious it was, nor did they realize Albino and Segel had been hit.

After looping around the Pizza Slice, the two vehicles turned right onto Route Elizabeth near the Blackwater Bridge, heading east, and the seriousness of the situation slapped Kim and Alexander in the face. The normally bustling, packed marketplace artery was completely empty. If tumbleweeds had blown across the street, this section of Fallujah would have looked exactly like a deserted town in an old spaghetti western.

"Jesus Christ," Alexander said.

"Where the fuck are they?" Kim yelled in frustration.

Suddenly they heard gunfire.

"There!!!" Alexander said, pointing at the besieged alleyway where two American Humvees were still being riddled by bullets.

As both vehicles stopped on Route Elizabeth facing east, the Marines jumped out and ran as quickly as they could—ducking as rifles continued to crack—toward their comrades. Kim then confronted an image that would stay with him for the rest of his life.

Travis was lying near the back driver's side tire of the Humvee he had been riding in, his eyes wide open but glazed over with emptiness. Kim saw no blood, but it was obvious that something horrible had occurred in that wretched, violent alley.

For the first time in the entire deployment, sheer panic seized Kim as he ran with Alexander up to Kubicki, who was kneeling by Travis while firing a 9mm handgun at one of the buildings after running out of rifle ammunition.

"What the hell happened?" Kim asked, firing his own rifle. "Where do you need us to go?"

"Get the wounded," Kubicki said. "Get them out of here!"

"Who else is hit?" Alexander said.

"Segel and the Doc," Kubicki said before moving to another position to continue firing.

Swinging open the passenger's side back door for cover as he fired, Kim saw Segel, who had avoided being shot again but was still in great pain, lying in the backseat. Despite being on his back, he was reaching down to the floor trying to find more ammunition for the turret gunner. His left wrist was bleeding profusely.

"The major ordered us out," Kim said. "Do you need help?"

"I can make it," Segel said. "You gotta get Lieutenant Manion. . . . I think he's dead."

"My vehicle is right over there," Kim said, pointing toward Elizabeth. "Go!"

Now that reinforcements had arrived, the sniper was gone, and the insurgents were pulling back.

Segel, mustering all his strength, exited the Humvee on the passenger's side and hurried to Kim's vehicle, where he collapsed in the backseat. He knew he had been shot in the stomach by this point, and wasn't sure if he would make it. But even as Segel ran to the intersection, the wounded Marine's thoughts were focused on the unforgettable scene he had just witnessed.

Segel didn't see Travis get shot by the sniper. But after dragging himself to the driver's side of the vehicle, the lance corporal was shocked to see the first lieutenant lying facedown and motionless, his arms stretched toward the curb with his feet facing toward the bullet-riddled vehicle.

When Segel pulled himself toward Travis and asked where he had been hit, he got no response. He realized Travis was seriously wounded and started feeling underneath his fellow Marine's body armor with his left hand, despite the hole in his own aching wrist. He found a bullet wound on the left side of Travis's rib cage.

He whispered in Travis's ear.

"Hey, Travis," said Segel, who normally would have addressed him as "lieutenant" or "sir." "I'm here for you."

Travis didn't respond.

Even without realizing that the sniper's bullet had struck the first lieutenant from the right side and exited at the spot he was covering with his left hand, Segel knew the situation was grave when Travis began jerking with convulsions.

"Is he dead?" Kubicki yelled over to Segel while continuing to fire at enemy positions.

"Not yet, but he will be soon if we don't do something," the lance corporal said, his voice shaking.

Segel turned to Travis, whose eyes were still wide open.

"I'm here for you," Segel repeated over and over into his ear.

Those words echoed in Segel's ears as he later lay in the Humvee, thinking for the first time about a horrific episode that would haunt his dreams for years to come. As the twice-wounded Segel reflected inside the vehicle, Kim motioned to its driver to come help him get Travis into the Humvee he was still lying beside. Alexander, also shaken by the shocking tragedy, was helping move his friend as well. Travis was far too bulky for one man to carry, and with both Kubicki and Marang running out of ammunition as they fired at the dispersing enemy, now was the time to get the wounded back to base.

As soon as Kim and Alexander had carried their unresponsive friend into the vehicle, Kubicki ran over and dove into the smoke-filled Humvee, where he clutched Travis to begin trying to identify his wounds, stop the bleeding, and perform CPR. He ordered Petty to start driving toward Camp Fallujah, while Wilson fired his last rounds from the turret. This was probably Kubicki's last chance to save his fellow Marine.

As remnants of the patrol headed east to Camp Fallujah, unsure whether they would encounter more insurgents or IEDs, Kim, who was numb after seeing Travis's blank, lifeless eyes, asked Segel, who was wracked with pain from his wounded gut, what had happened.

"We got ambushed. . . . They had us surrounded," Segel gasped. "It's Manion. . . . I think he's gone."

As a seriously wounded Doc Albino struggled to breathe in the other Humvee and continued to think about his mother, Kim thought about Travis's mother, a woman he had never met. On that night when Travis had told him how much this deployment was wearing on his mom, Kim couldn't imagine what his friend's death would do to her. As the vehicle roared across an empty Route Elizabeth, Kim put his hands over his face and lowered his head.

As four American vehicles sped toward Camp Fallujah, Father John Gayton, a Marine Corps chaplain from Pennsylvania, sat in his tiny office on the makeshift American base. He was reading e-mails from home while sipping from a large bottle of water to keep hydrated on the steamy Sunday afternoon.

A few minutes later his phone rang.

"We've got two WIA [wounded in action] and one possible KIA arriving at the field hospital," a nurse reported.

As the chaplain ran over to the wooden complex, he saw a group of Marines—Kim, Alexander, Kubicki, Marang, Petty, Marquette, Wilson, and Bryner—huddled like a team on a football field. As he jogged by, one of them turned around and looked at him. Father John saw the redness in the eyes of this Marine, who had obviously been crying. It was clear that something terrible had happened.

"Any Marines with Type O positive blood: report immediately to field hospital room 4," a voice said over the base loudspeaker.

Could Travis survive? The announcement gave the Marines a brief moment of hope.

Albino was badly injured but would ultimately make it, and Segel, who was doubled over in pain, would also return home, with physical and emotional scars. As the corpsman and lance corporal received emergency care, Travis was in a different wood-paneled room, surrounded by doctors and nurses working frantically to save his life.

As they tore off his bloody fatigues before finding the wounds on each side of his rib cage and trying to resuscitate him, crowds began to form in the hallway outside the operating room. Word was quickly spreading that First Lieutenant Travis Manion, the heart and soul of the MiTT team, was badly wounded.

Father John anointed Travis's feet and said a prayer as the medical staff tried feverishly to revive him. If only the Marine could show the doctors some sign—any sign—of life.

About ninety seconds later, the physician in charge announced a time of death. For the next minute, the only sounds heard in the operating room came from the hallway outside.

As doctors and nurses watched in silence, Father John, standing above the fallen US Marine, broke the silence.

"God the Father of mercies, through the death and resurrection of your son, you have reconciled the world to yourself and sent the Holy Spirit among us for the forgiveness of sins," he said, looking down at Travis. "Through the ministry of the Church, may God grant you pardon and peace. And I absolve you of your sins, in the name of the Father, and of the Son, and of the Holy Spirit."

The war in Iraq was in one of its bloodiest chapters in the spring of 2007. Heavy casualties were the norm. But that didn't stop several nurses from crying.

"Amen," the priest whispered, gently placing his hand on Travis's head.

From the Marines gathered in the hallway to the MiTT Marines huddled outside the building, word spread that Travis was dead. After a few minutes, a Marine asked Kubicki if the MiTT team wanted to come inside the operating room to pay final respects to their fallen team member.

The major, still in disbelief about Travis and concerned about Albino and Segel, simply nodded.

The packed hallway grew silent as the MiTT team Marines, all covered in sweat and dirt and some in blood, entered the operating room to see Travis. A sheet covered the fallen Marine's entire body, except for his thick, shaved head.

One by one the Marines filed past their fallen brother. Kubicki, the senior officer who had desperately administered CPR in the

Humvee, was the first to walk by. Marang was next, then Wilson, Marquette, and Bryner.

When Petty looked at the fallen first lieutenant's face, he saw an officer who had given everything to the Marine Corps. From the 2005 referendum to ratify Iraq's constitution to the hellish events of April 29, 2007, Travis had been his leader during two deployments. Petty would never forget him.

When Alexander approached the operating table with tears streaming down his face, he put his hand on his friend's head. He didn't know how the mission could carry on without him.

Kim approached the table with weak knees and a broken heart. He paused to take one last look at his friend, who had saved his life by volunteering to go on a patrol he knew would be far more dangerous than a school supply drop.

Kim steeled himself, looked directly at Travis's now-closed eyes, and said good-bye. "This should have been me," he whispered before walking outside in tears.

As news of the sniper attack began to filter through Camp Fallujah, many Marines from the 1st Reconnaissance Battalion, Travis's permanent unit, began filing into the hospital. As Marines tried to find out what had happened to their friend, Kim went behind the building and found a good spot to cry.

After about twenty minutes of weeping beside a trailer, he looked up to find the third "amigo," Alexander, doing the exact same thing about thirty feet away.

Kim approached his friend, gave him a hug, and told him what he was feeling.

"Travis took my place," Kim said. "This is all my fault."

"No, it's the sniper's fault," Alexander said. "Don't do this to yourself."

Pausing for a moment, Kim pondered the story that was already spreading throughout the hospital complex. Without thinking twice, Travis had leapt squarely into enemy crosshairs to direct gunfire away from his patrol.

"I don't think I could have done what Travis did," he said, wiping away tears. "If it had been me, maybe more guys would have gotten hit."

As two of the three amigos walked back to the front of the hospital, the Iraqi interpreter who had joined them on the hellish mission stood by himself near the Humvee Travis once rode in, which was covered with dirt, sand, and bullet holes. Petty, an angry, determined look on his battle-hardened face, was washing blood out of the backseat.

If the first lieutenant had been able to give one last order to the Marines of 3-2-1 MiTT, it might have resembled the final decree issued by King Leonidas in *300*. Instead of letting the day's events break their will, Travis would have wanted his death to strengthen their resolve.

"Remember us," the king told his messenger. "Remember why we died."

As First Lieutenant Chris Kim and Second Lieutenant Scott Alexander stood next to the interpreter, the Iraqi native uttered the only Arabic word he could think of to describe a valiant Marine who had genuinely cared for the Iraqi people.

"Asad," he said.

On April 29, 2007, a lion of the Iraq war was struck down by a single bullet. It cut through Travis's aorta, causing massive internal bleeding that couldn't be controlled.

Though the fallen Marine's loved ones would undoubtedly suffer, everyone else on the Pizza Slice patrol was still alive. Indeed, by fearlessly protecting his Marines and the Iraqis serving beside them, First Lieutenant Travis Manion had done his part.

7

THE WAR COMES HOME

Brigadier General Dave Papak had been a close friend of Tom Manion for nearly two decades. Ever since they first served together in the Marine Corps Reserve, they had kept in close touch, no matter where they were stationed. The general's wife, Kate, was also close to Tom's wife, Janet.

On April 29, 2007, in New Orleans, where General Papak was commanding the 4th Marine Aircraft Wing, the Papaks had already attended a morning church service when the general sat down at his computer to check e-mail over a cup of coffee. His wife was out running a few errands, and before another busy work week began, Papak was looking forward to a relaxing day. Though life in the Big Easy still hadn't returned to normal less than two years after Hurricane Katrina, it was certainly a beautiful Sunday morning.

After scanning some AOL News headlines, the general logged into his e-mail and did a double-take. A forwarded message was waiting from his boss, three-star Lieutenant General Jack Bergman, which contained the latest list of Marines killed in action in Iraq.

"Is this Tom's son?" General Bergman, who knew the Papaks and Manions were close, inquired in the e-mail.

A tough military man who had endured his share of difficult moments over the course of a long, distinguished career, Papak, nearly spilling coffee all over his desk, felt genuine fear as his eyes moved down the casualty list.

"MANION, T.," he read moments later.

After briefly trying to convince himself there could be another "Manion, T." deployed to Iraq's Al Anbar province, he accepted that Travis, the young man he had watched mature into a Marine officer, was dead.

Without thinking, Papak picked up the phone next to his computer and began dialing Tom and Janet Manion's number. Yet just after entering the 215 area code, the general hung up.

After briefly pausing to collect himself, Papak behaved the same way he had as a young helicopter pilot suddenly faced with an emergency. The disciplined Marine let his training override the instincts of human emotion.

Instead of dialing the Manion house, Papak called retired Lieutenant Colonel Corky Gardner, one of his best Marine Corps buddies, who was also very close to Tom. They had been the "three amigos" long before the affectionate nickname was bestowed on Travis, First Lieutenant Chris Kim, and Second Lieutenant Scott Alexander in Iraq.

Lieutenant Colonel Gardner had known Tom's son since Travis was in the seventh grade. He had watched Travis wrestle in high school, and by sheer coincidence wound up becoming his battalion commander at the Naval Academy.

Gardner often thought about the day that he had initially refused to accept Travis's resignation as a midshipman, and how happy he was when Travis later decided to reapply. One of his proudest moments, in fact, was attending Travis's 2004 Naval Academy graduation and watching him become a respected Marine officer.

While Gardner was a recipient of the mass e-mails Travis often sent from Iraq to dozens of relatives and friends, they also e-mailed back and forth personally. He had last written Travis in early February and remained concerned about how the Marine was faring in what he knew was a particularly violent, unstable area of Iraq.

"Take care, Travis," the retired Marine had written in the last paragraph. "We're keeping you in our prayers. Please keep up the great work you're doing for us!"

Travis had responded on the morning of Saturday, February 17, ten weeks before his final battle in the Pizza Slice:

> Sir,
>
> It's good to hear from you again. Sounds like things are going well in PA. I didn't get to see the Super Bowl, but my parents said they had a good time.
>
> We're still pretty busy here as the team tries to figure out its role. I feel pretty confident in what I'm trying to accomplish and how I want to operate with the Iraqis, however, some of the guys on their first deployment are still trying to figure it out. As a small team out here it takes a lot of initiative to make this work, so I hope our team comes around soon.
>
> We've done some pretty good things so far, but there have definitely been some intense days so far. I'm really relying on my past experience with Recon (Battalion), and those guys' examples have really helped. We're almost two months down and the time is going pretty fast.
>
> I'll be sure to send another update soon. Please tell the family I said hello, and I appreciate all your support and guidance.
> Semper Fi,
> Travis

Not a day went by that Gardner didn't think about his dear friend's son and the sacrifices he was making on the streets of Fallujah. This Sunday morning was no different.

Gardner was about to leave his Ardmore, Pennsylvania, church when he felt his cell phone vibrating in his right pocket. Since the service was over, he flipped open his phone to see who was calling. "Dave Papak," the screen said.

Gardner and Papak were close friends, but a Sunday morning call was out of the ordinary. The retired lieutenant colonel realized that if Travis were killed in action, the general would probably be among the first to know.

Listening to the voice mail on the walk out to his car, he sensed the discomfort in his friend's voice.

"Yeah Corky, it's Dave," the General said. "I need you to call me back as soon as you get this."

After Gardner got into the car with his wife, Renee, he looked her in the eye and told her about the voice mail.

"Dave Papak just called," he said. "And I think I know what it's about."

"Oh, no," said Renee, thinking of her dear friends Tom and Janet. "Please God, no."

After the short drive home on a beautiful Pennsylvania Sunday morning, Gardner solemnly sat down to return his friend's call.

"Hello, Corky," Papak said. "I don't know how to say this, but Travis is down."

"I had a terrible feeling this is why you called," Gardner said. "Does Tom know yet?"

"That's actually what I wanted to ask you about, old friend," the general said. "I was wondering if you'd be willing to assist the young Marine who's going to notify Tom and Janet."

"Of course," Gardner said. "Absolutely."

Though the retired lieutenant colonel was swamped by a flood of emotions as he remembered Travis and his dad, both in uniform, smiling and laughing on Travis's graduation day, it was time to buckle down and be a Marine. Gardner would perform a difficult job with dignity and respect, because the Manion family deserved nothing less.

About thirty miles away in Doylestown, the sunny afternoon was shaping up to be even more beautiful than a morning that had seemed perfect. Other than the stress and worry of Travis being in Iraq, it had been a refreshing Sunday for Janet, who was spending time with her only granddaughter, Maggie. Janet's daughter, Ryan, who lived about an hour away, was back in town looking at some space for a store she was planning to open when she and her husband, Dave, moved back to the area.

Janet's sister, Annette Arcuri, had also come over with their mother, Rose Lemma. Janet's brother, Frank Lemma, and his wife, Maria, arrived shortly afterward. Tom's brother, Chris, and his wife, Susan, were also spending the afternoon at the Manion house.

Sunday afternoon family get-togethers were not uncommon, but this was a particularly large gathering. With her son deployed to Iraq, "the more the merrier" was not a cliché for Janet, who was always trying to distract herself with the company of people she loved.

Janet had called Annette a few hours earlier and insisted that she come over. Having just returned from a weekend on the Jersey Shore, Annette didn't really feel like going anywhere, as she wanted to rest and relax at home. But because of the e-mail Janet had received from Iraq two days earlier, she knew her sister needed to be surrounded by as many familiar, caring faces as possible.

Two days earlier, Janet had heard from Jill Kubicki, wife of Travis's commanding MiTT team officer, Major Adam Kubicki.

> Janet,
>
> I know that as of the last message I received (today) that everyone on the team is fine. However, I think that they've had a bit more exposure to the real hardships of combat of late, and given the timing of it (mid-point of the deployment), now's probably a good time for some support from their loved ones.
>
> Finally, I do know that there are good reasons for you to be proud of your son, that he is a fine and honorable man. I don't know much of the details, but I do know that he has been important to setting the right sort of examples for the rest of the Marines and for the Iraqis with whom they are working.
> Best,
> Jill

After receiving that e-mail, Janet had told Annette she had a horrible feeling about this deployment. It was different from the first one, and she could hear it in Travis's voice every time they spoke. He didn't share most details with his mother, but it was obvious that he was in the middle of the fight.

As Janet handed six-month-old Maggie to her sister so she could finish making salads, Tom was preparing hot dogs and chicken on the deck for their visiting relatives. He was talking to another relative about Senator Biden's *Meet the Press* appearance before heading out on the deck to fire up the grill.

As sounds of life filled the Manion house, Gardner sat just outside their driveway. As on the day he had encouraged an emotional Travis to reconsider his decision to leave the academy, he was giving a pep talk to an extremely nervous Marine who happened to be a member of Travis's graduating class at the Naval Academy. First Lieutenant Eric Cahill didn't know Travis personally, but he had heard stories about his fellow Marine's prowess, on both the battlefield and wrestling mat.

"There's no way to know exactly how this will go, son," said Gardner, who had once had to tell a close friend's wife that her husband was killed in Korea. "But remember how important it is that we do this the right way."

"Yes, sir," First Lieutenant Cahill said.

For the ninety-sixth time in the first twenty-nine days of April 2007, the military would inform an American family that their son or daughter had made the ultimate sacrifice in Iraq. Though Cahill had the unique privilege of having a retired lieutenant colonel by his side, the burden of delivering this devastating news still fell squarely on his shoulders.

With their cars parked on the street, the young Marine, in his green uniform, khaki shirt, and matching tie, walked toward the house with Tom's close friend, who was still wearing the same navy blue blazer he had worn to church. Renee Gardner followed closely behind as they walked up the driveway, which went straight to the house's "front" door, actually on the spacious home's right side.

Cahill and the Gardners weren't sure the Manions were home until they heard voices coming from inside the house.

Janet was at the kitchen sink when she heard the doorbell ring. Thinking it was two relatives who had gone across the street to pick up more food, she looked out the window and was pleasantly surprised to see Corky and Renee Gardner standing on her porch.

"Oh look, Tom," said Janet, drying her hands and starting to walk toward the front door. "Corky's here!"

That's strange, Tom thought. He didn't remember Janet telling him she had invited the Gardners over for dinner. In fact, he hadn't talked to Corky in a couple of weeks.

As Janet reached for the door's brass knob, she saw part of the young Marine's uniform through the window. Everyone in the house, including Annette, who was still holding baby Maggie, flinched as Janet let loose a piercing scream.

After opening the door and seeing the looks on Corky and Renee's faces, Janet slammed the heavy white door shut as her sister and other relatives sprinted toward the foyer. When Gardner gently reopened the door and attempted to come inside, Janet slammed it again, this time so hard that the hinges broke.

As Travis's mother collapsed on the floor in shock, with utter chaos overtaking the Manion home, Tom stood motionless as one of the most horrible scenes any husband and father could witness unfolded before his eyes. Though he hoped for a fleeting moment that his son was missing in action or wounded, the colonel was well aware of the Marine Corps' notification procedure. Travis was almost certainly dead.

Slapping both hands on the sides of his legs, Tom lowered his head and said the only words that came to mind.

"No," he said. "No."

Shrieks, along with the hysterical cries of a confused baby, filled the quiet neighborhood as the Manion home emptied into the front yard. Startled neighbors also began to come outside, including a Navy captain who lived next door. Annette, who was also screaming, helped her sister into the yard before realizing she had to get Ryan's baby out of this nightmarish setting.

As the Gardners tried to maintain their composure, Tom was the last person to walk out the door.

Gardner had known Tom since 1994. He had never seen anything like the current expression on his face. Travis's father wasn't crying, but nearly all the color had vanished from his face.

As Gardner's eyes met those of his devastated friend, Tom, in a daze, looked straight through him before wandering out onto the lawn. First he hugged and kissed Janet, then he walked around with his hands on his head and both arms covering his face.

"Why?" Travis's father yelled to the treetops. "WHY?"

As Annette took Maggie inside, where the baby's great-grandmother was weeping in the living room, Janet stood bawling in the driveway in front of the garage. She pointed at her sister.

"I knew it," she said, clearly referencing Jill Kubicki's e-mail. "I knew it, I knew it. . . ."

Tom, who was aimlessly circling the front yard, approached his old friend.

"Dead?" he asked, to which Gardner nodded with his eyes closed. After shaking his head in disbelief, Tom had started walking away, when his friend put his arm around him.

"Tom, I know this is the worst possible news," he said. "But I have this Marine over here who must give you the official notification. Let's just compose ourselves for a minute and let him do his job so he can get back to base. Can you please do that for me, Tom?"

When Tom looked over at Cahill, who was probably twenty-five or twenty-six, he saw his own son. Having served in the Marine Corps for a quarter century, he knew how tough this young man's assignment was. No matter how painful, Tom had to take a deep breath and let the Marine do his duty.

He stood quietly as Gardner motioned the visibly shaken Marine over to face the fallen hero's father.

"Okay, Eric, you can begin," Gardner said.

"Colonel Manion, sir, the Commandant of the Marine Corps has entrusted me to express his deep regret that your son, First Lieutenant Travis Manion, was killed in action in Al Anbar province, Iraq, on April 29, 2007, while conducting combat operations," Cahill said. "The Commandant extends his deepest sympathy to you and your family in your loss."

It was official. Travis was gone.

"Thank you for telling me," Tom said. "Can you tell me anything more about what happened?"

"I'm very sorry, sir, but this is all the information I have at this time," the Marine said.

"Okay," Tom said, putting his right hand on Cahill's right shoulder as tears began to flow. "Thank you."

As the young Marine walked back to his car, Gardner turned around and called his name.

"Lieutenant Cahill," he said. "You did a fine job."

Moved by the retired lieutenant colonel's words, Cahill promptly saluted him. After walking back to his car, getting inside, and putting on his seat belt, the young Marine put his elbows on the steering wheel and lowered his head into his hands.

When Annette got inside the house with Maggie, she smelled something burning. It was the hot dogs and chicken Tom had been cooking on the deck when the doorbell rang. With the sliding glass door wide open, smoke was pouring in from the deck. Annette handed Maggie to her sister-in-law, Maria, and turned off the smoldering grill. Nobody knew that earlier that day, Travis had enjoyed a final barbeque with his fellow Marines. Though they knew Travis was dead, the family still had no idea what had happened.

Travis's sister Ryan was just about to leave her prospective store when her cell phone rang. The caller ID said it was from her parents' house, so it was probably just her mom asking when she would be over for dinner.

"Hello," Ryan said in an upbeat, confident tone.

The inarticulate screaming of someone who sounded like her mother filled her left ear. Ryan, as anyone would, began to panic.

"Mom? MOM? What's wrong?" she said as her stomach shriveled into knots.

Ryan heard shrieks and sounds of people sobbing.

"Mom, you have to calm down and tell me what's wrong," Ryan said. "Is it Maggie?"

All she heard was more screaming.

"Mom, did something happen to Maggie?" Ryan repeated.

Suddenly the line was quiet.

"You need to come home," the voice said.

"Did you call an ambulance?" she said.

"Yes," the voice said before Ryan could even finish her question.

In complete shock, Ryan hung up the phone and asked her friend to rush her over to her parents' house. The drive was the most tense, frenetic five minutes of the twenty-seven-year-old mother's life, as she asked herself what could have possibly happened to her baby daughter.

Did she fall? Did she stop breathing? Did Dave, her husband, who was working about an hour away over in West Chester, Pennsylvania, already know?

As the car pulled up to the mailbox at the end of the long driveway, Tom and Gardner stood alone on the front lawn, with all the guests waiting inside near the broken front door. Ryan flung open the passenger's side door and started running toward her dad.

Where is Maggie? Where is the ambulance? What are Corky and Renee Gardner doing here?

As a totally confused, panicked young mother demanded to know what in God's name was going on, Tom met her near the end of the driveway and wrapped his arms around his little girl.

"Travis was killed," her father said in a solemn monotone.

It was Aunt Annette, not Janet, who had made that frenzied phone call to Ryan. She could now hear Maggie crying inside and knew her baby was okay. But Travis was dead, and just like her mom a few minutes before, Ryan fell to the ground, picturing his face.

"It's not fair," Ryan screamed in agony while lying in the driveway. "It's not fair!"

Ryan's husband, Dave, who nearly got in an accident after receiving the news while driving, had already made about half of the hour-long drive to Doylestown when he pulled over onto the shoulder of Interstate 276. He was sick to his stomach as he pictured Travis, his brother-in-law and very close friend, returning home from Iraq in a flag-draped casket. Dave had already lost a brother to bone cancer at a young age, and losing Travis felt like the same nightmare all over again.

As he wiped sweat from his forehead and got back onto the road, Dave thought about that night with Travis at the Eagles game in December, just before Travis left for his second deployment. When he had joked with Trav about coming up with a way to avoid another deployment to Iraq, his brother-in-law had suddenly grown serious and uttered those five words Dave had never forgotten: "If not me, then who. . . ."

Travis's death was a punishing, inconceivable blow, but Dave realized his brother-in-law had backed up his words.

As he pulled up to his in-laws' home, like his wife and her parents, Dave still had no idea what had happened in Iraq.

The front lawn was now empty, although several neighbors were still outside talking about the tragedy that had just struck their town. Because of a sniper in Fallujah, Iraq, the peace of Sunday in this quiet Pennsylvania community had been shattered.

When Dave hurried inside, he found his wife sitting on a living room chair, shaking, staring blankly in front of her. Janet was on the couch to Ryan's left, with loved ones on each side and her devastated mother also close by.

Travis's mom was sobbing as she held a glass of whiskey in her right hand. She hadn't taken a sip, as she knew she'd throw it up. Instead, with her eyes wide open, she prayed in silence.

God, please wrap your arms around my baby boy. Please don't let him suffer. Please welcome him into your arms.

For a moment Janet was calm, until baby Travis's face once again flashed through her mind. Each time she saw that enduring image, the agonizing spasms of pain would resume.

After hugging his wife and telling his mother-in-law he was deeply sorry, Dave walked into the kitchen, where he saw through the window his father-in-law on the porch. The smoke from the burning chicken and hot dogs was starting to dissipate, and Tom was standing near the grill, blankly staring into the tall trees behind the house as Gardner tried to console him. Without saying a word, Dave, tears streaming down his face, walked up to Tom and gave him a big bear hug.

As word spread and the night drew in, the house quickly began to fill with relatives, neighbors, and friends, almost overwhelming the family as they wandered through the house in shock. When Dave went downstairs to feed his daughter a warm bottle and whisper soothing, reassuring words in her ear, Tom, suddenly in full military mode, summoned his wife and daughter to the master bedroom, which wasn't far from the living room on the middle level of the house.

"Look, I'm not sure how we're going to get through this nightmare, but the one thing I know is we need to stick together," Tom said. "From this point forward, we need to be there for each other, no matter what."

Janet and Ryan didn't say anything, but they didn't have to. America's newest Gold Star family, now three instead of four, embraced in a hug that each of them would always remember.

Across the country, in Coronado, California, Brendan Looney was moving into Building 602 of the BUD/S compound, where he would soon start initial courses that would eventually lead to the grueling first phase of training to become a Navy SEAL.

After mostly quiet deployments to Korea and Iraq, Brendan was determined to become a SEAL, despite facing the most physically demanding training known to man. Moving into the barracks was the first step in an odyssey that would last more than a year, starting with the upcoming twenty-four-week BUD/S training regimen and culminating with another seven-month SEAL Qualification Training (SQT) program.

Brendan and his new roommate, fellow Naval Academy graduate Rob Sarver, whom he had known for nine years, were almost finished moving in their personal items when Rob's phone rang. On the other line was a good friend and fellow midshipman, Kacey Kemmerer.

"Rob, is Brendan with you?" Kemmerer said. "I just tried to call him."

"Oh, sorry man, I think Brendan left his phone out in his car," Rob said. "What's up?"

"Shit, man, I really don't know how to say this," Kemmerer said. "It's Manion. . . ."

The reception was terrible in the barracks, and the phone cut out before Kemmerer could finish his sentence.

With a suddenly bleak look on his face, Sarver looked at Brendan, who instantly knew something was wrong.

"It's Trav," Sarver said to Brendan, who immediately sat down on his bed. "Something happened."

After Sarver helped Brendan stand up, nothing else was said as Brendan walked to the parking lot to call Kemmerer back and find out if his friend was alive. While heading outside to get his cell phone, Brendan's legs began to wobble, so much that the ocean breeze from the nearby beach, where SEAL candidates endure

BUD/S training, nearly knocked him over. Brendan then realized he probably wasn't going to make it to his car.

"You call him," Brendan said so quietly that Sarver could barely hear him over the waves crashing outside the Coronado base's fortified perimeter.

With Brendan standing a few feet away, Sarver dialed Kemmerer's number to get the news.

"Hey," he said. "What happened?"

"We're not sure on the details," Kemmerer said. "But Travis was killed earlier today in Fallujah. Please tell Brendan I'm sorry."

Brendan knew Travis was gone before Sarver hung up the phone. Tears welled up in the SEAL candidate's eyes as Sarver gently delivered the shocking news.

"Trav didn't make it," he said. "He passed away."

In nearly a decade of friendship, Sarver had never seen anywhere near this level of emotion from Brendan, who clasped his hands behind his neck and wandered dazedly into the parking lot. He was breathing so heavily that even as he got farther and farther away, Sarver could still hear him huffing and puffing over the usual coastal noise.

As Brendan walked back toward his friend, his eyes engulfed with tears, Sarver handed him his cell phone so he could call his two brothers, Steve and Billy, who also knew Travis well from their days at the Naval Academy. When they heard the stunning news they were devastated, as were their parents and sisters.

Next it was time to call Amy, who had spent countless days and nights hanging out with Travis during the Annapolis years. Amy, who was still living on the East Coast, wasn't just linked to Travis through Brendan. She was his friend as well.

While Brendan dialed Amy's number, great memories from Annapolis and other fun times he had had with Travis filled his mind. In the instant that Amy's phone rang, Brendan panicked.

After saying "hello" and quickly realizing it was Brendan calling, not Sarver, Amy began trying to coax an explanation out of her boyfriend, who had become hysterical. Even after five years of dating, Amy was shocked to hear him crying.

"It's . . . Trav . . . ," he gasped. "He's gone."

"What?" asked Amy, confused and having trouble understanding Brendan's words. "What are you talking about?"

"He's gone," Brendan repeated. "He's gone."

"Who?" Amy said. "Brendan, you have to tell me what happened."

After another deep breath and a long, painful pause, Brendan said it: "Travis is dead."

As confusion turned to heartbreak, Amy listened helplessly to the man she loved crying uncontrollably three thousand miles away. She was crying, too, thinking about Travis and the agony the Manions must be experiencing.

The rest of the conversation didn't make much sense, but Amy longed to hold Brendan on the eve of his long journey to become a Navy SEAL.

"I love you," she said as the painful call concluded.

"I love you, too," Brendan said. "I'll see you later."

"See you later," Amy said.

After Sarver informed the BUD/S class leader that an Annapolis classmate and dear friend had been killed in Iraq, he and Brendan were excused for the next few days and permitted to leave the base. A few minutes later the aspiring SEAL retreated to the house they had been sharing on San Diego County's picturesque Imperial Beach.

Back in Doylestown, the number of people inside the Manion house had quadrupled since the Gardners and young Marine first arrived on their doorstep. As the sun set on the worst day of Tom, Janet, and Ryan's lives, neighbors were bringing over trays of food, while close friends and relatives were pouring in to offer condolences and hugs and to ask Tom and Janet if there was anything they could do.

As Travis's dad sat on the deck surrounded by concerned friends, Gardner stepped out the front door to dial Papak, who was sitting with his wife in the Louis Armstrong New Orleans International Airport, where they were waiting to board their flight to Philadelphia. They had spoken briefly after the notification, but Gardner hadn't reached Papak to tell him how Tom and Janet were doing.

"Dave, things are still rough here," Gardner said. "Tom, Janet, and Ryan are taking it very hard, but Renee and I are here, and we'll make sure to take good care of them."

"Thanks, Corky," Papak said. "Please just tell Tom we'll be there as soon as we can."

Janet was still in the bedroom, lying motionless on her bed and crying into her pillow. She couldn't stop thinking about the first time she had held her little boy in the hospital at Camp Lejeune. Baby Travis was so sweet, innocent, and helpless, and all Janet wanted was the chance to hold him one more time.

Ryan sat in the hallway bathroom, makeup smeared on her face. Ever since she had collapsed in the driveway, she was barely aware of her surroundings. *This has to be a bad dream.*

The Manions' phone had been ringing off the hook since the news began to spread. The official casualty notice had been released to the public shortly after the family was notified, prompting calls from some Philadelphia TV stations and area newspapers. Most of the calls, however, were from relatives and friends, who spoke to Janet's sister, Annette.

When the phone rang for what had to be the hundredth time, Tom picked up the cordless, which was sitting next to him on the patio table.

"Hello," he said in a subdued monotone.

"Mr. Manion, sir, is that you?" a young man said on the other end of the line.

"Yes, it is," Tom said.

"This is Brendan. I'm so sorry."

Getting up from his chair, Tom walked inside the house and toward the bedroom as he thanked Brendan for calling and told him there were still no details about what had happened. All they knew was that Travis was killed in action in Al Anbar province.

"Janet," Tom said, opening the door. "Brendan is on the phone."

Tom and Janet shared the phone as they listened to the emotions of Travis's former roommate on the other line. For the first time all day, Janet and Tom were the ones lending comfort.

"Brendan, we love you," Janet said, her voice shaking. "You are such a good friend."

"I love you, too," Brendan said. "I am coming out there to be with all of you."

Tom knew Brendan was about to start BUD/S training and realized it wasn't something an aspiring Navy SEAL could simply leave and return to.

"No, buddy, you need to stay focused on what you're doing out there," Tom said. "You gotta do your training or they might never let you back in."

"Sir, I understand, and I'm not going to quit," Brendan said. "But I have to fly east and be there for Travis. . . . I'm sure they'll let me come back."

"Brendan," Janet said in the most motherly, authoritative voice she could muster given the tragic circumstances. "You need to stay there and finish what you've started."

"I understand what you're going through," Tom said. "We haven't even like . . . made sense of all this yet."

"But you've got to think about what Travis would want," Janet said.

Hanging up after one of the most difficult conversations of his life, Brendan told Sarver he was ready to head over to the house on Imperial Beach. As they left Naval Amphibious Base Coronado and crossed over the bay, it began to hit Brendan that he would never get to hang out on the island with Travis, as they had excitedly discussed via e-mail in February.

As night fell in Pennsylvania, Janet and Tom lay next to one another in their bed. Silence filled the room, but both were still wide awake. For moments at a time, they each pondered the uncertainty of the next few days.

When will Travis's casket arrive at Dover?

Will we get to see his body?

What in God's name happened to our son?

Yet this was not a night for reasoning or logic. It was a time for grief.

"Mom, Dad?" Ryan asked, slowly cracking open her parents' door. "Is it okay if I sleep in here?"

As April 29, 2007, came to a close, a married, twenty-seven-year-old mother lay between her parents, just like when she was a little girl. A single combat patrol in the notorious Pizza Slice of Fallujah, Iraq, had changed everything for Tom, Janet, and Ryan Manion.

•———•

Sitting at the Imperial Beach house's shared computer with an untouched beer that had been out of the refrigerator for hours, Brendan Looney thought about his fallen friend and his heartfelt conversation with the Manions. The house was quiet, except for the ocean waves and the barely audible sound of music playing on the kitchen radio.

His eyes still red from crying, Brendan looked through the care package he had been preparing to send Travis, which included dozens of sports and fitness magazines. He then reread the last e-mail he had received from Travis, sent a week and a half before from Camp Fallujah:

> Friends and Family,
>
> We are a little over the halfway point of deployment. We have been pretty busy and working hard. It seems I have less

free time than I did last year, but I do take the time to read all the e-mails and open all the packages sent. Thanks for all the support (my guys, the Iraqis, and I really appreciate the packages). Also, it's been good to see a lot of familiar faces as new units are rotating in. My Battalion (Recon) has arrived and they're ready to get to work-It was great to see them as well as some other Marines I know.

Our Iraqi battalion has had some tough times lately but they are getting back on track. My company has really done well bouncing back and showing their dedication to the mission. I have attached some pictures from a recent operation.

Again, it's definitely been busy (and I apologize for the delay between updates), but the hard work definitely makes the time go by and keeps us all focused on the job at hand. I'm excited to see the deployment end strong and leave the Iraqi battalion at a higher level than when we arrived. I miss you guys and I'm looking forward to seeing you soon.
Semper Fi,
Travis

Taking a deep breath, Brendan sat down on a couch across from where Sarver was studying his BUD/S training manual. Brendan hadn't said a word in several hours. He suddenly spoke up, prompting Sarver to put down the manual and focus squarely on his roommate.

"It hurts, man," Brendan said. "But Trav would want us to go out there and get after it."

"Damn right," Sarver said with a nod. "Let's do this."

• —————— •

As the morning of Monday, April 30, dawned in Pennsylvania, the Pentagon issued one of the day's ten press releases about US troops killed in Afghanistan and Iraq:

The Department of Defense announced today the death of a Marine who was supporting Operation Iraqi Freedom.

1st Lt. Travis L. Manion, 26, of Doylestown, Pa., died April 29 while conducting combat operations in Al Anbar province, Iraq. Manion was assigned to 1st Reconnaissance Battalion, 1st Marine Division, I Marine Expeditionary Force, Camp Pendleton, Calif.

From Doylestown, Pennsylvania, all the way to Wichita, Kansas—the hometown of twenty-one-year-old US Army Sergeant Alex Funcheon, who was killed in a Baghdad IED attack alongside two fellow soldiers on the same day as Travis—the horrors of war transported a multitude of American families to desolate islands of confusion, anger, and grief.

As the Manions lay in bed without having slept a single wink, birds started to chirp outside the master bedroom window and the local paper boy was making his early morning rounds. Without knowing it was his day's most significant toss, he flung a newspaper into the driveway of Tom and Janet Manion's home. On the front page was Travis's smiling face.

8

LIVE FOREVER

Except for stirring sounds of bagpipes and occasional gusts of wind, Hangar 680 of Naval Air Station Joint Reserve Base Willow Grove was silent on May 3, 2007. On this sad Thursday afternoon during one of the Iraq war's most violent chapters, the flag-draped casket of First Lieutenant Travis Manion was coming home to Pennsylvania. Hundreds joined Tom, Janet, Ryan, and Dave for the ceremony, and all could feel its mixture of trepidation, sorrow, and pride.

It was a different atmosphere than earlier in the week at Dover Air Force Base in Delaware, when the grief-stricken Manion family had first welcomed Travis to American soil. Rather than being surrounded by loved ones, the Manions had stood alone in a massive hangar as six US Marines slowly carried Travis out of a large military jet. In 2007, no media coverage of these solemn ceremonies was allowed at Dover. The fallen hero's return to eastern Pennsylvania, the Manions decided, would be different.

Four days after the death of his only son, Tom stood in the front row of a large, hushed crowd in his clean, crisp Marine Corps uniform. Wearing his dress blue pants, white hat, and Navy blue jacket, Tom would have gladly traded his colonel's rank and every medal on his uniform to have one last conversation with Travis.

The father's anguish was matched only by his determination to honor Travis the right way, while showing the world that no sniper could ever gash the vein of his son's fighting spirit.

Tom's hand was clasping Janet's, who stood to his right with her head bowed. Wearing all black except for a Marine-colored scarf and a pair of gold earrings shaped like the Corps' distinctive Eagle, Globe, and Anchor, she had barely slept since the Gardners had arrived on her front doorstep with the nervous young Marine. Still, she shared her husband's resolve to honor Travis, even if seeing her son's casket for the first time in Dover had been the most painful moment of her life. All Janet wanted to do was hug her little boy, and hopefully, someone would soon let her.

Ryan, wearing a turquoise blouse and black skirt with dark sunglasses, held a small American flag in her right hand and her mom's hand in her left. Travis's older sister was also looking down as she awaited his return home, but she occasionally looked up with her tearful eyes at the many signs guests had made to honor Travis. One bright poster, held by Ryan and Travis's cousin Lauren Gretz said "Welcome home Travis!" in red cursive handwriting.

The warm messages of support helped replace the cold feeling Ryan had felt in Dover. She also noticed reporters from every major Philadelphia-area television station and newspaper, which helped the audience appreciate the significance of the heartrending moment they were about to witness.

Dave, who wore an American flag pin on his dark suit, thought again of what his brother-in-law had said after the Eagles game in December—"If not me, then who . . . "—and marveled at the quote's unmistakable meaning. Though Travis had said it in passing, without the slightest hint of bravado, he had backed up his words with decisive, selfless actions.

Nobody in the packed hangar knew what to expect as an anxious calm blended with what would have been an ordinary, comfortable spring day. From eastern Pennsylvania to Iraq, where the Marines of 3-2-1 MiTT and their Iraqi counterparts were holding a memorial service for their brother in arms, this was a time of utter uncertainty.

Janet heard the faint sound of helicopters approaching, gasping as she looked toward the partly cloudy skies. She squeezed her husband's arm in anticipation.

Tom also looked up at the sky, which he had shouted at in anger four days earlier after realizing Travis was dead. Ever since that excruciating moment, however, he had been determined to hold the family together.

When the sound of the choppers grew louder, Tom stood at attention and tried not to cry as the helicopters appeared over the distant treetops. Janet gripped both her husband's and daughter's arms. In a few agonizing moments, Travis would finally be home.

The audience's heartache was palpable as the helicopter carrying Travis flew over the treetops, descended slowly, and landed gently on the warm Pennsylvania concrete.

To Tom and Janet, the helicopter was carrying a beloved son. To Ryan and Dave, it was carrying a trusted brother. To Travis's relatives, it was carrying a grandson, nephew, or cousin. To the Marines standing at attention, it was carrying a brother in arms. To everyone else, the chopper was bringing home a young man who was willing to sacrifice everything to protect others.

When the helicopter's rear hatch opened and six Marines carried Travis back to the place where most of his formative years had been spent, onlookers saw a young man's casket covered with the flag that so many heroes of current and prior generations have fought to preserve.

Major Steve Cantrell, who had taken Travis to the Rescue One firehouse in lower Manhattan and comforted the twenty-six-year-old Marine after the first time he struck down an enemy fighter on the battlefield, rode in the back of the helicopter that brought Travis back to Pennsylvania. He had spent the previous night guarding Travis and even slept in front of his casket. From Fallujah to Doylestown, the fallen Marine was never alone.

As Cantrell watched his fellow Marines march Travis toward his loved ones, a bagpipe played the first, dramatic notes of "Amazing Grace." The timeless hymn echoed through the hangar, causing Tom, Janet, Ryan, Dave, and almost everyone else in the audience to weep.

Many who watched in person and on Philadelphia-area television sets were shocked to see such an emotionally visceral ceremony. Since Vietnam, the public had been largely sheltered from seeing the toll of war unfold before their eyes. But as Tom and Janet often said, Americans had to see war's consequences in order to grasp the burden military families were enduring. While Ryan and Dave chose to shield Maggie from the confusion of seeing her uncle's coffin being carried off the helicopter, older children in attendance got their first glimpse of the military community's enormous sacrifices.

Brigadier General Dave Papak, who had immersed himself in every detail of Travis's homecoming since first receiving the devastating e-mail from his commanding officer in New Orleans, summed up the ceremony's meaning in three words: "Welcome home, warrior."

The Manion family was exhausted by the time they collapsed into a limousine to follow the hearse to the funeral home. That's when Krista Brown, a close family friend who had grown up with Ryan and Travis, looked up with a blank expression after receiving a shocking text message.

"Colby Umbrell was killed today in Iraq," she said.

"Oh, my God," Ryan said. "We went to high school with him."

"What?" Janet said, covering her mouth with both hands. "Oh no, it can't be . . . that poor family."

After a moment of silence, Janet took Ryan's and Krista's hands.

"Let's all lower our heads and say a prayer," she said.

Twenty-six-year-old US Army First Lieutenant Colby Umbrell was killed in action on May 3, 2007, by an enemy IED in Musayyib, just south of Baghdad. In a cruel twist of fate, two sons of the small community of Doylestown serving in Iraq were killed just four days apart.

"Two in one week," Tom said before rephrasing his sentence as a question. "Two in one week?"

Shock and disbelief gripped Bucks County, Pennsylvania, during the difficult days that followed. But as stores sold out of American flags and schoolteachers brought children outside during both funeral processions, there was a sense of pride and patriotism not seen in the Philadelphia area since the entire nation rallied in unison on September 12, 2001.

The day after learning of Umbrell's death, Ryan, who had never met her onetime classmate's parents, went with her Uncle Chris to the family's house to pay her respects. They exchanged hugs, tears, and stories about their loved ones.

For US Marine Captain Brian Stann, who had seen the horrors of war up close on the bloody, bombed-out streets of Iraq, Travis's death was another devastating blow.

From May 8–14, 2005, then Second Lieutenant Stann was instrumental in holding down a bridge after his unit was ambushed by enemy fighters using IEDs, machine guns, and rocket-propelled grenades. The Scranton, Pennsylvania, native had also directed casualty evacuations that helped save the lives of several wounded Marines.

"Inspired by his leadership and endurance, 2nd Lt. Stann's platoon held the battle position on the Euphrates River for six days protecting the Task Force flank and isolating foreign fighters and insurgents north of the river," read Stann's Silver Star citation.

Stann rarely spoke about his gallantry in combat and consistently refused to take any credit, even after receiving the military's third-highest honor. He had told Travis about those hellish events, however, to help prepare his friend for what he would soon encounter in Iraq.

The Marine officer had endured the loss of Naval Academy friends, explained to weeping mothers that sons under his command weren't coming home, and seen the limbs of fellow Marines blown off by roadside bombs. But when Stann arrived at the Reed-Steinbach Funeral Home in Doylestown, he felt lost.

As the Iraq war hero waited in a long line that stretched outside the funeral home, he turned to his wife, Teressa. During his first deployment, Travis had e-mailed Stann from Iraq to congratulate Brian and Teressa on their engagement. He couldn't wait to see them again upon returning from his second deployment.

Shaking his head, Stann said to his wife, "I can't believe Travis is gone. I can't believe it."

As Stann waited, he saw everyone from Naval Academy buddies and fellow Marines to Travis's high school friends and grieving relatives. Police officers and firefighters were everywhere, and the Patriot Guard Riders, pledging to protect the fallen hero's farewell from any potential protests, surrounded the premises with Harley Davidson motorcycles and American flags. Though Stann could hardly bear the day's emotions, it was heartening to see the solemn event being handled with so much dignity. The patriotism was palpable.

Stann recalled how, after returning from Iraq, he would calmly and patiently listen when Travis called from Fallujah during his first deployment to voice frustrations about not being able to leave his base to go outside the wire on a daily basis. While Stann knew how much it hurt Travis to be stuck mostly on the sidelines, he had encouraged the young Marine in the same way Travis had inspired him to push toward becoming a professional mixed martial arts fighter.

"Keep after it, Trav," Stann often repeated.

The tragedy wouldn't seem real to Stann until he saw Travis's body for himself. He was sick to his stomach upon seeing the buttons, ribbons, and medals on his buddy's uniform. The sight of

Travis, with his "wrestler ears" and closed eyes, made grief's cold hands grab Stann by the throat like an opponent's crushing head-lock. He broke down.

"Travis wanted a family someday," Stann said through tears. "Travis wanted a wife and children."

As his wife consoled him, Stann quickly pulled himself to-gether before going to speak to Tom, Janet, Dave, and Ryan. They were standing next to Krista, who was keeping the line organized and making sure the family had everything they needed.

Upon greeting Krista at the front of the line, Stann extended his hand to the steely, composed colonel, who was determined to put on a brave face to honor his son.

"Sir, I just want you to know how much Travis meant to me and how sorry I am," Stann said. "I'll spend every day of my life trying to be like him."

Tom hugged his son's friend and thanked him. Stann's condo-lences meant a lot. After Stann told Janet how sorry he was for her loss, she also expressed her gratitude.

Janet took solace in the endless stream of well-wishers. During an earlier, private viewing she had sobbed uncontrollably.

When she first saw Travis, Janet held her son's hand, kissed him, and finally got to give Travis the hug she had been longing for since receiving the painful news.

"I love you," Janet told Travis, whose eyes were closed just like when he was a baby. "I am so proud of you."

Before the public viewing started, Janet said a prayer, as she often did in difficult situations.

"Lord, help me to remember that nothing is going to happen today that you and I together can't handle," she whispered. Even with her son's casket just steps away, Janet managed to compose herself and hug every single mourner.

Ryan took intermittent breaks after becoming panic stricken during the private viewing. After rubbing his head, much like when they were little kids, Ryan secretly hoped Travis would wake up, then realized that he never would. Without Dave and Krista at her side and the relatives who had volunteered to watch Maggie, Ryan, who told Stann she couldn't believe Travis was gone, never would have made it through the morning viewing and early afternoon funeral services.

As Stann stood over his friend's body, he thought of all the times Travis had been there for him, starting with the night at the Naval Academy when they watched *Vanilla Sky* and were the only two guys who admitted that they liked the occasionally sappy film.

"Isn't that what being young is about? Believing secretly that you would be the one person in the history of man that would live forever?" says the movie's main character, played by Tom Cruise.

Few possessed a better understanding of mortality than Captain Brian Stann. But in that moment, as he again marveled at a line that stretched well outside the funeral parlor's front door, Stann realized that Travis had died doing exactly what he had written as they flew to their mutual friend's funeral: standing for what was right.

"You earned it, man," Stann said, channeling one of his and Travis's favorite *Saving Private Ryan* quotes. "Good-bye, Trav."

Though too humble to admit it, Stann, like many of his classmates and fellow warriors, had also earned it. Just over a year before his death, Travis had been ecstatic when his friend was singled out for some well-deserved praise.

"I appreciate the service of people like Marine 1st Lt. Brian Stann, a former Navy linebacker who was awarded the Silver Star last month for his actions and his bravery in Iraq," President Bush had said on April 25, 2006.

After serving as a pallbearer at Travis's funeral, Brian Stann would become a champion mixed martial arts fighter, television analyst, author, and president of Hire Heroes USA, which helps veterans find employment. Before and after Travis was killed, Stann knew he would always be in his corner.

Along with Stann, Mike Bigrigg, Steve Brown, Sean Kent, Steve Kovach, Carlo Pecori, and Croft Young, Brendan was listed as a pallbearer. Not being able to pay his respects in person hurt more than any of the punishing challenges he would soon experience in BUD/S training. Instead Amy, who was also devastated by Travis's death, attended the funeral and burial with her boyfriend's immediate family. She had never lost a close friend and didn't know how she would handle saying good-bye to Travis.

The procession to and from Our Lady of Mount Carmel Catholic Church was the most inspiring sight that Amy, Stann, or anyone else who witnessed it had ever seen. All along Highway 611, from Doylestown to the Pennsylvania Turnpike junction at Willow Grove, fire truck ladders joined together to hang huge American flags over Pennsylvania streets and highways. Parents, teenagers, children, and the elderly all put their hands over their hearts and waved American flags. Veterans and active duty troops stood in silence to salute a fallen brother in arms. Pennsylvania governor Ed Rendell ordered a section of the Pennsylvania Turnpike closed to support the fallen Marine's massive procession, which included at least three hundred slow-moving vehicles.

"Look at all these people," said Janet, who cried all the way to the church, pointing toward the seemingly never-ending stream of supporters. "This is unbelievable."

At the church Travis's uncle, Chris Manion, spoke about the boy, wrestler, young man, and Marine who had inspired him so much:

> From wonderful parents to the sister and brother in-law that he so deeply loved and so deeply loved him, to the niece he cherished and was so protective of, to the grandparents he doted over and who doted over him, to the family he was so proud of and to the many extraordinary friends whose friendships he was blessed with, from his beloved La Salle High School, from the Naval Academy, from his Marine Corps family . . . from this great circle of love,

Travis learned all that he knew and all that he was to become. And Travis learned well.

"Travis Lemma Manion was no accident," Chris continued. "He did not just magically appear and suddenly become who he became. Look around . . . here in this church, in this congregation, are the family and friends and the mentors that filled his life with so much love, so much happiness, and so many fond memories."

Chris Manion closed his speech with a call to action: "Let us not just mourn our loss today and in the days ahead. But as Tom and Janet have requested, let us cherish his memory, act with love, and celebrate his life."

Across the country in Imperial Beach, California, Brendan sat in silence, holding his cell phone. The Navy SEAL candidate may not have heard the stirring eulogy delivered by Travis's uncle, but he was already heeding its selfless message.

Suddenly his cell phone rang. It was Amy, and like Brendan a few days earlier, she was too hysterical to make much sense. She was overcome with emotion not only from seeing Travis's coffin, but also after seeing Ryan spend most of the afternoon crying behind thick, dark sunglasses.

"I . . . I . . . I don't know what to say," she said. "Travis. . . ."

"Sweetheart, please take a deep breath and try to calm down," Brendan said quietly. "Can you tell me how it's going there? How are the Manions?"

"I don't . . . I don't know what to say," Amy repeated. "I feel so horrible for them, Brendan."

That was Amy's last comprehensible sentence before she started to sob. Realizing that hearing his girlfriend's anguish would likely make Brendan even more upset, Billy Looney gently took the phone from Amy and told his brother that though the ceremonies were very emotional, Travis was being memorialized with a perfect, fitting tribute. Brendan, who would have given almost anything to witness the day's events, thanked his brother for being there.

First Lieutenant Travis Manion was laid to rest with full military honors. In one of the burial's most powerful moments, uniformed US Marines presented Tom and Janet with the American flag that had covered their son's coffin ever since he was struck down in Fallujah.

"On behalf of the President of the United States, the Commandant of the Marine Corps, and a grateful nation, please accept this flag as a symbol of our appreciation for your loved one's honorable and faithful service," a Marine told Tom and Janet.

Tom, Janet, Ryan, and Dave trembled when TAPS was played and shivered as a twenty-one-gun salute shattered the calmness of the spring air over Calvary Cemetery in West Conshohocken, Pennsylvania. By the end of the service, they were almost completely numb.

The Manions had considered burying their son at Arlington National Cemetery before Janet told Tom and Ryan that she wanted Travis nearby. Though West Conshohocken was about thirty-five minutes away from Doylestown, Janet could still go see him often and make sure the flowers on her son's grave were always fresh. Amid the fog of grief that dominated the ensuing weeks, when some of Travis's final wishes were revealed, the Manions decided to put off making a final decision about whether it would be Travis's permanent resting place.

●————————●

Brendan couldn't see from afar that his friend's place of rest was marked only by a simple wooden cross. After his conversation with Amy, he slowly opened the door to his room and was greeted by Rob Sarver.

"Hey buddy, are you alright?" Sarver asked.

Brendan was still shell shocked after hearing Amy's voice. Following a brief pause and a sip of water, he managed to utter a few words.

"It's like we said the other day," Brendan said. "We've gotta go out there tomorrow and get after it."

"I hear you," Sarver said. "What do you say we hit the gym?"

"Let's do it," Brendan agreed.

After that day, Brendan rarely mentioned Travis to Sarver or any other military friends. But the words and deeds of his fellow warrior, Naval Academy roommate, and dear friend would live forever in his heart.

9

HONOR MAN

Before sunrise on the first day of BUD/S, Brendan and Sarver drove onto the island of Coronado, blasting an intentionally comical hip-hop song, Fat Joe's "Make It Rain." In what would become an early morning tradition, the new roommates shouted the over-the-top lyrics to the song to get fired up before a seemingly impossible day of mental and physical challenges.

It was the first time that Brendan had laughed since Travis died, and Sarver knew how important that was before the relentless BUD/S instructors started trying to break them and every other Navy SEAL candidate down. For the next six months Brendan's emotional, mental, and physical strength would be tested as never before.

BUD/S got off to a rocky start. Every candidate's room, uniform, and appearance were required to be spotless and were routinely subject to rigorous inspections that could sometimes last several hours. For twenty-four punishing weeks, nothing mattered more than attention to detail.

Brendan first faced an instructor's wrath because of his haircut. The night before, Sarver had accidentally nicked his neck with the clippers they used to shave each other's heads.

"HAVE YOU SEEN THE BACK OF YOUR NECK?" the instructor shouted directly into Brendan's left ear. "WHO DID THIS?"

Brendan was silent.

"WAS IT SARVER?" the instructor said.

Brendan quickly glanced at his roommate, who nodded.

"Hooyah," Brendan said. The word is often used as a battle cry inside the Navy, and sometimes as a substitute for "yes, sir."

"Sarver, you pass inspection," the instructor said. "Looney, you fail. NOW GET OUT ON THAT BEACH!"

"Hooyah," Brendan said.

Brendan spent the next ninety minutes doing God knows how many push-ups and other exercises in cold "BUD/S Beach" water. When he returned to the barracks almost completely covered in sand, Sarver wasn't sure if Brendan would crack a joke or punch him in the face.

"You owe me, bro," said Brendan, walking in the room, wiping off his face, and throwing his gear on the bed.

"Anything you want, Brendan," Sarver said. "Just name it."

"Ice cream," Brendan said. "After this day is over, you're taking me to get some ice cream."

His first run-in with the instructors behind him, Brendan attacked the island of Coronado, where all Navy SEAL candidates train but very few graduate, with the same intensity Travis had brought to the streets of Fallujah. At almost two hundred pounds of muscle, Brendan was running 5½-minute miles. Aspiring SEALs were shocked by Brendan's physical prowess.

"That guy is a beast," one trainee told another. "What's Looney's story, anyway?"

"I talked to his roommate, Sarver, the other day," the other SEAL candidate responded. "Looney just lost one of his best friends in Fallujah."

Except on weekends, when candidates were usually permitted to rest, Brendan hardly slept during his six months of BUD/S training and was rarely able to communicate with Amy. But after one particularly arduous day of running, being sprayed with ice-cold water while doing push-ups, and shivering while carrying logs over his head with teammates through merciless waves, he described to Amy how Travis was still pushing him.

"When Travis died, I think it gave me that extra motivation to make sure I got out there and did everything I could," Brendan said.

Amy exchanged "see you laters" with Brendan after he yawned and told her the SEAL candidates had to be awake in three hours. She was proud of her boyfriend's resolve.

Across the room, Sarver was talking on the phone to his girlfriend, Heather Hojnacki.

"Honestly, I'm just trying to keep up with Brendan," Sarver said when his girlfriend asked how his training was going. "He is a machine."

One of Brendan's favorite quotes was one he rarely spoke out loud, but always kept in the back of his mind: "Be strong. Be accountable. Never complain."

Sarver, as Brendan's BUD/S roommate, was watching his friend live out every word.

Fiercely committed and quietly confident, Brendan would have excelled in training even if Travis had still been alive. From spending eight consecutive hours stenciling his number on his gear to sometimes staying up all night doing additional administrative duties, he brought an exceptional, sincere brand of dedication to a special operations group that was already among the US military's most revered.

Despite being tough, smart young men, candidates all around Brendan were quitting or being dropped from Class 265 by the time "Hell Week," a fierce combat simulation during which sleep is not an option, started after two already grueling weeks of training.

On Saturday, May 26, 2007, three days before the Manions would mark one month since Travis's passing, Brendan wrote an e-mail to Janet:

Mrs. Manion,

Hi, sorry it has taken me so long to write back. I do not get a chance to check my e-mail as much as I would like.

Things out here are going well so far. We started with 203 guys and are now down to 80. Hell Week begins tomorrow night, so we are all getting geared up for that hurdle. Right now I am not too nervous about it because I know I have Travis looking out for me and that will give me strength when I need it. He is probably laughing at me too with all of the crazy stuff they have us doing.

Other than that, not much else is going on, we have long days so that leaves time only to sleep when we finish. I have lost a few pounds, but still continue to eat everything they put in front of me. Anyways, that is about it for now. I'll be sure to send you all an e-mail when I finish Hell Week next Friday to let you know that I finished.
—Brendan

That Friday an instructor walked up to Brendan and told him what he thought of his Hell Week performance.

"Looney, you crushed Hell Week," he said. "You beasted it."

Brendan, who never wanted special attention, simply said "hooyah," nodded his head in acknowledgment, and headed back to barracks to spend the next few days resting and sleeping. His mom, Maureen, had timed a cross-country trip to help Brendan and Sarver recover before they resumed the first phase of BUD/S training: another month of difficult conditioning exercises. After first phase they would move on to the second and third, which focused on combat diving and land warfare, respectively. Each lasted about eight weeks.

The weekend after his mom's stay, Brendan welcomed Amy to San Diego for her only visit of the summer. She arrived in Imperial Beach on a Friday night, anxious to see her boyfriend not only because she missed him, but also because she wanted to discuss where their relationship was headed after he became a Navy SEAL.

After a nice Saturday night dinner at an ocean-view restaurant in nearby La Jolla, Brendan asked Amy to join him on the beach.

"I had some time to think after Hell Week," Brendan said. "That's when I realized that I couldn't think about my life without you in it."

"So I really wanted to ask you something," he continued. "I've been trying to do this all night."

Kneeling in front of Amy, Brendan pulled a box out of his pocket.

"I got you this ring," he said. "Do you think you would marry me?"

"Yes," Amy said. "I love you."

"I love you, too!" said Brendan, awash with relief. He then kissed his new fiancée.

When Brendan and Amy got back to Imperial Beach, Sarver was waiting to congratulate them. After opening the bottle of champagne that the elated couple had bought on their way home, Sarver proposed a toast to his two friends, who he said were perfect for each other.

After Sarver went to his room, Brendan told Amy about a conversation he had had with his mom while she was in town after Hell Week.

"I told her that after Travis died, I realized there was no reason for you and me to wait any longer," Brendan said to Amy. "Life is short. . . . Just look at what happened with Trav. I don't want us to have any regrets."

The next evening, Amy left San Diego sporting a smile big enough to light up the entire harbor. Although moving from Maryland to the West Coast would be challenging, she couldn't wait to start her new life. But first, Brendan would have to finish training to become a Navy SEAL.

At BUD/S, officers train alongside enlisted personnel, which gave the Naval Academy graduate a chance to start blossoming as a leader. Before grabbing paddles and starting boat exercises, Brendan would underscore what the instructors were always hammering home: teamwork and paying attention to the small things. Whether it was lacrosse, football, the classroom, Iraq, or Korea, Brendan's experience helped guide other candidates through the choppy seas. Even Sarver, who knew Brendan better than any other trainee, marveled at how instinctively his roommate adapted.

Before embarking on long beach runs through the island's chilly morning wind, guys would sometimes gripe, understandably, about lack of sleep, persistent hunger, or physical exhaustion. One time Sarver himself was commiserating with a group of SEAL candidates about the consistently tough training conditions.

"Okay guys, it's time to shut up," Brendan said. "Let's get started."

During the third phase of what seemed like six years of BUD/S training rather than six months, Brendan once joined his team on the beach for a morning "ruck" run, during which each SEAL candidate would carry forty pounds of gear in his backpack. Brendan, who had been up more than thirty straight hours after working his administrative job all night, didn't have time to pack his bag before the five-mile run started at 5:30 a.m. Instead, he arrived at the beach a few minutes early and found a huge rock that he thought would satisfy the ruck's weight requirements.

As he had done in his races through Annapolis with Travis, Brendan ran as if his life depended on it. The ocean breeze didn't affect his tired eyes, nor did the wet sand slow his aching feet. When Class 265 crossed the five-mile mark, Brendan finished first, standing at the finish line shouting words of encouragement to every fellow SEAL candidate who followed.

"Looney, what the hell is in your pack?" one fellow trainee asked.

"It's a rock," Brendan said. "I didn't have time to pack up."

"Well that's one big fucking rock!" said another classmate, who thought the rock looked much heavier than forty pounds.

Though downplaying his own toughness, Brendan grinned and admitted that the rock felt "pretty damn heavy." When a few of his teammates later put the rock on a scale, it weighed fifty-five pounds.

"Hooyah!" the guys shouted.

For instructors and trainees, the easiest part of BUD/S was determining who would finish at the top.

"Now we will announce the Honor Man of Navy SEAL BUD/S training Class 265," an instructor said. "This award goes to a leader who not only excels in physical training, but makes every Frogman [as SEALs are nicknamed] around him better. I'm proud to name Brendan Looney the Honor Man of your class."

After twenty-four weeks of a meticulous, exhausting regimen that had encompassed physical conditioning, diving, and land warfare, Brendan, who had almost missed the chance to train at Coronado because he was colorblind, received the ultimate recognition from his instructors and peers.

All fall 2007 graduates of BUD/S would almost certainly go to war at some point in the next few years after completing SEAL Qualification Training (SQT) and receiving their tridents. Brendan and Sarver would have to wait longer than the enlisted BUD/S graduates to complete their twenty-six weeks of SQT, however, as all SEAL officers are held back one class to complete the required Junior Officer Training Course (JOTC). But as the valiant men of Class 265 gathered one last time on BUD/S Beach, they applauded Brendan for not only overcoming the loss of a close friend, but also inspiring all of them with his sheer willpower, ability, and character.

"In times of war or uncertainty there is a special breed of warrior ready to answer our nation's call," the Navy SEAL ethos and creed begins. "A common man with an uncommon desire to succeed.

Forged by adversity, he stands alongside America's finest special operations forces to serve his country, the American people, and protect their way of life. I am that man."

Brendan said only "thank you" when he received the rare, coveted award, and he didn't even tell Amy until she later discovered the "Honor Man" plaque in a drawer. When she asked Brendan what it was, he said it was "no big deal."

Since he was a little boy, when his mom would find ribbons and tests with A+ grades crumpled up in his backpack and trophies hidden in his drawers, Brendan had never been interested in recognition. Sure enough, when Amy later asked some of her husband's peers about the Honor Man award and discovered its significance, Brendan had already mailed it to his parents' house in Maryland.

The Honor Man of BUD/S Class 265 sent his plaque home as a symbol of appreciation and respect. In Brendan's mind, no award was ever his; it belonged to the people who had sacrificed to give him a chance at success. Indeed, there was no one prouder of what Brendan overcame the odds to accomplish than Kevin and Maureen Looney.

•————•

Though also proud of Brendan, those same six months were brutal for Tom and Janet Manion. Since Travis's death they had attended two more funerals for US service members killed in Iraq. The first was for First Lieutenant Colby Umbrell, the Doylestown soldier who had died four days after Travis, and the second was for a Marine and Naval Academy graduate who was killed in Baghdad less than two weeks after their son.

Major Douglas Zembiec, the "Lion of Fallujah" from Albuquerque, New Mexico, whom Travis knew, worked out with, and deeply respected, was killed on May 11, 2007, in Baghdad. Due to his already famous battlefield heroics, Zembiec's death received a high level of attention inside and outside military circles.

"After the Battle [of Fallujah], he said that his Marines had 'fought like lions,' and he was soon himself dubbed the Lion of Fallujah," Defense Secretary Robert Gates said to a large group of Marines on July 19, 2007. "He volunteered to deploy again, and was sent back to Iraq earlier this year. This time, he would not return to his country, or to his wife and his one-year-old daughter."

Gates, who had been nominated by President Bush to replace Donald Rumsfeld at the Pentagon less than a year earlier, paused before continuing. He was clearly moved by the thirty-four-year-old Marine's courage.

"In May, the Lion of Fallujah was laid to rest at Arlington, and he was memorialized at his Alma Mater in Annapolis," the defense secretary said, his voice cracking with sadness. "A crowd of more than a thousand included many enlisted Marines from his Beloved Echo Company. An officer there told a reporter: 'Your men have to follow your orders. They don't have to go to your funeral.'"

Gates concluded his speech with a touching tribute.

"Every evening, I write notes to the families of young Americans like Doug Zembiec," he said. "For you and for me, they are not names on a press release, or numbers updated on a Web site; they are our country's sons and daughters."

For Tom and Janet, the months after their son's death were filled with devastation and daily reminders of their enormous loss. They were lifted up, however, by the many visits from Travis's friends and Marine Corps brothers.

The Manions were also getting hundreds of messages on a Legacy .com page set up to memorialize Travis. During many late, sometimes sleepless nights, Tom, Janet, Ryan, and Dave would scroll through the words of support, and they were particularly moved by posts from men and women inside the circle of 3-2-1 MiTT:

I was with Travis when he was killed. There is no doubt in my mind that he saved my life and the lives of all of us that were there that day. Know that Travis is missed and remembered. He was one of the best Marines and men I have ever had the luck to meet and I'll never forget his gift.

~1st Lt. Jonathan Marang

I've been getting stronger. I see the progress every 2–3 weeks or so. I'm pushing to get back to full duty status before April [2008] is over. I know that when I take the PFT [Physical Fitness Test] I'll think of what we talked about, of how we could look back on the days spent in Iraq and know that we did our part. We wouldn't be the ones wondering about whether we had an effect or not.

R.I.P. brother,

~Ed ("Doc") Albino

I served with Travis during his first tour in Iraq as his battalion surgeon. Last year when I heard of his death I was deeply saddened due to the loss of an exceptional man and Marine.

Travis built our gym in Fallujah and this is where I had most of my conversations with him.

Every day I work out now, even in a gym far away that he has likely never been in, I remember Travis and am grateful to have had an opportunity to know him.

~Reagan Anderson

I am the wife of 2nd Lt. Scott Alexander, a member of Travis' MiTT team and his great friend. I want to let you know what joy Travis was able to bring to the team. Scott called last night and for an hour relayed stories of all the ways Travis would make the guys laugh and keep up the morale of the team. Throughout the deployment he spoke of Travis with the utmost regard and he was a true mentor, friend, and brother to my husband. Thank you for raising such a wonderful young man, I know he impacted each one of our guys out there and is now watching over them. My sincerest apologies for your loss.

~Catherine Alexander

Although her husband made it home safely, Catherine Alexander, who served in the Navy Reserve, would lose her brother,

Marine Lieutenant Colonel Thomas Budrejko, almost five years later on February 22, 2012, in a helicopter training accident near Yuma, Arizona. Six fellow Marines were killed in the crash, which along with tragic events in Afghanistan, Iraq, and around the world, served as a painful reminder of the military community's continuing post-9/11 sacrifices.

On one quiet day in September 2007, the phone rang at the Manion house. It was Brendan, who asked Tom how he, Janet, and Ryan were holding up.

"It's great to hear from you, Brendan," Tom said. "We're doing alright up here. . . . How was BUD/S? . . . Did you make it out in one piece?"

"Yes, sir," Brendan said. "It was tough, but I made it, and I think you know who was looking out for me the whole time."

"Congratulations, buddy, and I also heard you got engaged, so congratulations to you and Amy, too," Tom said. "Janet and I are proud of you, and I know your parents are, too."

Brendan told Travis's father that he was in Maryland to visit his folks, and if it was alright with Tom and Janet, he would like to drive up to Pennsylvania and spend time with the Manions. After agreeing on a day, Tom invited Brendan to stay the night on the same downstairs couch next to the bar and pool table that Travis had loved to sleep on when he visited from California.

"Brendan, it really means a lot to us that you'd come up here," Tom said.

After hanging up Tom went into the kitchen, where his wife was immersed in the roots of what would later become the Travis Manion Foundation. Hearing that Brendan was coming to visit, Janet smiled for the first time in weeks.

"It will be so great to finally see Brendan," she said.

Many other friends and fellow Marines who knew Travis had made the pilgrimage to Doylestown, and Tom, Janet, Ryan, and Dave appreciated every visit. But few, if any, came without their spouses or significant others and spent the night. It was obvious that Brendan cared deeply about his friend's family and wanted to personally ensure that they were okay.

After opening the front door, which the Manions had not fixed since Janet had broken it six months earlier, one of America's newest Gold Star mothers embraced the soon-to-be Navy SEAL. With tears in her eyes, she profusely thanked her son's dear friend for making the trip.

Brendan, who felt guilty for being stuck in California during the funeral services, started apologizing to Travis's grieving mom.

"You can stop that right now," Janet said, patting Brendan on the back. "We all know you would have been here if you could have."

A collection of medals and letters, including one from the president, was sitting on the living room piano. Brendan paused to look at them for a few seconds, then took a deep breath and went inside.

Tom and Brendan exchanged a firm handshake and quick hug. Janet brought Tom and Brendan beers before they headed to the lower level to sit at the Manion bar, where they discussed BUD/S, Brendan's family, and Amy.

Surrounded by more of Travis's medals and mementos, sitting at the bar felt like having a drink in a Marine Corps museum. It was the first time Brendan had spent time with the Manion family since before Travis was killed.

Janet and Tom told Brendan they were proud of him and asked him to explain his upcoming SQT training, which would take him to Kodiak, Alaska, to simulate combat in bitterly cold weather. As she would have said to Travis, Janet told Brendan to take his heaviest winter coat. With a smile that evoked laughter, Brendan assured her that his own mom had been telling him the same thing.

After talking more about Brendan's next round of training and learning that he would likely become a Navy SEAL in June 2008, Janet proposed a toast.

"Let's have a drink for Travis," said Janet, pouring three shots of Patrón tequila. "He cared about you so much, and you were always—and still are—such a great friend."

"To Travis!" Brendan, Tom, and Janet said in unison.

● —————————— ●

The next time Brendan saw Travis's parents was the Friday night before the 2007 Marine Corps Marathon in Washington, DC, which was held on the Sunday just before Halloween. At long last Brendan had his chance to pay his respects to Travis, while spending the weekend surrounded by his buddy's relatives, friends, and fellow Marines. But he was also confronted with the full breadth of the mark that Travis's passing had made on people from all walks of life.

Before Brendan ran Sunday's Marine Corps Marathon with the Manions, his brother Steve, and their uncle, Chris Parker, the soon-to-be Navy SEAL attended a prerace "Team Travis" Saturday night dinner banquet in Arlington, Virginia, with his parents and Amy. Janet and Tom, who had created the special marathon group along with relatives and friends, began the emotional evening by standing at the podium to thank the hundreds in attendance. Nearly six months after an enemy sniper ended their son's life in the Pizza Slice, the grief on the Gold Star parents' faces was clear. But as Tom began to speak, their strength was even more apparent.

After expressing his gratitude and talking about how his son's constant desire to push himself further could serve as a theme for Sunday's 26.2-mile run, Tom talked about a significant moment earlier in the day.

"Janet and I went over to Arlington [National Cemetery] this morning," Tom said with his right arm around his wife. "We spent some time over there, and if you get a chance, that's a place to go and visit. . . . It's a special place. You feel a certain energy . . . when you go over there and see what's there and certainly feel all the brave men and women who've given their lives for our freedoms. You feel their spirits there, and it's really a special place and a special time. And this is really all about getting behind those who are over there now, continuing to fight for our freedoms, and those who have given their lives and made the ultimate sacrifice."

Family friend Bob Schumaker, who had helped organize the event with his wife, Kit, then introduced Steve Brown, a close friend of Travis's since elementary school. Steve, who is African American, stepped up to the podium and told a childhood story that very few in the audience had ever heard.

"A time that stands out to me the most was the summer between sixth and seventh grade when we set out to get a slice of pizza from a local pizza parlor," Brown said. "I remember stepping up to the counter and asking for a slice of plain, and was ignored. I asked again, and still no response.

"But before I knew it, the man behind the counter was already asking Travis for his order," Brown continued. "Travis, without hesitation, replied and said 'what about my friend? . . . What about my friend?' The man stood there in silence, and Travis quickly processed the situation and ordered three slices, and then handed two to me."

Brown finished the story, beginning to smile.

"He then looked the man in his eyes, and said with his 12-year-old voice: 'What you're doing here is wrong. He's just the same as me.'"

Brown ended his remarks by saying how much he missed and loved his friend. He received enthusiastic applause, then introduced one of Travis's best high school buddies, Sean Kent. After making the audience laugh with several creative lines, including "you can't send a boy to do a Manion's job," Kent introduced the next speaker.

"At this time, I'm going to hand it over to Brendan Looney, who was Travis's roommate at Navy," he said.

Brendan, who hadn't been nervous before Hell Week or during a deployment to Iraq, had confessed to Amy that he was petrified about speaking that night. He was worried not about himself or his image, but about adequately honoring Travis in front of so many loved ones and friends.

Amy had also been surprised when Brendan, who didn't care about fashion and usually dressed in a relaxed style when he was out of uniform, had asked her to take him shopping earlier in the day. He had bought a new button-down, blue-striped dress shirt and a pair of brown khaki pants.

"Amy, what if I break down up there?" Brendan had asked as they walked through the mall.

"Then you cry, Brendan, and everyone will cry with you," Amy had replied. "There's nothing wrong with crying."

But the aspiring Navy SEAL never wanted to show weakness, especially while paying tribute to Travis, who in Brendan's mind defined what it meant to be a warrior.

Brendan looked solid, handsome, and lean as he settled into the podium, which had a gold poster on the front that read "GO TEAM TRAVIS."

Looking out over the hotel ballroom, Brendan suddenly felt pressure building in his throat after wishing everyone "good evening." Despite spending the entire day figuring out how to avoid becoming emotional, seeing everyone sitting in front of him, especially Tom, Janet, Ryan, Dave, and Maggie, hit him harder than any explosion he had experienced during combat simulation exercises. Less than a year earlier, Travis and Brendan had still been hanging out, laughing, and going to Redskins-Eagles games. Now he was giving a speech after Travis's death.

As Brendan looked down and briefly covered his mouth, the only sound in the room was a barely audible whimper from little

Maggie, who was up past her bedtime. Everyone else was quiet and motionless as the sorrow on Brendan's face became more evident.

Almost no one in the room knew this young man was about to become a Navy SEAL. They just knew he was a very close friend.

After beginning by thanking the Manion family and again looking toward their table, Brendan stopped. To his astonishment, tears were starting to form. In that moment he realized, as he never had before, that Travis really wasn't coming home from Iraq.

After again covering his lower lip, gently shaking his head, and taking a breath so deep it was audible through the microphone, Brendan continued his speech.

"I was lucky enough to room with Travis at the Naval Academy for two years," he said, pausing and taking a deep breath. "Throughout our time, we became very close."

Brendan was now on the verge of tears, and many could hear it in his voice. Though Brendan believed he was showing weakness, those watching him marveled at his courage in stepping up to the microphone. Clearly this young man was in pain after losing someone so close.

"I think it was mostly because we had very similar views on many things and enjoyed a lot of the same activities," Brendan said. "In a very short time, he became another brother to me."

Still fighting tears, Brendan began to hit his stride, launching into a story about taking a trip to Texas with Travis for a wedding. Slowly but surely, he was overcoming his emotions, taking a few more deep breaths in between speaking.

"It was on this trip that Travis solidified his position in my family . . . as an extended member of my family," said Brendan, who added that his mom, sister, brother, and fiancée were all there.

After sharing several humorous anecdotes involving his brother Billy and his unique rapport with Travis, Brendan had the tearful audience laughing. He showed them a funny picture of Billy and Travis from the trip, which helped everyone smile, including Brendan.

"It reminds me of all the good times we had," Brendan said of the picture. "I think it also shows how easygoing and likable a person Travis was."

As his voice began to crack, Brendan's well-guarded emotional levee finally broke.

"He was a great friend, and I'll never forget him, and I miss him," Brendan said.

The ensuing ovation was universal, heartfelt, and lengthy. As Brendan stood there listening to the applause, he may have realized that his fiancée was right. If there was ever an appropriate time to reveal his emotions, this was it.

"Your speech was beautiful, Brendan," Janet said afterward as Tom nodded in agreement. "I know Travis was up there smiling.

"We also brought two things that we thought you should have," she continued. "We meant to give them to you that night at the house."

"This is Travis's knife," Tom said. "He got this when he first joined First Recon and took it with him both times to Iraq. . . . It was given back to us with his things. I couldn't think of anyone who deserved this more than you."

Before Brendan could say "thank you," Janet put her arm around him to give him the second memento.

"And here's a bracelet we had made to honor Travis," she said. "It's the same one that we all wear, and when things get tough or dangerous, I want you to make sure you're wearing it."

The bracelet was black and engraved with three lines of silver lettering:

1ST LT. TRAVIS MANION, USMC
SPARTAN, HERO, LEADER
KIA IRAQI FREEDOM, 29 APR. '07

"Always remember," Janet said. "Someone is looking out for you."

Brendan hugged Janet, shook Tom's hand, and thanked them both, then held up the bracelet and promised, "I'll wear this every single day for the rest of my life."

———•————————•———

Two days later, on the Monday morning after the Marine Corps Marathon, Tom, Janet, Ryan, and Dave stood in the Oval Office as President George W. Bush opened the door and walked straight toward Travis's mom.

He gave her a hug.

"Janet, I am so sorry," the president said. "Your loss is my loss."

"Thank you, Mr. President," Janet replied.

After hugging Ryan and shaking Tom's and Dave's hands, President Bush expressed his appreciation for the men and women who had served so bravely overseas, including Travis.

"Today, I'm not the commander-in-chief," the president said. "I'm the consoler-in-chief."

As the visit concluded, Ryan gave President Bush a T-shirt from Sunday's Marine Corps Marathon.

After thanking Ryan for the shirt, the president said he would make sure it was stored in a safe place. Ryan then shared a detail about the marathon.

"Travis was going to run the marathon this year and actually signed up for it before he left," she said. "So after he was killed, we all started training."

Ryan told the president that her dad wore both his and Travis's numbers during the race. At the marathon, she explained, runners are given computer chips to put in their running shoes so they can accurately record race times.

"My dad had both his and Travis's chips, but before the race started, he forgot to note which chip was on which sneaker," Ryan said. "He wanted Travis to finish first, but now we're not sure how it turned out. . . . We're going to check tonight."

The president, who was moved by the story and the Manion family's courage, met with and wrote letters to thousands of military families during his eight years in office. With no end to the wars in Iraq or Afghanistan in sight, President Bush would soon pass the torch to his successor, who would be thrust into the dual wartime role of commander and consoler-in-chief.

●━━━━━━━●

After giving an emotional speech on Saturday night and running the full Marine Corps Marathon on Sunday in the nation's capital, Brendan reported for duty first thing Monday morning on the Southern California island of Coronado. SQT was just a few months away, and in the meantime, he and Sarver would tackle JOTC and Survival, Evasion, Resistance, and Escape (SERE) training. Though Brendan had cleared a major hurdle toward becoming a Navy SEAL, much hard work still lay ahead.

As Monday began, few of those stationed at NAB Coronado knew that just twenty-four hours earlier, Brendan had been running 26.2 miles on the East Coast. While he drank a lot of coffee and took plenty of Advil that day, not once did Brendan complain about being weary, achy, or exhausted. No matter what it took, he was going to salute Travis by running the entire marathon.

In the shadow of the Iwo Jima Memorial, Brendan could picture Travis running next to him as he summoned his last ounce of strength to cross the finish line. The marathon may have symbolized their last race, but no matter what was on the horizon, Brendan knew Travis would always push him forward.

Later, when the Manions got the official results of the 2007 Marine Corps Marathon, they learned that Tom had finished in 7,567th place. Sure enough, Travis finished 7,566th, a split second before his dad.

10

MAGGIE'S PRAYER

"God bless Uncle Travis," a blonde-haired, two-year-old girl said in her soft, tender voice.

A step down from her family's kitchen, where little Maggie Rose Borek was saying her prayers at the dinner table, pictures of Travis hung on the living room wall. One photo showed the smiling Marine holding her when she was a baby.

Old enough to comprehend that her uncle had gone to heaven, Maggie finished her nightly prayers on a muggy summer evening in Doylestown, Pennsylvania. Fourteen months earlier, flag-carrying mourners had solemnly filled Doylestown's quaint streets to honor Travis after he was killed on April 29, 2007.

As Maggie prayed for her fallen uncle on July 12, 2008, the city and surrounding Bucks County were bustling with life. Malls and movie theaters were packed; hoagie and ice cream shops had long lines; and most television screens portrayed the 2008 presidential campaign, along with Philadelphia Phillies games, instead of the daily struggles and accomplishments of US troops serving in Iraq and Afghanistan. After Travis died, things went back to normal for almost everyone except the Manions, whose lives had not been the same since two Marines arrived at their door on a horrible Sunday that Maggie was mercifully too young to remember.

Maggie's mom and Travis's sister, Ryan, had been aware of the risks of her younger brother's post-9/11 military service, but never really thought Maggie would grow up learning about her uncle through stories and pictures. Ryan had even dismissed Travis's attempt to bring up the possibility of not coming home from Iraq, preferring to imagine a world in which tragedy couldn't reach her family's doorstep.

Ryan and Travis's parents, Tom and Janet, weren't in Doylestown that night. They were in Annapolis, Maryland, for the wedding of Amy and Brendan, who were getting married not far from the dorm where Brendan and Travis had roomed together. Ryan had spoken to her mom earlier that day, who had said she was dreading her first overnight stay in Annapolis since Travis's death. But seeing Brendan for the first time in almost a year would make the pain worthwhile.

Ryan knew how close Travis had been to Brendan, his now twenty-seven-year-old, former US Naval Academy roommate. She also knew that Travis should have been one of Brendan's groomsmen, which weighed heavily on her mind as the sun set during a mild Pennsylvania thunderstorm.

After putting Maggie to bed Ryan, who was six months pregnant with her second child, watched the rain from the window of her darkened upstairs bedroom. The Marine's pretty older sister, who always wore a bracelet bearing Travis's name, pictured what should have been happening that night: her brother, her parents, and Brendan laughing up a storm and doing shots of Patrón, just like at their friend Ben Mathews's wedding shortly before Travis was killed.

Ryan still spoke about her little brother in the present tense and usually immersed herself in long hours at work to avoid thinking about losing him. But on this Saturday night, there was no escape.

Sitting in a beautiful, bright Catholic church, Ryan and Travis's parents were watching Brendan marry Amy Hastings. Now twenty-seven, Amy knew that being the wife of a Navy SEAL would require resilience, which was one of her defining characteristics. Amy had been working full time since she was fifteen years old. Since she had met Brendan during her college years, Amy had also weathered his deployments to Iraq and Korea. Without Amy's emotional toughness, she and Brendan may have never reached the altar.

While it was hot and humid in Brendan's home state of Maryland, the night was foggy for the Manions, who were still in shock from losing their only son. As the wedding festivities kicked off, they felt as though they were looking into the church from the nightmare they had been living outside its walls.

With the Manions and about 250 other guests watching, a nervous Navy SEAL waited at the altar. Beads of sweat formed on Brendan's forehead as the tall, bulky, brown-haired groom stood in his black, gold-trimmed US Navy "mess dress" uniform. Awaiting Amy's grand entrance in her gorgeous ivory gown was even more anxiety invoking than a lengthy room inspection at the Naval Academy or BUD/S training.

There was no clock in the church, but Brendan may have still been able to hear one ticking. In forty-eight hours the Navy SEAL would deploy to Iraq, where Travis had been killed just fourteen months before.

If he looked to his left, Brendan would think of his dear friend, who would certainly have stood up in the wedding if he had made it back from Iraq alive. Brendan had already told Amy that he couldn't handle seeing an empty spot for his departed groomsman next to the altar and his two younger brothers, "best men" Steve and Billy. He also didn't want to risk upsetting Amy, who was also mourning Travis.

To the Manions and virtually everyone else, Amy appeared calm and composed as she glided toward the altar and the man she was so excited to be marrying. As Father Damian started the Mass, Amy whispered her love in Brendan's ear.

As they held hands, Amy saw the bracelet bearing Travis's name, which Brendan hadn't taken off since it was given to him by Travis's mom in October 2007.

There were some lighthearted moments as the priest told stories of Brendan harmlessly misbehaving in high school. While pointing out the beauty of the bride, he also recounted a conversation he'd had with Brendan after being introduced to Amy.

"It was a pleasure meeting your fiancée," had said Father Damian, who once taught Brendan, his brothers, their father, and several uncles and cousins at DeMatha Catholic High School. "But I'm wondering how a guy like you got so lucky?"

Everyone laughed, including the Manions, who had barely managed a chuckle in fourteen months.

"Ladies and gentlemen, I present to you Mr. and Mrs. Brendan Looney," the priest said.

Brendan looked into Amy's big brown eyes, which he had admired since the day they met, and kissed his bride as applause echoed through the church.

While clapping, Janet's tear-filled eyes met her much taller husband's. The Manions would never be able to see their only son get married, but they were thrilled to witness Travis's close friend experiencing such a special moment.

After pictures had been snapped and hugs exchanged with Brendan's parents, Kevin and Maureen, the Manions weren't sure what to do next. They had managed to avoid stopping at their second home just outside the Naval Academy gates before the wedding. The house had so many memories, and they weren't sure if they wanted to go inside to spend the couple of hours before the reception started at a nearby hotel. Travis, along with Brendan and many other buddies, had spent countless weekends at the house. Janet hadn't been inside since her son was killed.

Tom, who had been back a few times, thought visiting the house would be a big step and gently encouraged his wife to take it. Still, Janet was trembling as they sat in their parked car in front of the bed and breakfast next door. Through the sunlight she could still see Travis sitting on the back porch with his group of friends, which often included Brendan. *He was just here.*

Janet stayed in the car, nervously straightening her short, dark hair, while Tom opened the front gate and then the wooden, creaking "front" door, which was on the right side of the house. As Tom gently waved her inside, his wife took a deep breath and said the same quick prayer she had recited after Travis died: "Lord, help me to remember that nothing is going to happen today that you and I together can't handle."

Even though Travis had been killed thousands of miles away, going inside the house felt like returning to the scene of a horrible accident. Janet struggled to breathe at first, but was determined to get through it as Tom put his arm around her. She looked right toward the kitchen, where Travis used to sit and play cards. She looked left toward the living room, where he had watched football games with his dad.

Travis's mother then walked upstairs, where she saw a small pile of clothes.

She collapsed.

A few of Travis's T-shirts, including a Navy wrestling shirt he had worn in school, were lying on the floor. Cries of sorrow could be heard that summer evening near downtown Annapolis as an anguished mother longed to hug her son. *He was just here.*

Arriving at the Marriott hotel on the waterfront for Brendan and Amy's wedding reception was another challenge. In December 2006, just before their son had left for his second deployment to Iraq, they had been with Travis at the same Annapolis wedding that Ryan was thinking of earlier in the evening. On that occasion Travis, looking lean, muscular, and strikingly handsome in his full Marine Corps dress uniform, had caused a stir by carrying two bridesmaids into his buddy Ben Mathews's reception. As Janet and Tom stepped inside the ballroom, they could still hear the laughs and applause of friends, including Brendan, when Travis had made his memorable entrance. *He was just here.*

Despite the difficult memories the Manions, determined not to let their grief spoil a special evening for the Looneys, couldn't wait to chat with Brendan. Where was he taking Amy for their honeymoon? Did he have any news from his SEAL commanders on when he'd go to Iraq?

The Manions didn't know he was just hours away from deploying. Brendan was still waiting for the chance to tell them.

Although Janet and Tom saw Travis everywhere, they still marveled at the reception's ambience. Light from the setting sun glistened off the water and straight through the balcony doors, where it met the dance floor. Custom floral centerpieces, arranged by Amy's mom, were on every table. Handsome military men were everywhere, many holding the hands of dazzling dates in gorgeous gowns. It was almost perfect.

As is the case at many weddings, the bride and groom breathed a sigh of relief when the church ceremony was finally over and the time came to eat, drink, and be merry. Naval Academy guys who weren't in Iraq, Afghanistan, or some faraway base already had drinks in hand and were ready to party.

When it was time to snap a few pictures of Brendan and his side of the wedding party, the groom made a beeline toward Tom.

"We're taking some pictures outside and you're going to take Travis's place," Brendan said.

"No, that's alright buddy, you don't have to do that," Tom said with a smile.

"Respectfully, sir, you're getting in these pictures," Brendan said. Though not accustomed to receiving orders from officers junior to his rank, there was no way Tom was turning down the SEAL's request.

Amy was also determined to make this a fun night, and anyone who started asking Brendan about leaving for Iraq was politely asked to "check it at the door." For one Saturday night there would be no war, except for two special, unexpected moments that the Manions would never forget.

As Brendan and Amy made the rounds of their guests, Brendan excused himself to have a private talk with Tom and Janet that he had been rehearsing in his mind. He hadn't had a long conversation with Travis's parents since ten months earlier, when he gave that stirring speech honoring his roommate before the 2007 Marine Corps Marathon. Keeping his emotions in check, Brendan finally told the Manions where he was headed in forty-eight hours.

"I'm leaving on Monday for Iraq," he said, afraid to look into the eyes of his best friend's grieving mother.

"What?" Janet said. "You're not going on a honeymoon?"

"No ma'am, although we do hope to take one eventually," Brendan answered.

There was a brief moment of silence until Tom, sensing Brendan's uneasiness, spoke up.

"You stay safe over there, buddy," said Tom, drink in one hand and patting Brendan on the back with the other.

"And you stay in the back of the fight," Janet said as her emotions swelled.

"I think you know me better than that," Brendan, forcing a smile, said candidly before hugging a tearful Janet and saying he'd be right back. It was time for his brothers to give their joint best man speech.

Steve and Billy Looney had bonded even further with their brother as teammates on Navy's men's lacrosse team, which made the improbable run to the 2004 NCAA national championship game. They also grieved for Travis, but were determined to ensure that Brendan's wedding night—the last time they would see him before he left for Iraq—was fun and memorable. So when it came time to team up for their mutual speech, the Looney brothers, both of whom bore a striking resemblance to Brendan, made light of their twenty-seven-year-old brother's stoicism in a chandelier-lit ballroom.

Steve and Billy kidded their brother for being "a man of few words." After he met Amy, they explained, he wouldn't stop talking about her. They told a story about the first time they heard Brendan tell Amy he loved her, which reinforced that their older brother and fellow midshipman was serious about the pretty Johns Hopkins student he had met in Baltimore.

Their parents and three sisters, Bridget, Erin, and Kellie, smiled as Steve and Billy proposed a toast to their big brother and the new sister-in-law they were welcoming into the Looney family.

"Stay happy, stay healthy, and stay safe," the brothers said as applause and the clinking of spoons against glasses filled the room.

After the audience-requested kiss and subsequent speech by the maid of honor, Amy and Brendan made more rounds to thank their guests for coming. Brendan approached the bar, where Travis normally would have been waiting to hand him a Guinness, to spend a few minutes with some friends. He declined to do a shot with his buddies, not wanting to risk getting drunk on his wedding night or spending Sunday hung over. For all he knew, it could be his last full day with the woman he had just married.

"Seriously, bro," said one of his Naval Academy friends, who had started drinking earlier in the day at Pusser's, the downstairs bar. "Let's have a drink for Travis."

Brendan nodded and took a few small sips of beer while talking about lacrosse and football with the guys. But in that moment, all he could think about was his earlier conversation with the Manions and the pain they were feeling.

Suddenly Brendan realized that the Lonestar song "Amazed" was about to play, meaning it was time for his first wedding dance with Amy.

Even though they wanted to see the dance, Tom and Janet—still rattled by learning that Brendan was leaving for Iraq—retreated to a balcony overlooking the harbor. They knew Travis's friend would soon face considerable danger as a Navy SEAL.

As the Manions stared into the water, Brendan stared into Amy's eyes back on the dance floor. Fittingly, the song's lyrics describe the emotions of two lovers looking squarely at each other.

Amy rested her head on Brendan's broad shoulders and squeezed him tightly as the song's chorus—"baby I'm amazed by you"— soared through the crowded ballroom. She was so proud of her new husband, who had overcome an enormous obstacle—the death of a dear friend at the start of his BUD/S training—to become a Navy SEAL.

Next came a moment Brendan would always treasure: a dance with his caring, compassionate mother. From always being there for Brendan while he grew up to flying across the country to cook his meals and do his laundry after he finished Hell Week at BUD/S, there was nothing Maureen wouldn't do for her children. Brendan felt truly blessed to call her his mom.

Janet, who was standing just a few feet off the dance floor, couldn't help but think about all the special moments she would never get to enjoy with her own son. But she also was genuinely happy that Maureen got to see her son marry a wonderful woman and mature into such an honorable young man. No wonder Travis always thought the world of Brendan and his family.

Tom, meanwhile, was still standing outside on the balcony. He was looking at the boats and reflecting on the sacrifice he knew Brendan was making by leaving so soon to go to war. After spending more than a quarter century in the Marines and watching his only son leave for Iraq twice, Tom understood what thousands of young men and women were giving up by volunteering to spend years of their lives in dangerous places. Tom knew how much Brendan wanted to be a Navy SEAL and marveled at how hard he had worked to become one. But still, he worried about his son's good friend going into harm's way.

As the mother-son dance ended, the entire audience applauded when Brendan kissed Maureen's cheek. They shared more hugs, laughs, and smiles before Brendan started walking back to Amy so the couple could resume greeting and thanking guests.

That's when Brendan saw Janet, who was about to go back out on the balcony to find her husband. Having just shared such a special dance with his own mother, he thought about the grief Travis's mom was still experiencing. Almost instinctively, Brendan reached into the pocket of his mess dress uniform and then got Janet's attention.

"If you don't mind, there's something I want to give you," he said.

Inside Brendan's pocket was the gold trident pin that every Navy SEAL makes almost impossible sacrifices, during many months of training, including Hell Week, to earn. But to Brendan it also represented Travis. In front of more than 250 people, he took out the trident and gently placed it in Janet's right hand.

"This is the pin they gave me last month at graduation," Brendan said. "I want you to have it."

"Oh, Brendan," Janet said. She began crying, not for herself, but for the heartache this young man was experiencing on his wedding night.

"Whenever things got rough, Travis was always there to keep me going," Brendan said. "I never stopped thinking about him."

Also becoming emotional, he hugged his friend's grieving mother.

"No matter what, Travis will always be in my heart," he said. "Amy and I would do anything for you."

Very few guests could hear what Brendan and Janet were saying, but several in the ballroom understood the significance of a moment usually seen only in movies. This was the real thing.

After Brendan and Janet's tearful embrace, it was time for the dancing to resume as Brendan and Amy's families, as well as their guests, enjoyed one of the most jubilant wedding receptions anyone could remember. But after that night, the SEAL trident would be with Janet, just as the bracelet bearing Travis's name would be on Brendan's wrist.

Brendan was the first of the Looney kids to get married, and that night he laughed and sang with his brothers and sisters just like on those memorable summer days growing up in suburban Maryland and hanging out in the "cool room." They knew how hard it was for Brendan to leave his new wife and deploy overseas and were determined to make him happy by welcoming Amy into the cool room, too.

After dinner was over, Janet went back out to the balcony to call her daughter.

"Hi, Ryan," Janet said. "Did you put Maggie to bed?"

"Hey mom, yes, she said her prayers and went to sleep," Ryan said in her strong, distinctive voice. "How's the wedding? Are you and dad holding up okay?"

Janet's voice, normally strong like her daughter's, began to crack.

"It's been hard, honey," her mom said. "Brendan told us he's going to Iraq on Monday."

"Mom, Brendan's going to be okay," Ryan said. "Trav won't let anything happen to him."

"He gave me his trident pin," she said. "He said Travis will always be in his heart."

After they said their good-byes, Ryan sent a text message to her dad. The father and daughter had grown even closer after Travis was killed, and the three surviving Manions had all sworn to stay strong together as one tight-knit family unit.

"Is mom okay?" she wrote.

"Tough night," Tom wrote back a few minutes later.

Tom and Janet, worn down emotionally, went downstairs to Pusser's, the large waterfront bar and restaurant below the ballroom, to bid farewell to Brendan and Amy as the new couple joined the after-party. The Manions navigated through the loud, crowded bar, where a large wedding group was laughing, drinking, and telling funny stories.

They discovered Brendan, Steve, and Billy's Navy lacrosse coach, Richie Meade, buying drinks for the entire wedding party. He gave Brendan and Amy a bottle of champagne, which neither intended to drink that night but wound up sipping from anyway. But when they saw Tom and Janet Manion walk in, almost everyone in the loud bar area, especially those who knew Travis, rushed to offer them a drink.

When the shots of Patrón were brought, Brendan proposed a toast.

"Let's have a drink for Travis," he said.

"Naah, let's have one for you and Amy," Tom said to Brendan. "Travis would have wanted this night to be all about you."

Janet, reaching deep down for one last bit of strength after an exhausting day, somehow came up with the perfect toast.

"Brendan and Amy, we know Travis is here celebrating with you tonight," she said. "He loves you, we love you, and we wish you all the best."

"Hear, hear!" Brendan, Amy, and the wedding party said in unison.

After the toast, Janet couldn't help but peek over at the table where Travis, Brendan, and their friends had drunk and sung until 2:00 a.m. after the Mathews's wedding in December. *He was just here.*

This time, the Manions retired for the night long before 2:00 a.m., when Brendan and Amy finally left Pusser's. Had it been a normal wedding night, the new couple probably would have headed upstairs earlier, but with Brendan on his way to Iraq, they wanted to have as much fun as possible with friends and family. Later, when her husband embarked on his SEAL missions, Amy would return to San Diego to become one of the thousands of young military spouses with a loved one deployed to Iraq or Afghanistan.

Waking up late on Sunday morning, Brendan and Amy lay in bed watching a movie, refusing to answer their phones or look at the clock. A wedding brunch with relatives downstairs at Pusser's was scheduled, and the newlyweds knew they would spend most of the day going through gifts to make sure Amy knew who to send thank-you cards to while Brendan was away, but these couple of hours would be for them and them only.

As they watched TV, the new bride began to sense that something was bothering Brendan, who was much quieter than usual. When she asked him what was wrong, Brendan described his emotional conversation with the Manions at the wedding. After comforting her husband, Amy told Brendan that she was proud of him.

Despite their best efforts to stop the clock, Monday arrived, and it was time for the Navy SEAL and his new bride to separate their aching hearts by thousands of miles. As Amy prepared to leave first for a work-related conference, she tried to keep her composure because Brendan and several of his family members were to accompany her to the airport. Still, these were the last few minutes the bride and groom could spend alone, and Amy couldn't help but shed some tears.

Amy knew Brendan was intelligent and extremely well trained. Like Travis, her husband was a compassionate warrior who deeply respected the Iraqi people. But Amy also knew Brendan's deployment to Iraq would be dangerous, and she felt that she had to say something before he left.

"Don't try to be a hero over there," Amy said. "Just be my husband."

Brendan embraced his new bride and promised to be careful.

"I don't want to leave, even though it has to be done," he said. "But I wouldn't want to come home to anyone but you."

After telling each other "I love you" and sharing one last hug and kiss, it was time to go to Baltimore-Washington International Airport. When they arrived Amy, with tears filling the eyes Brendan would dream about in the months ahead, spoke three words before heading inside. "See you later," she said.

"See you later," the unusually emotional Navy SEAL responded.

—————•————•—————

Back in Doylestown it was once again dinnertime, which meant little Maggie was about to say her prayers. Right after she asked the Lord to bless her Uncle Travis, Ryan asked her to add another prayer for Brendan.

Maggie nodded her head and smiled at her mom.

"God bless Uncle Travis," she said. "And God bless Brendan too."

A few hours later Brendan sat on a plane, unable to communicate with Amy. Surrounded by married couples on the commercial flight, Brendan was filled with the same empty feeling that often consumed him whenever he and Amy were apart.

This would be the toughest challenge yet. Forty-eight hours after marrying the woman he had met and quickly fallen in love with five years earlier, Brendan was on his way to Iraq. Though leaving his bride was difficult, Brendan was thankful he had been able to marry the girl of his dreams. Travis, who had often spoken of someday meeting the right woman and starting a family, never had that opportunity.

With the plane ascending, Brendan looked down at his shiny new wedding ring, which signified the love he shared with Amy. Then he looked at the black-and-silver bracelet on his right wrist, which signified the memory of a close friend he would never forget.

11

MOVING FORWARD

"As a warrior, he strode like a giant across the battlefield of the eastern portion of Al Anbar Province."

In 2008, then US Marine Lieutenant General John Allen visited Doylestown to present the Silver Star and Bronze Star with Valor to First Lieutenant Travis Manion's family.

"When his unit was ambushed on that fateful day in April in Fallujah, when the Doc and his fellow Marine were shot down, Travis went forward," General Allen said. "Under fire, Travis, absolutely fearless in his resolve to save his fellow warriors, left the safety of a covered position to suppress the enemy and extricate his wounded, and when he was hit, Travis was moving forward, selflessly exposing himself to enemy fire."

Brendan never had the chance to say good-bye to Travis in person. General Allen, who had been leading US Marines in Fallujah on April 29, 2007, did. As Commandant of the US Naval Academy from 2001 to 2003, Allen knew Travis and shared another connection to the Manion family through Tom's good friend General Dave Papak.

"I was unprepared for seeing Travis that day," Allen later wrote to Papak, who had helped with the notification process and Travis's homecoming. "Not unprepared for the circumstances or the human pieces of this, but seeing one of these young mids lying there. For me, the circle is now complete."

In 2007, Travis left an indelible mark on a general who would later assume command of all US forces in Afghanistan.

"2007 was a remarkable year in Al Anbar. . . . It was the year that began the turning of that province, and in many ways the remainder of the war in Iraq followed what began in Al Anbar," General Allen now said. "Travis was a part of that . . . a big part of what became known, and what historians are now calling 'The Turning.'"

In 2008, Brendan picked up where his Naval Academy roommate had left off.

Lieutenant Brendan Looney, Honor Man of US Navy SEAL BUD/S Class 265 and a recent graduate of SQT Class 266, was tracing the footsteps of Travis, who the general said "strode like a giant across the eastern portion of Al Anbar province." Newly married and in peak physical condition after earning his gold trident, Brendan eagerly joined SEAL Team Three in the middle of the elite special operations group's Iraq deployment.

"Congratulations to the groom," said Lieutenant Rob Sarver, who was already deployed and had not been able to leave Iraq to attend his friend's wedding. "It's really good to see you."

"It's good to be here," Brendan said. "Let's get to it."

Brendan and Sarver had deployed to Fallujah before, but under vastly different circumstances, in 2006 as Navy officers. After transferring to special operations and enduring the rigors of BUD/S and SQT, being back in Iraq together as Navy SEALs was a special experience. Sarver, who had broken the tragic news after Travis was killed, also knew that for Brendan, being in Fallujah carried added significance.

Thanks to the sacrifices of Travis's MiTT team and countless more American, Iraqi, and coalition troops who served in Al Anbar, the streets of Fallujah were much quieter than in the previous year. To be sure, some insurgents and terrorists still remained in the city and surrounding region. But the progress made was remarkable, and Brendan could now see the fruits of his Naval Academy roommate's labor, which General Allen had noted in his presentation speech, up close.

"His training skills, his leadership, his personal example of heroism. . . . All these influences helped shape an entire battalion of this division," General Allen had said. "And when Travis was killed in action, fighting alongside his beloved Marines and Iraqi warriors, the Iraqis reacted by naming one of their combat outposts for Travis. In all the time Americans have served with Iraqi forces, this has only happened twice."

One of Brendan and Sarver's primary responsibilities was meeting with key Iraqi leaders at various combat outposts to ensure that the critical area continued on a positive track. While most Americans probably don't think of Navy SEALs as sitting down for meetings with foreign soldiers or politicians, the two officers spent many hours listening to Iraqis and giving them advice on how to work not only with US troops, but also with rival tribes and factions. Like Travis, Brendan cared for the Iraqi people and wanted to see the country succeed, which would be impossible without a relatively stable Al Anbar province.

Brendan e-mailed Janet from Iraq on September 10, 2008, the day before the seventh anniversary of the 9/11 attacks:

> Mrs. Manion,
>
> It was great seeing you guys at the wedding. I am glad you guys were able to make it. It meant a lot to both me and Amy to see you both there.
>
> I am doing ok over here. Since arriving I have been tasked reviewing all the evals [evaluations] and awards for the command as well as work in the TOC [tactical operations center]. I am sure you have heard about the decreased violence out here and PIC (provincial Iraqi control) taking

place in Al Anbar. To see how much different it is over here
since last time is a true testament to the work that everyone
over here has done.

I have not had the opportunity to get out to COP [Combat
Outpost] Manion. On a trip out west to Al Asad [Airbase]
though, while myself and Rob Sarver—another USNA '04
guy who knew Travis—were waiting for our helo to show up,
struck up a conversation with a young Lance Corporal. This
young Marine was a MiTT member and had mentioned that
he had just come from COP Manion.

When we heard that, I let him know that Travis was a
good friend of mine and roommate during college. He said
that he did not know him, but had only heard great things
about [Travis]. He also said that there was a room at the COP
dedicated to him with pictures. I just thought that you would
like that story since Travis is still influencing the men and
women over here.
Love,
Brendan

Sarver never asked Brendan what it felt like to be serving in
the city where Travis had died, but he didn't have to. He could
see the significance in Brendan's eyes.

Amy could also sense the impact being in Fallujah was having
on her husband. She asked Brendan what a normal patrol was like
and what he had to bring with him.

"Well, I always make sure I wear two things over here," Brendan said. "I wear the bracelet Mrs. Manion gave me on my right
wrist and my G-Shock watch with my wedding band attached to
it on the other.

"You're always with me here," he continued. "And so is Trav."

Brendan and Sarver, two of SEAL Team Three's newest members, patrolled the city. Bonding with officers and enlisted SEALs

alike, they were rotated into various assignments, much like rookies on a football team seeing their first playing time. The platoon that Brendan and Sarver accompanied on patrol would often have the new SEALs operate on the periphery to contain danger zones from the outside. If a firefight were to erupt, Brendan and his BUD/S roommate were always ready to strike with devastating, pinpoint effectiveness.

During the weeks when Brendan spent the most time on patrol, he and Sarver helped capture six suspected insurgents. With a calm, professional demeanor that quickly won the respect of his new teammates, Brendan ensured that the narrow streets Travis once helped rid of the enemy remained considerably safer than in previous years for Iraqi men, women, and children.

To SEAL Team Three, Brendan was bringing the mix of talent and determination that he and Travis had always pushed each other toward at the academy. Inside Fallujah gyms, fellow service members marveled at Brendan's workout routine and sometimes collapsed while trying to follow along. If there were no night missions scheduled, Brendan would watch movies on his laptop and read. But before he relaxed, he always e-mailed Amy, who had moved across the country from Maryland to California shortly after they were engaged.

———•———•———

For Amy, the hardest parts of the deployment were the days between her husband's e-mails or rare phone calls. She worried about Brendan and always wondered what he was doing, but was also supremely confident in the years of training that had prepared him for whatever could happen. Even in the hell of combat, there was no situation a Navy SEAL couldn't handle, and Brendan's constant refrain of "don't worry, I'm fine" reinforced what she always told herself to believe. Still, the vivid memory of Travis's funeral served as a painful reminder to Amy of the risks her husband was facing.

Even with more than 150,000 US troops deployed to Iraq and Afghanistan in 2008, only a tiny fraction of the population—less than 1 percent—had a spouse serving in a war zone. Not only was Amy part of a small community to which very few Americans could relate; she had watched Brendan leave for Fallujah, where Travis had died the previous year, less than forty-eight hours after a priest pronounced Brendan and Amy man and wife. As Amy, an East Coast native, settled into life and work in unfamiliar San Diego, the challenges she faced were extraordinary.

The new military wife also had several shining examples to follow. Amy could lean on the strength of her mother, Christina Palmer, who had raised Amy on her own while working full time. She also received constant support from the Looney family. In addition, Amy drew on the same approach that her husband brought to his duty as a Navy SEAL: "Be strong. Be accountable. Never complain."

Heather Hojnacki, Rob Sarver's girlfriend, was astonished by Amy's adjustment to life as a military spouse. Heather had moved to California after meeting and falling in love with Sarver around the same time that Amy had moved. Like Amy, she barely knew anyone on the West Coast, and she had only met Brendan's wife once, back in Annapolis. The second time they met was when Amy volunteered to pick her up at San Diego International Airport.

Amy took Heather under her wing right away. As Brendan and Sarver bonded in Fallujah, their significant others were growing closer in California, where Amy managed a retail store and Heather was starting law school a few hours away at Pepperdine University in Malibu.

Whenever Amy got an e-mail update or attended a meeting for the wives of deployed Navy SEALs, she would alert Heather, who as a girlfriend was not privy to the same real-time information. On most weekends, Sarver's girlfriend drove down to check on Rob and

Brendan's house in Imperial Beach. She then met up with Amy, who took Heather to downtown San Diego for relaxing evenings to distract them both from the constant worry they were experiencing.

Over drinks one night, Sarver's girlfriend expressed bewilderment at how Brendan's wife could cope so calmly with such a difficult set of circumstances.

"I don't know how you could have enjoyed your wedding," Heather said.

Before and after Brendan left, Amy said, she tried not to let his dangerous job creep into every aspect of their lives.

"I just want to make the best of it," Amy said. "We have to enjoy the time we have."

———•———•———

Brendan was silent during several rides through the Pizza Slice. On multiple occasions, he and Sarver operated near the infamous Blackwater Bridge while navigating narrow roads riddled with huge potholes, possibly from IED attacks during Travis's time in Fallujah.

Inside the once-hellish enclave where daytime patrols were once regarded as suicide missions, Sarver would occasionally look over at his fellow SEAL and wonder what he was thinking. Once again, he could see the impact on Brendan by simply looking into his steely, focused eyes.

For three and a half months Brendan, Sarver, and their fellow SEALs patrolled Fallujah's streets, where they confronted insurgents and terrorists with the same courage that Travis and his fellow Marines had displayed. As few could have predicted a year earlier, the sacrifices of 3-2-1 MiTT had made SEAL Team Three's current mission immeasurably safer.

Even though Travis didn't live to see the outcome of his sacrifice, Brendan made sure his friend's legacy was sustained in Fallujah and around the world. At the same time Brendan, as Travis had once predicted to Tom, was making his own mark as a Navy SEAL in the summer of 2008.

Stuck at a base in Iraq for nearly a week at the end of the deployment, Brendan and Sarver amused themselves by holding a "sleeping contest" to make up for the countless hours of lost rest during BUD/S and then Fallujah. Brendan then finally returned to California. When Amy ran toward him, Brendan embraced his wife and passionately kissed her.

It was the moment Amy had been dreaming about since the night of their wedding. At long last, her husband was home.

During the drive from Coronado to San Diego's W. Hotel, where they would stay that night, Amy asked Brendan about seeing where Travis had spent the last weeks of his life.

"This may sound strange," Brendan said. "But after being there and seeing the places where Trav spent those last few months, I felt a strong connection to him."

It didn't seem strange to Amy at all. It helped her understand what her husband had experienced in Iraq.

While serving his country in war, Brendan found peace. Gaining some closure didn't eliminate the pain of Travis's death, but as his wife understood, Brendan was learning how to deal with losing such a close friend.

A few months later, Brendan learned that SEAL Team Three would be heading to Afghanistan, where he would lead a platoon into dangerous, much more frequent combat missions than during his first deployment as a special operations warrior. He did his best to hide his emotions from Amy to keep her from misunderstanding his enthusiasm, but she knew Brendan felt like he'd just won the lottery.

The SEAL wasn't looking forward to being apart from Amy or being in the middle of violent clashes with the Taliban. He was eager to realize nearly a decade of intense, almost nonstop preparation by going to the country where 9/11 had been planned and having a positive impact on people's lives. After valuable experience in Korea and Iraq as an intelligence officer and a combat deployment to Iraq as a SEAL, Brendan knew that leading his fellow warriors into battle in Afghanistan was his best chance yet to make a difference, just as he and Travis had once discussed.

Brendan poured himself into readying his platoon for the mountains of Afghanistan, which would be vastly different than Fallujah's urban terrain. He read books, studied manuals, refined his already solid marksmanship, and worked out at levels that were unprecedented, even for him. He was quiet around the other SEALs, which made his words even more meaningful when he did speak up. Not only did Brendan give clear, constructive orders to those who looked up to him, he never asked anyone to do something that he wasn't willing to do himself.

For Brendan, the most difficult part of his combat assignment, which would start in the spring of 2010, was leaving Amy behind in San Diego during his fourth overseas deployment since they had started dating. By Valentine's Day, with Brendan's deployment quickly approaching, Amy was overcome by stress and a recent bout with flu-like symptoms. After being sick for several weeks, she finally felt well enough to go out to dinner, but still couldn't shake the uneasy feeling that in a few weeks, her husband would once again be risking his life halfway around the world.

"Look, if anything happens to me," Brendan said at almost the exact moment it was dominating Amy's thoughts. "The first thing you need to know is that you are never allowed to get remarried."

His joke provoked a nervous laugh, and after they shared an appetizer, Brendan put down his fork and looked straight into his wife's eyes, much like during their first wedding dance.

"Seriously, if anything happens to me, obviously you should know that you will always be part of my family and that they will always be good to you," the SEAL said.

Amy's eyes welled with tears as she tried to change the subject.

"There's just one more thing," he continued. "I also want to make sure you stay in touch with the Manions, and especially Ryan, since I've always thought you two would become good friends."

Amy always referred to Brendan as her "friend-finder," because he had introduced her to at least four of her very best friends since they had become a couple almost seven years earlier. But this conversation was getting too visceral—too real—for Amy to allow it to continue.

"Don't even say that, Brendan!" she said. "I don't know what I would do without you."

Brendan told his wife he was sorry, to which Amy nodded and said it was okay. She simply couldn't handle discussing the unthinkable.

On March 9, 2010, Brendan and Amy stood in a loving embrace as they kissed and reassured one another. It was three years to the day since Brendan had left the East Coast for Coronado to realize his dream of becoming a Navy SEAL. It was also Amy's birthday.

"I only have to get through six months," Amy repeated over and over. "It's just six months."

Brendan's tears welled up. Only in his most painful moments, like Travis's death, the Marine Corps Marathon speech, and leaving Amy after their wedding, did Brendan become this emotional. Though he was committed to his mission and defending the defenseless, the SEAL hated to see his beloved wife pay such a high price for his duty.

"Please try not to worry," he said. "I'll see you later."

Amy had to leave for work before Brendan had to head over to base for his flight. After taking a deep breath, she gave him another hug and kiss.

"Six months," Amy said. "See you later."

After a roller-coaster workday during which it was difficult to focus on anything other than missing Brendan, Amy collapsed on the couple's big, empty bed. She had spent the early part of the evening hanging out with her brother-in-law's future wife, but as the clock approached midnight, Amy was alone on her birthday.

As loneliness crept into the bedroom, the couple's two dogs jumped up on the bed to keep her company. Like thousands of military spouses, Amy was starting the long odyssey of trying to function while her life partner and best friend was deployed overseas.

While petting Hayley and Lexi and looking around the room, Amy spotted the card Brendan had given her on Valentine's Day. She picked it up and opened it, hoping that seeing Brendan's handwriting would help her feel as close to him as she had that morning.

Titled "For My Wife on Valentine's Day," the pink Hallmark card was self-deprecating and tongue-in-cheek:

> *When something needs doing, I don't always do it . . .*
> *When something needs fixing, I don't hop right to it . . .*
> *When the checkbook's a mess,*
> *I may throw a fit . . .*
> *When the going gets tough,*
> *I've been known to quit.*

After reading the next few lines, which were filled with similar soliloquies, Amy smiled and flipped back to the second page. In thick black magic marker, Brendan had crossed out the last two lines and replaced them with three words: *I DON'T QUIT*.

12

MISSION 59

On April 29, 2010, the third anniversary of First Lieutenant Travis Manion's death in Fallujah, Iraq, Lieutenant Brendan Looney, sporting a full beard almost two months into his deployment, sent an e-mail to Tom and Janet Manion from the mountains of southeastern Afghanistan:

> Mr. and Mrs. Manion,
>
> I just wanted to let you guys know that I am thinking about you today and every day. I also [wanted] to drop you guys a quick line from Afghanistan and let you know what was going on and give you an update.
>
> Things here are pretty slow, but by all accounts should pick up in the near future. It is interesting here for sure; we are more or less out in the middle of nowhere and are expected [to] protect the local nationals as well as rid them of Taliban.
>
> The biggest problem . . . is trying to be in 100 places at once . . . seeing that the villages are so spread out and the terrain is such that it allows many different avenues of approach. So it is very frustrating. We are optimistic, but often wonder what we are doing here when you have [Afghan President Hamid] Karzai making comments that he might

join the Taliban. Kind of crazy . . . but we are trying to chip away at it.

Other than that things are good for the most part I guess . . . weather has not been bad, not too hot.

I also wanted to let you guys know that I flew a flag here for you today. We do not have outgoing mail, so I will not be able to get it to you until I return. I hope all is well and I will talk to you guys soon.

—Brendan

Brendan's parents, Kevin and Maureen, worried every day about their son. For Tom and Janet, watching Brendan deploy to Iraq and then Afghanistan was like having another son in combat.

When Janet became anxious, she would take Brendan's gold Navy SEAL trident out of her handbag and say the same prayers she used to say for Travis. When Tom read or watched the news, which didn't include nearly as much reporting from Afghanistan in 2010 as it had from Iraq three years earlier, he wondered what his son's former roommate was working on at the same moment in the country where 9/11 was planned.

America had changed dramatically in the eight and a half years since Brendan, Travis, and millions of Americans had watched the Twin Towers fall on live television. On November 4, 2008, the American people elected Barack Obama as the first African American president in US history. In his January 20, 2009, inaugural address, the new president echoed his theme of change:

We are the keepers of this legacy. Guided by these principles once more, we can meet those new threats that demand even greater effort, even greater cooperation and understanding between nations. We'll begin to responsibly leave Iraq to its people and forge a hard-earned peace in Afghanistan.

With old friends and former foes, we'll work tirelessly to lessen the nuclear threat and roll back the specter of a warming planet.

We will not apologize for our way of life nor will we waver in its defense.

And for those who seek to advance their aims by inducing terror and slaughtering innocents, we say to you now that "Our spirit is stronger and cannot be broken. You cannot outlast us, and we will defeat you."

Although a Democratic president had replaced a Republican in the White House, the burden shouldered by military families was largely unchanged. Two days after the new commander-in-chief took office, twenty-one-year-old US Army Specialist Matthew Pollini, of Rockland, Massachusetts, was killed near al-Kut, Iraq, in a vehicle rollover. Two days later, twenty-five-year-old US Marine Lance Corporal Julian Brennan, of Brooklyn, New York, was killed while supporting combat operations in Afghanistan's Farah province.

Almost three years before the last US troops would leave Iraq, and with no end in sight for the ongoing struggle in Afghanistan, thousands of American service members still faced danger on a daily basis. At home, their loved ones continued waiting, worrying, and sacrificing.

As assistant officer in charge of his SEAL Team Three platoon, Brendan saw the terrorist threat firsthand in a way few Americans could in the spring or summer of 2010. He was driven not by ideology, but by the same promise he and Travis had made when they were called to action after 9/11. As long as evil men wished to do Americans harm and demonstrated the willingness and capability to do so, brave men and women like Brendan and his fellow US service members would step forward to confront them.

With the Taliban launching its annual spring offensive, Brendan and his platoon started to see more action in May, just as he had predicted in his e-mail to Tom and Janet. Surrounded by jagged cliffs, extreme poverty, and acute desolation, which many of the younger SEALs had never experienced, it was Brendan's responsibility to keep them optimistic, focused, and sharp. But considering that the SEALs were sleeping on an FOB "in the middle of nowhere," thousands of miles from home, setting a positive tone was never an easy task.

Rather than barking out orders to the SEALs under his command, Brendan was "Loon-Dog." The enlisted SEALs, or "E-Dogs," as they were nicknamed, loved working for the twenty-nine-year-old lieutenant, because even though Brendan was an officer, he still thought of himself as just one of the guys.

During his deployment, Brendan spent roughly the equivalent of two full weeks on "over watch" missions above three districts in northern Zabul province, where the lieutenant and SEALs under his command would look down from the cliffs to make sure their brothers in arms operating below were safe from lurking Taliban and al Qaeda fighters. But after only a day or two on the high ground, Brendan was concerned that his primary responsibilities as an officer and squad commander weren't enough of a contribution to his platoon. Upon returning to base, he started training on a .50 caliber sniper rifle so he could directly help his teammates blunt the enemy threat.

After only limited training, Brendan was a consistent shot from a thousand yards. Over the next few months he made some of the most accurate shots his teammates had ever seen to protect Americans and Afghans in the villages below.

Wearing a half-shell helmet and carrying heavy gear and the .50 cal sniper rifle in his huge backpack, the bearded warrior patrolled, exercised, ate, and hung out with his entire platoon. When there was extra gear to carry, the officer threw it on his back instead of ordering enlisted SEALs to carry it. Regardless of the command structure or rank, Loon-Dog treated everyone with the same respect.

When things got dicey on the battlefield, however, there was no mistaking who was in charge, like one day when gunfire rang out beneath the over watch position Brendan's SEAL team had established above a small, Taliban-controlled Afghan village.

"Incoming!" Brendan yelled.

As bullets pounded the mountain rocks that were shielding his team, who took cover as soon as they heard their leader's unmistakable voice, Brendan's commanding officer (CO) asked for a status report over the radio.

"We've got enemy fire coming from just outside the village," Brendan said. "Nobody's been hit, and we're prepping the counterattack."

"Lieutenant?" the CO asked.

"Sir?" Brendan repeated what he had said a few times before realizing the signal was dropping in and out, as it had been for most of the day.

"Lieutenant," the CO repeated. "If you copy, call me on the SAT [satellite] phone."

As soon as Brendan heard the order, he broke his crouch and stood up. The SAT phone was a few yards in front of the boulder that was protecting him.

"Whoa, Loon-Dog," exclaimed a surprised fellow SEAL, Petty Officer First Class Vic Nolan. "Be careful, sir."

Brendan knew his CO wouldn't ask him to call unless it was extremely important, and for all he knew, retrieving the satellite phone could be a matter of life and death. Without blinking, Brendan hustled toward the phone, picked it up, and returned to his position as bullets whizzed by.

"Loon-Dog . . . you alright?" Nolan said.

"I'm okay," said Brendan, acting more like he was taking an afternoon stroll than engaging in an intense firefight.

Brendan then told his CO that his men were ready to strike back at the enemy. Moments later he aimed his sniper rifle at the enemy position. When the day was over, the Navy SEALs had once again disrupted the Taliban's plans.

At night in the cold, largely uninhabited land where he was serving, Brendan usually returned to his FOB, where he would unwind by lifting weights. At the same time, Amy would be starting her day in warm, sunny San Diego.

Before Brendan called home, he would give his teammates a chance to call their wives and girlfriends first. He wound up calling Amy about once a week. On one particular night, he was relaxing after an all-day mission and called his wife.

Amy was running around getting ready for work, making a cup of coffee with the birthday present Brendan had given her on the day he left for Afghanistan. Instead of spending money on pricey lattes at Starbucks, her husband had said, she'd now have her own machine and enough coffee to last the full six months.

"Damn it, I just spilled my coffee," said Amy.

She told Brendan that nothing out of the ordinary was happening. But Brendan, who missed home, asked his wife to tell him anyway.

"Well . . . things are crazy," Amy said. "I can't figure out how to merge our bank accounts online, work has been nuts, and Hayley and Lexi keep tearing up the furniture and peeing on the rug because I'm usually not home in time to take them out."

Amy was dealing with the stress that military spouses across the country, including wives of Brendan's teammates, experienced every day. The young couple didn't have children, but managing a household, its finances, two dogs, a full-time job, car repairs, and life's daily curveballs was starting to wear on Amy after almost three months.

"It's just hard, Brendan," she said. "Sometimes I can't even think because there's so much to do. . . . . Things get so hectic."

With the same calmness he had displayed on the battlefield, Brendan offered a gentle retort.

"Just one quick question," he said. "Did you get shot at today?"

Amy abruptly stopped what she was doing and pressed the phone closer to her ear. After she asked Brendan if he was okay, the SEAL asked his wife to please answer the question.

"Of course nobody shot at me today," she said with a nervous chuckle. "What do you? . . ."

Stopping herself mid-question when she understood her husband's point, Amy felt bad for making such a big deal out of her relatively painless hassles.

"See? There ya go," Brendan said. "Believe me; I know it's hard on your own. I totally get it, but just remember . . . only three more months."

"Three more months," said Amy. "See you later."

"See you later," Brendan said.

After hanging up, Amy initially worried that she had upset Brendan, which she always told her friends was a big no-no during an overseas deployment. But when Amy checked her e-mail later that day, a PowerPoint presentation was waiting in her inbox. Brendan, who had a combat mission the next day, had stayed up late to send his wife instructions on how to merge their bank accounts online.

Even though Brendan saw the sun set while Amy watched it rise, the young couple, separated by thousands of miles, were closer than ever.

Later that night, when Brendan returned from his patrol, another assistant officer in charge, Lieutenant Steve Esposito, asked him what had happened during the day's mission.

"Nothing much," Brendan responded, as he often did. "It was good."

It wasn't until later—at the weekly Sunday dinner their CO scheduled to reinforce the platoon's motto of "brotherhood"— that Esposito heard what had really happened outside the wire. Along with stories of his predeployment mountain training exploits in Alaska and Utah, in which Brendan wowed his teammates with his dogged approach and sheer might, the SEALs liked to joke about Loon-Dog standing up in a hail of bullets because he needed to make a phone call.

Each Sunday evening before they broke bread, the SEALs, prompted by their CO, would go around the table and each say something nice about the teammate to his left. Though some

SEALs initially compared this to a classroom exercise, it boosted morale and made the team even closer, just as the CO intended.

Sitting to Brendan's right was Esposito, who was routinely impressed by his fellow officer's valor, character, and humility. Instead of pumping up his accomplishments or exaggerating stories from the battlefield, Brendan's "nothing much" response embodied what being a SEAL was all about: accomplishing remarkable things without caring who got the credit.

"So what do I like about Loon-Dog?" Esposito said. "Where do I start?"

With every ensuing Sunday dinner and combat mission, the platoon's motto of brotherhood was being woven ever more deeply into its fabric. Much of that was thanks to Loon-Dog, whom every SEAL on the FOB was starting to model himself after.

One day Brendan and his fellow SEALs went house to house clearing terrorists from a collection of tiny villages in a one-mile radius. As the combat mission wore on, the team was becoming exhausted from carrying its gear and dealing with the constant, heart-pounding intensity of the unknown. When they flung open the doors of houses or huts, enemy fighters could be waiting to ambush them. During most searches, however, they encountered civilians, including frightened, confused children still living in the grip of the Taliban's iron fist.

On this day Brendan made a surprise discovery while searching a mud hut. Instead of IEDs or AK-47s, they found a litter of puppies. Starving and thin, the brown and black dogs, which were probably around eight weeks old, would almost certainly die or wander around the war-torn village for the next few months as strays.

Thinking of his dogs back home, Brendan gave a unique order to Petty Officer First Class Nolan.

"Hey, can you put that pup in my pouch?" he said. "We need a camp dog, and this little guy is perfect."

"Yes, sir," Nolan said.

For the next three hours, including a tense stint just outside a village, where Brendan kept his rifle at the ready in case any Taliban fighters jumped out and fired on his fellow SEALs, the puppy peeked out of the greenish-brown pouch on Brendan's left side. Next to a first aid kit and box of ammunition, the Afghan puppy got its first taste of freedom.

Battle-hardened and more muscular than ever after ramping up his already fanatical workout routine inside the war zone, Brendan was a nightmare for insurgents and terrorists. But even as the Navy SEAL peaked as a warrior, he was still Brendan. Compassionate and caring, he shared Travis's view that a combat deployment wasn't all about killing bad guys. It was also about respecting different cultures and religions while bringing hope to distant, faraway lands.

Back at the FOB, Brendan knew the names of every Afghan local who worked on the base and became acquainted with several janitors and cooks. On or off the battlefield, Brendan didn't view civilians as an obstacle to accomplishing SEAL Team Three's mission. To Brendan and those around him, the Afghans truly mattered.

Brendan's soft spot for the locals meant he had no sympathy for the insurgents and terrorists trying to kill them. Three years after his friend's life was cut short by a sniper terrorizing Fallujah, Brendan used his own high-powered rifle to bring murderers of men, women, and children to justice. As a former intelligence officer who was now meticulously planning missions with SEAL commanders, Brendan knew whom to target before ever putting his eye to his rifle's scope. When he did, however, the results were clear, precise, and devastating for the enemy.

In the heat of battle, even the strongest, best-trained warriors become engulfed in chaotic, unpredictable dilemmas. Once, as SEAL Team Three held another over watch position near a cliff's peak, Brendan and his men were taking incoming fire from insurgents in the valley, which echoed with sounds of gunfire.

"Hey, I need you to grab that box of ammo," Brendan told a fellow SEAL, Petty Officer Second Class Joe Battaglia, while talking to his CO over the radio.

Bullets were smashing into rocks and tree branches, as well as ricocheting all around them, and if an American stuck his head out for even a few seconds, it could mean death. Unless they quickly regained the upper hand, every Navy SEAL on the mission was almost certainly in grave danger.

Brendan was out of ammo, as was almost everyone on his team. The problem was that the box was a few yards away, in an exposed position.

"I'll get it," Battaglia said. "But I'm waiting a minute or two until this shit calms down."

Putting down the radio, Brendan repeated his order.

"No, we need that ammo right now," he said.

Brendan, who never minced words, did not give an order unless it was for good reason. Nothing meant more to the lieutenant than the safety of his men, but as he worked with the CO to plan a counterattack, which would include air support, he simply did not have time to retrieve the ammunition himself.

"I'm sorry, sir, but that's suicide," Battaglia said as gunfire from the valley grew even louder. "Look behind you. . . . Rounds are landing right above our heads!"

Without speaking, Brendan put down the phone, stood up, and retrieved the ammunition. Looking at the SEAL who hadn't followed his order quickly enough, he slammed the box on the ground as insurgents shot at him from below. They missed.

"That wasn't so hard, was it?" Brendan asked before resuming the strategy call with his CO.

Far from showing up a teammate who he had no doubt was courageous, Brendan was demonstrating that he would never ask someone to do something that he wouldn't do himself. It was the last time anyone under his command ever hesitated before following an order.

"Loon-Dog, I'm really sorry about what happened today," Battaglia said after his team had eliminated the threat and returned to the FOB. "I fucked up."

"Don't worry about it," Brendan said. "I trust you, brother."

———•——————•———

Back home, Amy had invited several Navy SEAL wives, fiancées, and girlfriends on a "girl's trip" to Las Vegas. It was summer, and if everything went as planned, Brendan's platoon would be coming home soon.

Amy knew her friends were feeling the same tense, burgeoning sense of anticipation while waiting for their significant others. A Lady Gaga concert in Vegas was the perfect antidote to counting every hour and minute until their loved ones finally returned.

For the first time, Brendan was deployed in a war zone without Sarver, who was on a separate mission in Iraq. Amy, who had become even closer to Sarver's girlfriend, invited Heather on the Vegas trip.

On a lazy Sunday by the pool after the raucous Lady Gaga show the previous night, Amy, Heather, and their group were discussing "the boys." As the wives talked about whether they and their husbands might soon start families, Amy turned to Sarver's girlfriend.

"I think you have it so much harder than us," Amy said. "At least we know that when they come home, we're already married. . . . The future is pretty much set."

Sarver's girlfriend was touched by Amy's remark. Heather wondered how Amy could put the plight of others first while her own husband was fighting in the mountains of Afghanistan. Amy, Heather realized, was truly selfless.

After the Vegas trip, Heather called her boyfriend in Iraq. After seeing a brief news report about violence there, she was concerned for his safety.

"I'm not the one you need to worry about," Sarver said. "Brendan is the one you need to worry about."

Brendan? Heather remembered how Sarver had called him "a machine" during BUD/S, and she knew the larger-than-life reputation that had followed Brendan around ever since. Though she didn't doubt the seriousness of the danger Brendan faced, Heather mostly dismissed her boyfriend's remark. Brendan was invincible.

●────────●

With fifty-eight combat missions under his belt in Afghanistan, everyone trusted Brendan, and confidence was strong throughout the SEAL Team Three platoon. It was September now, and their six-month deployment would soon be over. Though still committed to their mission, their excitement about finally returning to Coronado to see their wives, fiancées, and girlfriends was palpable.

On September 11, 2010, the ninth anniversary of the 9/11 attacks, Brendan sent an e-mail from Afghanistan to Sarver in Iraq. Another SEAL team was about to arrive on Brendan's FOB, which meant that after a few weeks of getting them acclimated to the area and its terrain, Loon-Dog and his men would be going home.

"I am on the last damn flight out of here," Brendan wrote to Sarver. "I cannot wait to get back."

Brendan and Amy had big things to discuss upon his return to San Diego. They had just bought their first house, so perhaps it was time to discuss starting a family. The possibilities were endless, as both were young, bright, and successful. Most important, though, Brendan and Amy were in love.

The next time he went to Afghanistan or Iraq, Brendan would be his platoon's officer in charge, which carried even greater responsibilities that the SEAL couldn't wait to tackle. But first he needed to spend time with his wife, who had already endured two combat deployments during two short years of marriage.

On the Sunday before his fifty-ninth combat mission in Afghanistan, which would begin on Tuesday, September 21, 2010, Brendan called home an unprecedented three times. Amy hadn't heard this kind of excitement in her husband's voice since he and Sarver were about to come home from Iraq in 2008. She told him she was in the car with Ali, the wife of Brendan's brother Steve.

"We just got some ice cream, but we forgot my rainbow sprinkles, so we're stopping by the store to get some," Amy said.

As they drove through the palm-tree-lined streets of San Diego, laughter filled the car as Brendan responded with a joke.

"What's up with this?" Brendan said to Ali. "Are you trying to ruin my wife's figure while I'm stuck over here?"

"Oh whatever!" Amy said. "I'm doing Barry's Bootcamp right now, so I'll kick your butt when you get back!"

"Naah, I think I'll just have to come to one of your classes and show them a real workout," Brendan joked. "Seriously though, enjoy your ice cream and save me some of those sprinkles."

After another phone call in the middle of the day, Brendan talked to Amy again at night, which was already morning in Afghanistan.

"Hey, I meant to tell you, there's another SEAL here with me whose wife is dealing with his first combat deployment," Brendan said. "It's been tough on them while he's been away, so I was wondering if I could give him your e-mail address to give to his wife, just so you can give her tips on how to handle things."

Brendan was looking out for a teammate and his family, who were still adjusting to a demanding lifestyle that few outside the military and special operations communities could comprehend.

"Of course I will," Amy said. "Give her my e-mail address, and I'll make sure to get in touch."

"Thanks, you're the best," Brendan said. "I love you."

"I love you, too," Amy said. "See you later."

"Yep, see you later," Brendan said.

On Monday, Amy and Brendan exchanged e-mails. The six months that Amy dreaded were coming to a close, and finally they would be living together again as husband and wife. Brendan could barely contain himself during his last reply before the mission:

CAN'T WAIT TO GET HOME AND GO ON A LONG OVERDUE VACATION WITH YOU!! I'll call you when I get back from my op.
Love ya, Miss you
—Me

September 21, 2010, started like almost any other day. A front-page headline in that day's *San Diego Union-Tribune* read, "Recession's End Brings Little Joy: Official declaration that downturn ended in June '09 belies persistently high jobless rate, slow recovery." With millions still out of work after the previous year's economic meltdown, the wars in Afghanistan and Iraq had long since taken a backseat to what most Americans regarded as a more pressing, immediate concern.

Just after midnight in Afghanistan, Brendan's Tuesday started as normally as it could for a Navy SEAL at war. After putting on his camouflage uniform, backpack, pouch, and a tan ball cap that he wore backward, Brendan hooked up his radio; petted the dog that he had brought back from the war-torn village; and headed outside to meet his SEAL Team Three teammates, another group of US Army soldiers, and three UH-60 Black Hawk helicopters.

Several members of SEAL Team Four, who had recently arrived in Afghanistan to relieve Brendan's platoon at the end of their deployment, were also gathered near the choppers. After accompanying their successors on this mission, Brendan and his fellow SEALs were going home. After the mission the SEAL Team Three platoon would fly by helicopter to Kandahar, where they would be met by C-17 aircraft and flown out of Afghanistan.

Before most missions, Brendan's platoon would huddle for a quick prayer before giving each other high fives, hugs, and back slaps. Before the last few missions, however, the SEALs had forgotten to gather and say a few words, which prompted one team member, Petty Officer First Class Nolan, to ask for everyone's attention now.

Before saying a prayer, Nolan showed his fellow SEALs and soldiers the cover of a book written about Corporal Pat Tillman, the former NFL football star who turned down a three-year, $3.6 million contract offer by the Arizona Cardinals to join the US Army after 9/11. The twenty-seven-year-old Army Ranger was killed in a friendly fire incident on April 22, 2004, while serving in Afghanistan. Brendan had been moved by Tillman's courage and had spoken about the fallen hero several times with Travis, who had listed the football player turned warrior as one of his role models in his spiral notebook at Navy.

After Nolan read a short passage from the Tillman book and said a prayer, it was time for the mission to begin.

"Stay safe out there, Loon-Dog," Lieutenant Esposito said to Brendan.

"You too, brother," he said. "See you back here."

After boarding the chopper Brendan, who had shaved off his beard since blending in with the locals wouldn't be required during this final mission, was calm and alert. As long as he stuck to his training and looked out for his men, they would get through another challenging, unpredictable night. Soon, probably in about a week, he would be home in Amy's arms.

Brendan's assignment, in support of Operation Sea Serpent—an ongoing, joint antiterror assault—was to watch over the village of Ayatalah in the mountainous, southeastern Afghanistan province of Zabul. As on other tactical over watch missions, on this one Brendan and his team would serve as guardian angels, much like when Travis held the roof after the chlorine attack in

Fallujah. No matter what transpired in the darkness below, Brendan and his SEALs, equipped with night vision equipment, would be watching.

Quiet and focused, Lieutenant Brendan Looney flew above the skies of Afghanistan on the fifty-ninth combat mission of his fourth overseas deployment. As bright moonlight shined into the chopper through the war zone's soaring mountains, the words "Spartan, Hero, Leader" reflected from the bracelet Brendan always wore on his right wrist. Moments from landing on top of a mountain, the SEALs and soldiers aboard the chopper unhooked their safety belts and prepared to dismount.

Suddenly a terrible, piercing sound stunned everyone aboard the helicopter, which rapidly tumbled down a jagged, steep cliff before plunging into the darkness. The frantic moments that ensued were harrowing, dreadful, and tragic.

The next day the US military released two official reports to the American public:

> The Department of Defense announced today the deaths of five soldiers who died in a helicopter crash Sept. 21 during combat operations in Zabul province, Afghanistan, while supporting Operation Enduring Freedom. All soldiers were assigned to 101st Combat Aviation Brigade, 101st Airborne Division (Air Assault), Fort Campbell, Ky.
>
> Killed were:
>
> Lt. Col. Robert F. Baldwin, 39, of Muscatine, Iowa
>
> Chief Warrant Officer Matthew G. Wagstaff, 34, of Orem, Utah
>
> Chief Warrant Officer Jonah D. McClellan, 26, of St. Louis Park, Minn.
>
> Staff Sgt. Joshua D. Powell, 25, of Pleasant Plains, Ill.
>
> Sgt. Marvin R. Calhoun Jr., 23, of Elkhart, Ind.

As "Screaming Eagles" of the Army's storied 101st Airborne Division community mourned the tragedy, word was quickly spreading among Navy SEALs stationed in Afghanistan, Iraq, Virginia, and California that four of their warrior brothers were also killed during the combat mission. The Pentagon's official announcement left the entire US Navy special operations community reeling in stunned disbelief:

> The Department of Defense announced today the deaths of four sailors who died in a helicopter crash Sept. 21 during combat operations in the Zabul province, Afghanistan, while supporting Operation Enduring Freedom.
>
> Killed were:
>
> LT (SEAL) Brendan J. Looney, 29, of Owings, Md., assigned to a West Coast-based SEAL Team.
>
> Senior Chief Petty Officer David B. McLendon, 30, of Thomasville, Ga., assigned to an East Coast-based Naval Special Warfare unit.
>
> Petty Officer 2nd Class (SEAL) Adam O. Smith, 26, of Hurland, Mo., assigned to an East Coast-based SEAL Team.
>
> Petty Officer 3rd Class (SEAL) Denis C. Miranda, 24, of Toms River, N.J., assigned to an East Coast-based SEAL Team.

To Amy, Brendan was a loving husband, soul mate, and best friend.

To Kevin and Maureen, he was a loyal, brave son.

To Steve, Billy, Bridget, Erin, and Kellie, he was a trusted, caring big brother.

To fellow Navy SEALs, he was Loon-Dog.

To Janet and Tom, he was like a second son.

To Travis, he was the brother he never had.

To everyone, Brendan embodied the three words reflecting from his wrist during his final, courageous moments: "Spartan, Hero, Leader."

13

NO REGRETS

"If you make the most of what you are doing, there is no way to regret what you are doing," Brendan had often said.

The funeral of Lieutenant Brendan Looney was a time for grief, but not regrets. Just like his dear friend three and a half years earlier, Brendan had died doing exactly what he wanted to do in life: serving his country and protecting others.

The Looney house was already packed by the time Tom and Janet finished their numb, tearful drive from Doylestown, Pennsylvania, to Silver Spring, Maryland. The ride was mostly silent, as the death of Travis's great friend was a nightmare that neither had anticipated. Janet, who had fallen on the floor screaming "Not Brendan!" after getting off the phone with Brendan's mother earlier that day, still hadn't come to grips with the realization that lightning could indeed strike twice.

Tom and Janet spent time comforting Brendan's mom, Maureen, his dad, Kevin, and Brendan's five siblings. On the day Brendan's grief-stricken wife arrived on the East Coast, Janet went straight to the couch, where Maureen, Amy, and Amy's mom, Christina Palmer, were sitting quiet and still.

Upon learning of Brendan's death in San Diego, a fellow Navy SEAL whom Brendan had met in BUD/S training, Lieutenant

Flynn Cochran, had rushed over to Amy's house with his wife, Jamie, to help guide the stunned widow through the painful process, then flew with her to Maryland. Ever since Amy had first received the tragic news, she had been repeatedly asking to see two people in addition to her mother and mother-in-law. The first was Janet Manion, and the second was Rob Sarver, who was still deployed in Iraq.

Brendan's close friend and fellow Navy SEAL was preparing to leave Ramadi for a combat mission when he heard about a crash in Afghanistan that had killed nine NATO service members. After carrying on with his responsibilities, Sarver heard chatter on base about someone from SEAL Team Three being on board. A few minutes later, there were rumors that the fallen team member was, in fact, an officer.

There weren't many SEAL Team Three lieutenants deployed to Iraq and Afghanistan at the time, which first put the terrible thought into Sarver's mind that something might have happened to Brendan. Adding to Sarver's anxiety, all communication lines at his base were shut down until further notice due to ongoing security concerns. Even if Brendan had been killed or injured in the crash, there was virtually no way for Sarver, one of his best friends, to find out.

A few minutes later, a teammate tapped Sarver on the shoulder.

"Lieutenant, the XO [Executive Officer] wants to speak with you," he said.

Sarver, who had broken the terrible news of Travis's death to Brendan, slumped into his chair as the XO took a deep breath.

"Lieutenant Brendan Looney was killed in Afghanistan," he said. "We're very sorry for your loss, and we also apologize that it took so long for us to inform you, as we didn't realize how well you knew Brendan until a few minutes ago. The Looney family wants you in Maryland as soon as possible. What can we do to help?"

His mind racing and heart pounding, Sarver searched for something that made sense as his eyes welled up with tears. Somehow, some way, he had to reach Amy.

"Sir, I really need a secure telephone line and Internet access," Sarver said. "And I need to know when I'm getting out of here."

"We'll get you on the next flight," the XO said, again offering his condolences.

Still in San Diego before embarking on what would certainly be an exhausting, panic-filled cross-country flight, Amy didn't believe Brendan was dead, despite the words of her casualty assistance officer and both of Brendan's parents, who had also been notified. Surrounded by a distraught Steve Looney, his wife, Ali, Navy SEALs and their wives, and numerous friends, Amy focused on reminders of Brendan that filled their home, including the two confused, barking dogs. Brendan wasn't dead; this all had to be some sort of mistake. *He was just here.*

Suddenly Amy's cell phone rang. As the ringtone sounded, Brendan's wife looked at the screen and saw the same five-digit security code that appeared whenever her husband called from overseas. *He's alive!*

"It's Brendan!" Amy shouted as the others in the room paused and shot each other wide-eyed looks while gently shaking their heads. "I told you!"

"BRENDAN?!" Amy said after pressing the "talk" button.

"Amy, this is Rob," Sarver said. "I'm so sorry."

Hearing Sarver's voice was harder, in many ways, than listening to the casualty assistance officer's official notification of Brendan's death.

"Rob, . . . where is Brendan?" Amy sobbed. "Can you please tell me what the hell is really going on here?"

"I don't know the details yet," Sarver said, also starting to cry. "But my XO just told me that Brendan didn't make it.

"Amy, I am so, so, so sorry," he repeated over and over.

Screams, much like the horrible shrieks that had echoed in the Manions' neighborhood on the day Travis was killed, filled Brendan and Amy's San Diego home. The sound was horrifying, even to Navy SEALs accustomed to loud firefights.

Hearing Sarver's words did not fully dash Amy's hopes of getting a phone call from Brendan or even seeing him walk through the front door. Denial was the only wall separating her from the unthinkable.

Devastated after the most difficult phone conversation of his life, Sarver boarded a massive C-17 cargo plane, empty except for two pilots, bound for Germany and then the United States. For the next twenty-one hours, all he could think of was Amy's misery.

The second person Amy asked for was Janet. Her arrival in Maryland not only comforted Maureen and Kevin, who had asked her and Tom to come, but gave Amy a source of strength who could fully relate to her pain.

"Oh Amy," said Janet, in tears but holding herself together. "I am so sorry, honey."

"Janet," Amy said. "I still don't understand what's going on. Where is he?"

After a short pause and a few more tears, Janet took Amy's hand.

"Brendan is with Travis," the still-grieving mother said. "And now we're here with you, and we'll be here as long as you and Maureen need us."

The pain was unbearable. In her in-laws' family room, Amy collapsed into the arms of Travis's mother.

Janet and Tom were mindful of the periodic need for Amy and Brendan's family to grieve alone. Though they were at the Looney house by day, the Manions would retreat to their house in Annapolis at night.

Even three and a half years after Travis's death, staying there still made Janet uncomfortable. Now, after Brendan's passing, feelings of uneasiness were even more prevalent than during those difficult hours between the ceremony and reception for Amy and Brendan's wedding.

The house was like a haunted museum. Day and night, Janet could picture Travis and Brendan everywhere, especially on the back porch, where they would tell jokes and drink beer after long, competitive runs and bike rides. The boys were so much alike and such close friends. *They were just here.*

Upon returning to Silver Spring, Janet would hug Brendan's sisters and mother before sitting down next to Amy, Maureen, and Christina on the couch. Janet's right hand would then gently grasp Amy's. Janet's left hand would tightly clutch the gold Navy SEAL trident that Brendan had given her at his wedding reception.

Amy asked Janet how to function without Brendan, and whether it was even worth trying. Though sympathetic, Janet also struck a motherly tone when she reminded Amy that everyone in the house, including Maureen and Christina, would make sure she was never alone.

In one of the most dreadful, grief-stricken situations imaginable, something remarkable was also happening in the Looney family's Silver Spring home. Despite indescribable misery, one Gold Star family was comforting another.

After a long, punishing journey from the Middle East, Lieutenant Rob Sarver was welcomed with open arms by Brendan's family and friends. Sarver's girlfriend, who had flown in from California to help Amy, was also waiting to hug the tired, grieving Navy SEAL. Heather knew how much her boyfriend was hurting, and like Sarver, she was completely devastated for Amy. Just a few weeks earlier during their fun trip to Las Vegas, Heather had marveled at Amy's unselfish nature, as well as the hope she expressed for her future with Brendan. Suddenly across the country on this terrible, surreal day, Heather was watching Amy prepare to bury him.

After Sarver found Amy near the backyard pool and embraced her, the dazed young widow asked him to help the family handle funeral arrangements. Though exhausted after twenty-one hours of travel, the SEAL accepted without hesitation. If the situation were reversed, Sarver knew Brendan would have done the same for his family.

As they walked inside the house, Amy began telling Sarver where she wanted her husband laid to rest.

"I want Brendan buried next to Travis at Arlington," Amy said.

Before she left San Diego, Amy had conveyed the same wish during a phone call with Maureen, who then relayed it to Janet. After hearing Amy's comment to Sarver and shooting each other looks, Brendan's and Travis's parents walked across the room.

"Amy, honey, Travis isn't buried at Arlington," Maureen reminded her daughter-in-law.

"He's buried where we live, remember, sweetheart?" Janet said.

Of course Amy remembered. She had been at Travis's funeral and called Brendan in tears while driving to the Pennsylvania cemetery. But as bewilderment and panic dominated her normally structured state of mind, Amy was uncharacteristically defiant.

"I don't care . . . then bury him in Pennsylvania," Amy said. "Brendan would want to be with Travis."

Others attempted to convince the grieving widow that it would be far more sensible to bury Brendan closer to home. In response, Amy simply shook her head and said "no."

That's when Tom tapped Janet on the shoulder and whispered something in her ear. Janet then told Amy she would be right back and urged her to spend the next few minutes having something to eat.

"I'm not hungry," said Amy, holding a glass of wine.

"Amy, you have to eat some food and drink some water," Janet said, echoing the frequent pleas of Maureen and Christina.

As Amy nodded and sat down on the couch, Tom and Janet retreated to a nearby room so they could speak in private.

Unbeknownst to Amy or the Looney family, the Manions had long considered moving Travis from Calvary Cemetery in West Conshohocken, Pennsylvania—where his grave was still marked with a simple wooden cross—to Arlington National Cemetery.

"I'm okay with moving him, and I know Ryan is, too," Tom said before asking his wife what she wanted to do.

In the foggy days following Travis's death, Ryan had told her parents about Travis's desire to be laid to rest at Arlington. Weeks after her brother was buried close to home, where his mom could visit him at least once a week, Major Steve Cantrell, Travis's friend and mentor, had told Tom that he'd had a similar conversation with Travis. From that moment forward, Tom believed his son should eventually be reinterred at Arlington, but only if Janet was comfortable with the decision.

After struggling for some time over Travis's final place of rest, Janet had to decide whether her only son's grave would be dug up and moved about 150 miles south. Before answering, she closed her eyes and said her oft-repeated prayer.

"Lord, help me to remember that nothing is going to happen today that you and I together can't handle," she whispered.

Whether God answered was impossible to know. But in that heartrending moment, Travis's mom felt clarity and peace.

"Amy is right," Janet said. "This is the way it should be."

Janet paused and rubbed her eyes with a tissue.

"We can bring Brendan and Travis back together," she said.

After an emotional hug, Travis's parents left for Annapolis, where Tom started making calls to military contacts while Kevin and Maureen also contacted various officials. Trying to bury Brendan and Travis next to each other at Arlington was an arduous, painful process filled with red tape and uncertainty, but both families were determined to make it happen.

After learning of the extraordinary circumstances being faced by both grieving families, Arlington National Cemetery informed the Looneys and Manions that Brendan and Travis would be buried side by side.

When the Manions told Amy, she embraced Janet. "I don't know how I can ever thank you," she said. "I didn't want Brendan to be alone."

From that moment forward, the afflicted families felt a powerful sense of consolation intermingled with their profound sense of loss. Reunited on America's most revered burial ground, Brendan and Travis would once again be roommates.

First many distressing decisions had to be made about Brendan's funeral, with the most pressing being whether his casket would be open or closed. Sarver, who worked nonstop to ensure that all arrangements were flawless, was asked by Amy and the Looney family to view Brendan's remains and report back on the appearance of his body. They knew Brendan had trusted Sarver with his life, and now they asked him to help them make one of life's most excruciating decisions. They needed to know whether their husband, son, and brother was fit to be seen.

Viewing his friend's remains was a raw, jarring experience for Sarver, who would never get the image out of his mind. But after composing himself, the Navy SEAL turned his attention to the ribbons on his fallen brother's uniform. Brendan, who had carried himself with such honor, courage, and distinction during fifty-nine combat missions in Afghanistan, was being awarded the Bronze Star with Valor, along with many other medals.

"His heroism under fire directly resulted in significantly degrading insurgent operations in northern Zabul Province, as well as 56 enemy killed in action," read Brendan's Bronze Star with Valor citation, signed by Rear Admiral E. G. Winters, Commander of Naval Special Warfare Command. "Lieutenant Looney's extraordinary guidance, zealous initiative, and total dedication to duty reflected great credit upon him and upheld the highest traditions of United States Naval Service."

Even if nobody else saw Brendan's uniform, Sarver would make sure every inch of it was perfect.

As a special operations warrior, Sarver was often presented with questions of life and death that sometimes had no clear answer. After summoning all his inner strength, Sarver told the Looneys that he thought they should go see Brendan.

Amy initially declined to be involved in the most agonizing aspects of the funeral planning, until she overheard part of a discussion about covering Brendan's face, which would already be heavily layered in makeup, with a veil.

"Brendan would never want a veil over his face," Amy said. "Brendan was proud of what he was doing and I know everyone else here was too. So why hide anything? Remember what he always said: No regrets."

Like the Manions three and a half years earlier, the Looney family courageously invited the American public to see the sacrifices of war up close. Brendan's casket would be open, and on Sunday, October 3, 2010, thousands of mourners were invited to DeMatha Catholic High School in nearby Hyattsville to pay their respects.

Before Brendan's remembrance ceremonies officially began, however, Amy and the Looneys joined the Manions on Friday at Arlington. After an extraordinary collaboration among two grieving families, the US military, local and state leaders, and officials at Arlington National Cemetery, the remains of First Lieutenant Travis Manion were being reinterred in Section 60, where so many fallen heroes of the Iraq and Afghanistan conflicts are buried. Three days after Travis was laid to rest, Brendan would join him.

Though they never doubted their decision, Tom, Janet, and Ryan were concerned about the reinterment ceremony distracting from Brendan's burial. Invitations were limited to relatives and close friends, and news of the ceremony was kept quiet, even though a busload full of Marines from the recently dedicated Manion Hall—a barracks at The Basic School in Quantico, Virginia, named in honor of Travis—showed up anyway.

Before finalizing the plans, Tom had shared his family's concerns with Amy.

"We know what a painful time this is," said Tom, gently placing his hand on the young widow's shoulder. "Please don't feel like you have to be at the reinterment. The next few days should be all about Brendan."

"I appreciate that," Amy responded. "But you can count on all of us being there. . . . We want to honor Travis the right way too."

Rarely does a wife, mother, father, brother, or sister sit in full view of a loved one's eventual gravesite just three days before the funeral. But as compassionate, courageous Americans, that's exactly what Amy and the Looney family did.

Sitting directly behind Tom, Janet, Ryan, Dave, and Maggie on a serene fall afternoon, Amy was dressed in a black outfit with large, dark sunglasses similar to the ones she had seen Ryan wearing at Travis's first burial. She was totally numb by the time a Marine Gunnery Sergeant knelt in front of Tom and Janet and handed them a folded American flag.

"On behalf of the President of the United States, the Commandant of the Marine Corps, and this grateful nation, please accept this flag—once again—as a symbol of our appreciation," the Marine said. "It's a symbol of your son's honorable and faithful service to this country and his code."

As Tom put his arm around Janet, who was nodding her head in appreciation, the Gunnery Sergeant stood and slowly saluted the Manions and Looneys before kneeling down again. The ground beneath him was covered with a piece of artificial turf, as this hallowed portion of Section 60 was mostly dirt. Americans were still dying in Afghanistan and Iraq almost every week, and many more funerals were expected. The Marine then removed his white glove to shake the now-retired Marine Corps colonel's hand.

"You all have our deepest sympathy," the Marine said. "May God continue to bless you and your family, with a heavenly smile on each and every one of you. Thank you, and we love you."

Throughout the service, Maureen, Bridget, Erin, Kellie, and Ali took turns wrapping their arms around Amy. In a moment of profound sadness, each Looney also held a small American flag.

After remarks from the priest and the singing of a hymn, Tom stepped up to the podium next to a framed picture of his son. The spot where Travis would be reinterred, covered in flowers, was directly in front of him.

"I'd like to start off by thanking everyone for being here today as we move Travis to his final resting place," Tom said. "I want to also take this opportunity to acknowledge the Umbrells that are here. Their brave son Colby, the hero, is buried just a few yards away on this sacred ground."

After paying tribute to the family of the fallen Doylestown soldier and welcoming other relatives of departed military heroes, Travis's father said what was on everyone's minds.

"But most especially, I want to thank the Looney family for their presence here today," he said. "Our hearts go out to you as you deal with this incredible loss. Brendan represents the best this country has to offer. We mourn him now, and we will forever, the passing of this American hero."

The Manions were laying their beloved Travis to rest, but throughout the entire ritual, their paramount concern was the Looneys.

"There are so many mixed emotions for us as we move Travis to this place of honor," Tom said. "Brendan's loss fills all our waking hours, yet we're moving Travis to be next to his great friend, and together, with all their warrior brothers and sisters, who have paid their full measure defending freedom.

"This solemn place leaves us with a sadness for the sacrifices, but also extremely proud of these brave Americans who so unselfishly and courageously stepped forward to confront the evil that faces our world," he continued. "We, the families of these defenders of freedom, can't begin to describe the void that fills our hearts, but we can tell you how much our sons and daughters loved this country and all that it stands for. We are now their voice."

As Tom continued his moving address, he was interrupted by a plane flying overhead, presumably taking off from or landing at nearby Ronald Reagan Washington National Airport. In the anxious days after 9/11, as Travis and Brendan studied and trained in Annapolis, the mere sound of a jet had terrified many Americans, especially in Washington and New York. More than nine years later, however, most no longer feared a terrorist attack from the sky, largely thanks to the sacrifices of the men and women who had answered the call to serve.

"So Travis, as we lay you here today beside your brother, Brendan, and with all your fellow patriots, we will always remember the selfless service and sacrifice, and we will continue to rally in your honor with the call: 'If not me, then who . . . '" Tom said. "To make a difference for others and to always step forward to do what's right, no matter what the cost.

"God bless you, my son, and rest in peace with your warrior brothers and sisters," Travis's father concluded. "First Lieutenant Travis Manion, United States Marine Corps, Lieutenant Brendan Looney, United States Navy: warriors for freedom, brothers forever."

As Tom, Janet, Ryan, and Dave greeted dozens of mourners after the ceremony, someone gave Travis's mother a bouquet of flowers. Janet then pointed toward Amy, who was staring blankly at the dirt while still holding an American flag, and requested Maggie's help.

"Sweetie, would you give these to Amy?" Janet asked her four-year-old granddaughter.

Throughout the worst ordeal of Amy's life, Janet was there, along with Christina, Maureen, Bridget, Erin, Kellie, and Ali, to lend the type of support that only kindhearted, benevolent women can lend another.

That night, with Travis reinterred and Brendan's funeral on the horizon, almost everyone went out for a solemn evening in Annapolis. While many of Brendan's fellow SEALs drank Bud Light due to the "BL" initials on each bottle, Amy, Janet, Ryan, and Tom did shots of Patrón to salute Travis and Brendan at McGarvey's, which was always one of their favorite bars. There,

Brendan's wife and Travis's sister talked for hours, laying the foundation for a close friendship that would soon resemble sisterhood. Even in death, Amy's "friend-finder" was still at work.

On an otherwise quiet Saturday morning, Amy still jumped every time the phone rang or a door opened. Even after seeing the very spot in which her husband would be buried, which was just to the right of Travis's resting place, the SEAL's widow still believed an egregious error had been made and that Brendan would emerge, unscathed, from an undisclosed location in Afghanistan.

Her hopes ended when she walked out of the funeral home's elevator and turned the corner toward the room where her husband lay in his open casket.

When she saw Brendan's unmistakable profile, Amy felt like she'd been slapped in the face, punched in the stomach, and hit by a car all at the same time. In a moment of sheer anguish, she collapsed to the floor and cried harder than anyone in the room had ever seen.

The scene was excruciating for all to witness, especially Sarver, who approached Amy's mom a few hours later. He was worried that he had made the wrong decision by saying he thought it was appropriate to view Brendan, to which Christina replied that she believed he had made the right call.

Later, Kevin and Maureen also took Sarver aside to convey their gratitude. Not only was Sarver in Iraq when his close friend died, but in the tragic aftermath, he had spent almost three weeks helping arrange the funeral's every detail. A few months later, when the mist began to clear, Amy also thanked Sarver, sending him a framed picture of Brendan in Afghanistan, as well as the March 22, 2007, entry from her then boyfriend's journal.

"I am living with Rob Sarver also," Brendan had written. "Together he and I will crush BUD/S."

After the private viewing was Sunday's public wake at DeMatha, the high school alma mater of Brendan, his brothers, their dad, and several uncles. The turnout stunned even those who expected a large crowd, as people from every walk of Brendan's life drove, took trains, or flew in to view his casket and look at the many pictures, from boyhood to manhood, displayed nearby. On that Sunday there was no prouder, more patriotic setting than the packed DeMatha Catholic High School gym.

The heartbreaking backdrop also prompted several close friends and relatives to take breaks. At one point Ben Mathews, the Navy linebacker whose face was once bloodied by a bone-crushing hit from Brendan after he failed to hustle in football practice, was sitting outside the gymnasium with Ryan.

"I just have this picture in my head of Brendan and Travis at my wedding," a visibly shaken Mathews said. "I just can't believe this, Ryan. . . . I can't fucking believe it."

Ryan simply nodded. In the wake of a second inconceivable tragedy in less than four years, there wasn't much that anyone, other than those who would speak so eloquently at Brendan's remembrance services, could say.

With well over a thousand people inside, Brendan's parents were busy greeting mourners. Amy, still in shock after seeing her husband's body, could not handle doing that for more than a few minutes. When she wasn't upstairs taking a break, she usually stood next to her mom and Janet, who put her arm around Brendan's wife and held her upright whenever her knees began to buckle. During one particularly sad moment for Amy, both she and Janet realized they were facing DeMatha's wrestling room.

"Okay, let's go ahead and face the other direction," Janet said with her arm around Amy. The wrestling mat was a clear reminder of Travis, just as a lacrosse stick would naturally remind them of Brendan. When Amy started to cry, Janet spoke.

"Remember the story about how the boys went on a bike ride with that poor kid and basically left him out in the woods because they started racing?" Janet said. "They were always competing, those two."

President George W. Bush hosts Janet and Tom Manion, along with Dave and Ryan Borek, in the Oval Office on October 29, 2007, six months to the day after Travis died while fighting to shield his teammates inside the Pizza Slice. Janet brought a bag of Marine Corps Marathon "Team Travis" gear and presented it to the nation's 43rd commander-in-chief.

US Marine Lieutenant General John Allen, who served as Commandant of the Naval Academy while Travis and Brendan were midshipmen, presents Travis's posthumous Silver Star and Bronze Star with Valor to Tom and Janet Manion, along with Ryan, Dave, and Maggie Borek, during a 2008 Doylestown, Pennsylvania ceremony. Allen would later be promoted to four-star general and go on to lead all US forces in Afghanistan.

Maggie touches a plaque bearing her uncle's name outside Manion Hall at Marine Corps Base Quantico, Virginia. Manion Hall, which houses US Marine officers training at The Basic School, was named in honor of Travis.

Brendan Looney and Rob Sarver mark their successful
completion of Basic Underwater Demolition/SEAL (BUD/S)
training in Coronado, California. The BUD/S roommates
would go on to serve multiple combat deployments as US
Navy SEALs.

US Navy Lieutenant (SEAL) Brendan Looney visits with
Janet Manion on the night of his wedding in Annapolis,
Maryland. During the reception, Brendan gave his gold Navy
SEAL trident to the mother of his fallen Naval Academy
roommate.

Amy and Brendan Looney are married on July 12, 2008. Forty-eight hours later, Brendan left for his second deployment to Iraq and his first as a Navy SEAL. *Courtesy of Clay Blackmore*

Brendan, a member of SEAL Team Three, prepares for a combat mission in an undisclosed location.

The last page of the Valentine's Day card given by Brendan to his wife on February 14, 2010, less than a month before the Navy SEAL left for Afghanistan.

When the checkbook's a mess, I may throw a fit... ~~When the going gets tough, I've been known to quit~~. (I DON'T Quit)

Brendan, carrying his .50 caliber sniper rifle, conducts combat operations in Afghanistan's Zabul province in 2010. In his pouch is a puppy that "Loon-Dog" and a fellow SEAL rescued from a local village.

Even while missing his wife, parents, siblings, and friends, Brendan's spirits remained high during his 2010 deployment to southeastern Afghanistan.

Tom and Janet Manion receive a folded American flag symbolizing the ultimate sacrifice made by their only son. Travis was reinterred at Arlington National Cemetery on October 1, 2010, more than three years after the fallen Marine was originally buried in West Conshohocken, Pennsylvania.

In front of a group of US Marines who took a bus to Arlington National Cemetery from Manion Hall, Tom and Janet Manion, along with Ryan and Maggie Borek, lay flowers on the casket of First Lieutenant Travis Manion during his reinterment ceremony. *Alex Wong/Getty Images North America*

A fellow SEAL pounds his trident into the casket of fallen US Navy Lieutenant Brendan Looney at his October 4, 2010, burial service at Arlington National Cemetery.

President Barack Obama visits the graves of First Lieutenant Travis Manion and Lieutenant (SEAL) Brendan Looney following his Memorial Day address on May 30, 2011. A framed version of this photograph was subsequently placed in the West Wing of the White House.

Thanks to Amy's "friend-finder," Travis's sister and Brendan's wife became the very best of friends.

Travis's nieces, Maggie and Honor Borek, wear their respective Travis Manion Foundation and US Naval Academy shirts to honor their fallen uncle.

While icing her aching knee, Amy shows her Marine Corps Marathon medal to Maggie on October 30, 2011, in Washington, DC.

Maggie visits her Uncle Travis at Arlington National Cemetery.

Surrounded by fellow heroes, US Marine First Lieutenant Travis Manion and US Navy Lieutenant (SEAL) Brendan Looney are buried side by side in Section 60 of Arlington National Cemetery, where many fallen warriors of the Afghanistan and Iraq wars rest.
Matthew Sileo/Courtesy of Matthew Sileo Photography

"Gosh, I know, it's just like the first time I went for a quote-un-quote 'jog' with them and it ended up basically being a half marathon," Amy said, wiping away tears with a handkerchief. "I can almost guarantee that after shaking hands, the first thing Travis and Brendan did when they first saw each other again up there was go for a run."

"And someday, we'll see them again," said Janet, nodding in agreement.

When they went upstairs to take a break, Janet, Christina, and Amy saw Tom, Kevin, and several others in the room gathered around a small television screen. The Washington Redskins, led by former Philadelphia quarterback Donovan McNabb, happened to be playing the Eagles at Lincoln Financial Field. On that solemn Sunday above the DeMatha gym, where mourners were walking past Brendan's casket, it was only appropriate that Brendan's favorite team was playing Travis's.

"Brendan used to wear Travis's Eagles jersey at games because he was such a good sport," Janet said. "So for the first time in my life, I'm going to root for the Redskins today."

The Redskins beat the heavily favored Eagles, 17–12.

After thousands packed Washington's Basilica of the National Shrine of the Immaculate Conception on a drizzly Monday morning, Brendan's flag-draped casket, covered with a plastic sheet to protect it from steady early afternoon rainfall, arrived at Arlington National Cemetery.

About four thousand people, all saluting or with a hand placed over their hearts, lined the cemetery street as six white horses pulled the fallen Navy SEAL toward his place of rest. Four uniformed soldiers from the US Army's Old Guard, which handles Arlington funerals with such dignity, guided the horses forward until they quietly stopped, after which US Navy sailors carried Brendan toward Travis and the fallen heroes of Section 60.

Having flown in from Afghanistan, Brendan's entire SEAL Team Three platoon was at Arlington to bid farewell to the warrior affectionately known as "Loon-Dog." Indeed, as Defense Secretary Robert Gates had quoted while memorializing US Marine Major Douglas Zembiec, "Your men have to follow your orders. They don't have to go to your funeral."

Secretary Gates was also at Brendan's funeral. With a hand over his heart, he stood alongside many mourners, including Tom, Janet, Ryan, and Dave, as the remarkable ceremony unfolded. Those who witnessed the burial of Lieutenant Brendan Looney would never forget seeing US Navy SEALs, who had come from California, Virginia, Iraq, and Afghanistan to salute their fallen brother, filing past Brendan's flag-draped casket one by one. The SEALs included Lieutenant Flynn Cochran, who had trained with Brendan at BUD/S; Petty Officer First Class Vic Nolan, who had led the team in prayer just before Brendan's final mission; and Lieutenant Steve Esposito, who had said "where do I start?" when asked what he liked most about Loon-Dog.

Though the twenty-one-gun salute was technically louder, the sound of each Navy SEAL pounding his trident into Brendan's casket was thunderous. As the Looney family cried, Janet held Brendan's trident tightly in her right hand. Section 60 of Arlington National Cemetery may have been soaked by rain and tears on that gray fall afternoon, but as the SEALs paid tribute to one of their own, a communal sense of pride was overflowing. Brendan was taken too soon, but he was also being honored the right way.

When Lieutenant Rob Sarver clutched his right fist and thumped his Navy SEAL pin into Brendan's coffin, which had at least fifty gold tridents on it already, he took a deep breath and said good-bye. Brendan's funeral was complete, and he would now rest in eternity beside his Naval Academy roommate. But before Sarver went home for the first time since deploying to Iraq seven months earlier, he needed to give Brendan's personal effects to Amy.

After giving several of Brendan's medals, along with the bullet casings from the twenty-one-gun salute, to Kevin and Maureen, Sarver gave additional medals and personal items, including Brendan's wallet, to Amy. Later, when Sarver returned to Coronado, he would open his friend's locker and find Travis's knife, which Tom had given Brendan after the Marine Corps Marathon. On this day, however, the items he presented were from Afghanistan.

Sure enough, Brendan's wedding band was still attached to his G-Shock watch, which the Navy SEAL was wearing when he died. Seeing the ring she had slid onto Brendan's finger on the happiest day of their lives was another agonizing moment for the young widow. But at least they had found the treasured memento.

After shedding many tears and exchanging stories about each item, Amy suddenly rifled through everything Sarver had brought her and said, "There's something missing."

"I know, Amy," Sarver said. "I'm sorry to tell you this, but Brendan's jacket had to be cut off after the crash."

"No, not the jacket," Amy said. "Rob, remember the other thing he always wore?"

"Oh, of course," Sarver said. "You mean the bracelet."

"Yes," Amy said. "Do you know where it is?"

"I'm sorry," Sarver said, bowing his head. "It was never found."

Everything paused, including Amy's tears. Finally, after the most unbearable ordeal any military spouse could endure, something made sense.

Somewhere, most likely atop or below one of southeastern Afghanistan's tall, rugged mountains, a black bracelet with silver lettering lay covered in dirt and dust. Travis never got to serve there, but Brendan made sure that his fellow Spartan, hero, and leader also made his mark in the country where 9/11 was planned.

"No regrets," Amy whispered. "No regrets."

14

WARRIORS FOR FREEDOM

For Amy, the evening of May 1, 2011, was like many nights during the seven and a half months since Brendan had been killed. She was sad and lonely, but also surrounded by kindhearted friends in the tight-knit Navy SEAL community.

Still in San Diego, swamped by thoughts of what was and what could have been, virtually everything reminded Amy of Brendan. There was the coffee machine that ran out of coffee on the same week her husband would have come home from Afghanistan. There was the box of rainbow sprinkles she bought for her ice cream after one of their last phone conversations. There was the care package that Brendan planned to send Travis before he was killed in Iraq. Even though the magazines inside the box were old and outdated, Brendan could never bring himself to throw it away. Amy shed a tear as she flipped through them.

There was also a whiteboard in the garage where Brendan used to exercise that said "NFTM 4–29–07" in his handwriting. Amy, who hadn't previously noticed the initials while that particular corner of the whiteboard was hidden behind stacks of boxes, quickly realized it stood for "Never Forget Travis Manion, 4–29–07." Brendan had written it to inspire himself during grueling workouts, similar to the ones he used to have with Travis.

Day and night, Amy often felt like Brendan was still alive. *He was just here.*

The young widow spent that evening near the beach with a friend who was married to an active duty Navy SEAL. As spouses often did during deployments, and especially after a team member was injured or killed, Amy's friend Lindsey was cooking her dinner. Just like on the battlefield, no member of the SEAL community was ever left behind, and when Amy returned to California after three nightmarish weeks in Maryland, she was enveloped with love, support, and most of all, food. Amy could probably count the number of meals she had cooked for the first few months after Brendan's death on one hand.

Amy and her friend were eating chicken parmigiana and having a freewheeling, spirited discussion when they noticed that Sunday evening television programming had been interrupted by a special report. President Barack Obama was about to give a "major" address to the nation, and for at least a few minutes, nobody seemed to know what he was about to say.

"This is scary," Amy said, bowing her head to say a quick prayer. All the way across the country, Janet and Ryan were doing the same thing.

There was initially no way to know what was happening, but one thing was for sure: the president of the United States would not address the nation and the world well after 10:00 p.m. on a Sunday night unless the topic was potentially earth-shattering.

Before the topic of the president's speech was revealed on Twitter and in subsequent news reports, the country experienced some of its most suspenseful moments since Brendan, Travis, and millions more watched the horrific events of September 11, 2001, unfold on live television. The nation had since experienced several tragedies, from the explosion of space shuttle *Columbia* to Hurricane Katrina, but as rumors began to swirl, countless Americans wondered what the president was about to say.

The White House said the announcement was related to national security. Was it a massive terrorist plot? Had Moammar Gadhafi been killed or captured in Libya? What about Osama bin Laden? Was the country on the brink of war with Iran or North Korea? Were the American people in imminent danger?

The clock in the Del Mar, California, apartment read 8:35 p.m. when the commander-in-chief appeared in the East Room of the White House. It was 11:35 p.m. in Doylestown, Pennsylvania, where the Manions were busy preparing for the next day's memorial golf outing and dinner, which was held each year on the Monday closest to the anniversary of Travis's death. Several of Travis's closest Marine Corps buddies, in town for the event, were staying at the Manion house that night. They sat with Tom, Janet, Ryan, and Dave as the president walked to the White House podium.

"Good evening," President Obama said. "Tonight, I can report to the American people and to the world that the United States has conducted an operation that killed Osama bin Laden, the leader of al Qaeda and a terrorist who's responsible for the murder of thousands of innocent men, women, and children."

From San Diego to Philadelphia, Los Angeles to Washington, Seattle to New York, and Afghanistan to Iraq, millions of Americans rejoiced with a patriotic fervor not seen since the morning of September 12, 2001. President Obama, who had called President Bush shortly before making the startling announcement, spoke about the significance of bin Laden's death:

> For over two decades, bin Laden has been al Qaeda's leader and symbol, and has continued to plot attacks against our country and our friends and allies. The death of bin Laden marks the most significant achievement to date in our nation's effort to defeat al Qaeda.
>
> Yet his death does not mark the end of our effort. There's no doubt that al Qaeda will continue to pursue attacks against us. We must—and we will—remain vigilant at home and abroad.

In Del Mar, about twenty-five miles from the Coronado beach where Brendan was named Honor Man, Amy cried and hugged her friend. At Philadelphia's Citizens Bank Park, adjacent to Lincoln Financial Field, where Travis had attended countless Eagles games with Brendan, Dave, and others, a nationally televised Major League Baseball game between the Philadelphia Phillies and New York Mets was interrupted by enthusiastic chants of "U-S-A." In nearby Doylestown, the Manion family and several Marines who had served with Travis did a shot of Patrón at the same bar where Tom and Janet once raised a glass to their fallen son with Brendan. In the nation's capital, crowds celebrated into the night outside the White House. At the Pentagon, World Trade Center, and United Flight 93 Memorial in Shanksville, Pennsylvania, Americans lit candles and left flowers.

"We give thanks for the men who carried out this operation, for they exemplify the professionalism, patriotism, and unparalleled courage of those who serve our country," the president had said in his speech. "And they are part of a generation that has borne the heaviest share of the burden since that September day."

In Coronado and Virginia Beach, word was quickly spreading that the men who killed bin Laden were Navy SEALs, which the White House soon confirmed. Upon receiving many text messages from family members and close friends, including Janet and Ryan, Amy reflected on a moment that would have made her husband, who made the most out of every day he served as a sailor and SEAL, incredibly proud.

"I'm so happy they got him," Amy told her friend Lindsey. "But at the same time, my husband died and I know so many others are going to die too."

"This is a big deal," Amy's friend said. "But it's also only one slice of the pie."

Though the war wasn't over, that night was as close as America's post-9/11 generation would ever get to the unbridled elation of the World War II generation's V-J Day.

Amy smiled when she thought of Travis and Brendan laughing and drinking somewhere far above the Sunday night sky. Though proud of the role her husband and his close friend had played in America's struggle against terrorism, Amy still would have given anything to share the moment with Brendan before meeting up with Travis for an Annapolis-style celebration.

The day after President Obama's dramatic announcement, twenty-two-year-old Corporal Kevin White, of Westfield, New York, was killed by an IED in Afghanistan. Thirty-five American troops died in Afghanistan that month, as well as two in Iraq, from which the last US forces would withdraw that December.

As the sacrifices of America's military families continued after bin Laden's death, many controversial issues once again divided the country. In that month and many to follow, just about the only thing most Americans could agree on was the heroism of the military.

Whereas the first Monday in May 2011 was a time for bleary-eyed Americans to rejoice after bin Laden's demise, the last Monday—Memorial Day—was a time to reflect.

Amy was in San Diego when President Obama took the podium on May 30, 2011, to deliver his Memorial Day remarks. After receiving an invitation to join the ceremonies at Arlington National Cemetery, Tom and Janet Manion, along with Ryan, Dave, and their two daughters, Maggie and Honor, were in the audience to witness the president's address. Sitting beside them at Arlington were Kevin, Maureen, Bridget, Erin, and Kellie Looney.

Speaking at Arlington's historic Memorial Amphitheater on a bright, clear morning, the president closed his speech with a story about two young men who had made a difference:

Our nation owes a debt to its fallen heroes that we can never fully repay. But we can honor their sacrifice, and we must. We must honor it in our own lives by holding their memories close to our hearts, and heeding the example they set. And we must honor it as a nation by keeping our sacred trust with all who wear America's uniform, and the families who love them; by never giving up the search for those who've gone missing under our country's flag or are held as prisoners of war; by serving our patriots as well as they serve us—from the moment they enter the military to the moment they leave it, to the moment they are laid to rest.

That is how we can honor the sacrifice of those we've lost. That is our obligation to America's guardians—guardians like Travis Manion. The son of a Marine, Travis aspired to follow in his father's footsteps and was accepted by the U.S. Naval Academy. His roommate at the Academy was Brendan Looney, a star athlete and born leader from a military family, just like Travis. The two quickly became best friends—like brothers, Brendan said.

After graduation, they deployed—Travis to Iraq, and Brendan to Korea. On April 29, 2007, while fighting to rescue his fellow Marines from danger, Travis was killed by a sniper. Brendan did what he had to do—he kept going. He poured himself into his SEAL training, and dedicated it to the friend that he missed. He married the woman he loved. And, his tour in Korea behind him, he deployed to Afghanistan. On September 21st of last year, Brendan gave his own life, along with eight others, in a helicopter crash.

Heartbroken, yet filled with pride, the Manions and Looneys knew only [one] way to honor their sons' friendship—they moved Travis from his cemetery in Pennsylvania and buried them side by side here at Arlington. "Warriors for freedom," reads the epitaph written by Travis' father, "brothers forever."

In a cemetery where two American presidents—John F. Kennedy and William Howard Taft—are buried, the nation's forty-fourth commander-in-chief saluted two young patriots who could have become fathers, grandfathers, businessmen, doctors, teachers, professional athletes, police officers, firefighters, civic leaders, politicians, or even presidents. Like thousands of fallen heroes resting all around them, Travis and Brendan had the ambition, talent, and dedication to accomplish whatever they wanted in life. They chose to serve.

"The friendship between 1st Lieutenant Travis Manion and Lieutenant Brendan Looney reflects the meaning of Memorial Day: brotherhood, sacrifice, love of country," the president said. "And it is my fervent prayer that we may honor the memory of the fallen by living out those ideals every day of our lives, in the military and beyond."

Six months later Brendan's widow, exhausted and trying to overcome throbbing pain in her knee, passed the Iwo Jima Memorial while crossing the finish line of the Marine Corps Marathon. As her husband had run to honor Travis four years earlier, Amy had run 26.2 miles to honor Brendan, whom she would always hold in her heart.

Driven by love and grief, Amy met her goal, as did Brendan's equally courageous mother, Maureen, and sister, Bridget. When the Looneys crossed the finish line, Ryan and her two young daughters, five-year-old Maggie and two-year-old Honor, were cheering them on. Janet, who wasn't feeling well that morning, was being cared for by Tom back at the hotel.

After Amy iced her knee, she went to Arlington National Cemetery to see Brendan and Travis's headstones for the first time. Thirteen months after losing her husband, the Gold Star wife's emotions were still raw and fragile. Yet on this fall day, which had warmed up after a freak snowstorm the day before, Amy visited

Arlington with Travis's two young nieces. She was determined to hold herself together, although some tears were inevitable.

Staring at her husband's name, Amy kissed his tombstone before draping her Marine Corps Marathon medal around it. For the first time, she truly understood Brendan's emotions after Travis died, and in that moment, she missed her husband more than ever.

"I will always love you, Brendan," Amy said as Ryan kept the kids occupied nearby. "The reason I keep going is because I want to make you proud. I hope I am."

Suddenly, Maggie walked up to Amy and took her by the hand.

"Amy, why did you put your medal there?" Maggie asked.

Composing herself and wiping away tears, Amy smiled at the niece Travis had held when she was just a baby.

"I'm giving that to Brendan because I never could have finished that long race without him," she said. "And you know what, Mags? After your Uncle Travis passed away, Brendan ran that same race and went on to do some very important things. And no matter where he was, he could always hear Travis cheering him on."

"Are they in heaven?" Maggie asked.

"Yes," Amy said. "And no matter what you do, your Uncle Travis will always be cheering you on, too."

How had all this happened? Just a few short years before, Amy was making memories with Brendan and Travis in Annapolis. They were going to be friends for life, having each other's families over for Super Bowls and summer barbeques. *They were just here*.

"Don't be sad, Amy," Maggie said, breaking the silence. "Every night, I say my prayers and last night, I said one for you."

"Oh Maggie," Amy said, kneeling down and putting her arm around Ryan's little girl. "Thank you, sweetheart!"

After Amy and Maggie shared a hug, they said good-bye to Travis.

"Good-bye, Trav," Amy said.

"I love you, Uncle Travis," Maggie said.

With her arm still around Travis's niece, Amy then turned toward Brendan's place of rest.

"Bye, Brendan!" Maggie said, then skipped toward her mom and sister.

Amy, wiping away one last tear, looked down at her husband's headstone.

"See you later," she said.

As Amy caught up with Ryan, Maggie, and Honor and they walked through the cemetery, she looked at the gleaming white headstones of thousands of brave men and women who had fought in every American conflict since the Revolutionary War. There was a sense of awe here—and a true sense of community—that made her feel like Brendan and Travis belonged. During many subsequent visits to Arlington, Amy not only shared the story of her fallen heroes, but paused to listen to the stories of others.

Surrounded by their fallen brothers and sisters in arms until the end of time, Travis and Brendan are roommates who rest in peace after dying for their country in war. Called to action after the attacks of 9/11, they preserved liberty, defended the defenseless, and gave children like Maggie and Honor a chance at growing up in a safer, more just world.

At the bottom of Lieutenant Brendan Looney's headstone is an inscription: "US Navy SEAL, Loving Husband, Son & Brother." At the bottom of First Lieutenant Travis Manion's are the fallen Marine's words: "If Not Me, Then Who. . . ."

There is no inscription to define the meaning of their sacrifice. That mission is ours.

Epilogue

Maggie and Honor's Pledge

For the second anniversary of Brendan's death in Afghanistan, Amy—a widow at age thirty-one—challenged fellow citizens to perform ten random acts of kindness in honor of America's fallen heroes. Her stirring words appeared in an op-ed piece published by the *San Diego Union-Tribune*:

> In the two years since the Sept. 21, 2010, helicopter crash that killed Brendan and eight of his Navy and Army brothers, I have tried to live my life in a way that honors my husband and his fellow troops.
>
> I also want Americans to know that while Brendan was most certainly a warrior, he was also a kindhearted 29-year-old man who cared a great deal about America and the countries he visited.
>
> Brendan, like so many American heroes I've had the honor of knowing, was full of compassion. He didn't only risk his life during combat missions; he also put himself in peril to shield civilians. Seeing the plight of children in Afghanistan and Iraq impacted my husband profoundly, and Brendan did all he could to help them.
>
> Lt. Brendan Looney was proof that one could be a warrior for freedom and ambassador of kindness at the same time. By following

the selfless examples set by courageous men and women who volunteer to serve, many of the world's problems might not seem as impossible to solve.

The response to Amy's call to action was swift and overwhelming. The moving newspaper item mirrored Amy's response to her husband's death, which included helping and inspiring loved ones of fallen Navy SEALs. Amy even traveled to Europe with a group of military survivors to swim the English Channel in honor of America's departed heroes.

Amy also became head of the Travis Manion Foundation's San Diego office. While leading the nonprofit organization's Survivor Services effort, she has helped many Gold Star spouses, fiancées, parents, siblings, and children cope in the wake of incomprehensible loss.

Every day, Amy has changed lives while living out the bold words Brendan wrote on their last Valentine's Day card: *I DON'T QUIT*. Simply put, she has made her husband proud.

Brendan would also be proud of America's Navy SEALs, who not only electrified the world by bringing Osama bin Laden to justice, but spend every waking hour protecting their country.

Lieutenant Rob Sarver grew to embody Brendan's motto: "Be strong. Be accountable. Never complain." After his honorable discharge from the Navy in 2013, Sarver was hired by Goldman Sachs upon completing the company's innovative Veterans Integration Program. Sarver also asked his girlfriend, Heather Hojnacki, to marry him.

After happily accepting the proposal, Heather thought of the adoring, unbreakable love shared by Brendan and Amy. By devoting themselves to one another, Rob and Heather Sarver will honor two of their closest friends.

Although Travis's entire MiTT team was deeply affected by the harrowing events inside the Pizza Slice, none faced uphill battles quite like Navy Hospital Corpsman Edwin "Doc" Albino and

Marine Lance Corporal Chuck Segel, who were seriously wounded during the April 29, 2007, firefight. They both survived, and like so many of our nation's wounded veterans, they motivate those around them with their determination, dedication, and strength.

Nick, the Iraqi interpreter who told Travis that he hoped to one day leave his war-torn country and move to the United States, saw his dream become a reality. The week before he died, Travis had written a letter of support on Nick's behalf.

Like thousands of fellow Gold Star families, the Manions and Looneys are shining examples of our country's strength during wartime and beyond. Kevin and Maureen Looney, along with their five surviving children, responded to Brendan's death with selflessness and courage. They spearheaded the Brendan Looney '99 Memorial Scholarship Fund at DeMatha Catholic High School, which helps students who want to follow in Brendan's footsteps by always making the most of what they are doing.

Steve, Billy, Bridget, Erin, and Kellie Looney have all run the Marine Corps Marathon. Like their older brother, the Looney siblings push themselves and those around them to keep moving forward. Their example is one for every young American to follow.

Travis's sister, Ryan, became president of the Travis Manion Foundation, which carries the lasting imprint of her mom, Janet. The foundation and its rousing call to *honor the fallen by challenging the living* not only provides families of the fallen and veterans with direct assistance, but gives them a chance to take the next step forward in their lives.

Janet, Ryan, and the organization's dedicated staff and volunteers quickly turned "If not me, then who . . . " into a rallying cry for the military community. To date, the Travis Manion Foundation has provided support to almost twenty thousand veterans and families of the fallen.

It was out of Janet's passion for engaging younger Americans that the Character Does Matter program, which empowers veterans and families of the fallen to deliver inspirational presentations to emerging leaders, was born. Character Does Matter engages the next generation to serve and directly impact their local communities while carrying on the legacies of our nation's fallen heroes. To date, thousands of schools and organizations across the United States have signed up for these unique presentations, many of which Ryan has led.

The 9/11 Heroes Run, which started as one group run in Doylestown and spread to more than fifty locations across the country and around the world, quickly became the Travis Manion Foundation's most recognizable footprint. As the national race series to honor victims of the 9/11 attacks, fallen service members, and heroic first responders achieved unprecedented participation, Janet continued pushing those around her to make an even bigger difference.

Janet Manion died of cancer on April 24, 2012, just five days before the fifth anniversary of Travis's death in Iraq. Her funeral events were held in the same locations as her son's and carried with them sadness and disbelief, but also extraordinary pride.

At Janet's memorial service, Ryan closed her mom's eulogy with an assurance:

> Mom, now it's time for dad, me, and the rest of us to carry on your fight. Enjoy your time with your beloved son and your wonderful parents, and we'll join you a little later.
>
> Until that day comes, I will wake up every morning repeating my brother's words, which so deeply inspired my mom.
>
> "If not me, then who. . . ."

That evening on the lower level of the Manion home, Ryan hugged her husband, Dave, her two daughters, Maggie and Honor, her dad, Tom, and her dear friend Amy, before heading upstairs for the night. As she made the short walk through the main level on her way upstairs, Ryan passed Travis's medals and Brendan's gold Navy SEAL trident, which sat on top of the living room piano.

A few moments later, young Maggie stood up in the middle of the room and asked for everyone's attention.

"My Nan and my Uncle Travis and his friend Brendan loved our country a lot," the little girl said. "So could everyone please put your hands on your hearts and say the Pledge of Allegiance with us?"

Almost everyone's eyes welled up in unison as Maggie and Honor, along with several little cousins, spoke:

> I pledge allegiance
> To the flag
> Of the United States of America
> And to the Republic
> For which it stands
> One nation
> Under God
> Indivisible
> With liberty and justice for all.

Janet would soon be buried next to Travis and Brendan at Arlington National Cemetery. On the determined military mom's wrist when she was laid to rest—and for all time—was a silver bracelet engraved with black lettering:

1ST LT. TRAVIS L. MANION, USMC 04.29.07 IRAQ
LT (SEAL) BRENDAN J. LOONEY, USN 09.21.10 AFG
WARRIORS FOR FREEDOM, BROTHERS FOREVER

Acknowledgments

COLONEL TOM MANION, USMC (RET.)

My wife and I lost our only son, US Marine First Lieutenant Travis Manion, on April 29, 2007, in Fallujah, Iraq.

Soon after Travis's death, I set out to share his sacrifice through a book that would help more Americans understand the profound commitment that these young men and women have made to our country. After many who served with Travis mentioned his close bond with the Iraqis who he helped train, I traveled to Fallujah in the spring of 2010 to speak personally with several of the Iraqi Army soldiers whom he fought alongside.

I was overwhelmed by the pride that these people had in their country and inspired by their continuing quest for freedom. I saw firsthand what Travis must have experienced working so closely with the Iraqis, and I left the country with a better understanding of the struggles and the determination of these proud people.

As I flew back from Iraq, the caskets of five fallen American heroes were being carried home to their families on the same plane. The solemn moment reinforced how much this young generation of Americans had sacrificed so future generations of Iraqis could grow up in a land not gripped by fear, terrorism, and war.

My son's US Naval Academy roommate, US Navy Lieutenant (SEAL) Brendan Looney, was subsequently killed in action. Immediately after the death of this courageous warrior, I realized the story of service and sacrifice stretched beyond Travis and his efforts in Iraq to a bigger story about all who serve.

While mourning Travis and Brendan, it became clear that the story of these two American heroes was representative of an entire young generation of men and women who answered the call to serve after the attacks of September 11, 2001. Whether in Iraq, Afghanistan, or other volatile areas around the globe, our military and their families have taken on an immense burden for our country. At war for longer than any prior conflict, many with two, three, or four tours in a combat zone, the patriots of this all-volunteer force have continued to step forward without hesitation. Their selfless service is a shining example to all Americans of the price of freedom.

Throughout our history, generations have continued to answer the call to defend our nation, and none more proudly than today's volunteers. This book is for them.

There are countless people to thank for helping this project come together, particularly Travis's fellow Marines and Brendan's fellow Navy SEALs, who spent many hours helping us understand the heroism of their brothers in arms. Thanks for your service to our nation, and for helping us tell a story that we hope will enable more Americans to understand your generation's courage and sacrifice.

To our literary agent, E. J. McCarthy: thank you for your belief in this project. You helped make this book a reality, and we are enormously grateful for your efforts.

To our editor, Robert Pigeon: thank you for your guidance and wonderful ideas. You are the best in the business.

To our publisher, Da Capo Press and the entire Perseus Books Group: thanks to your team for your enthusiastic support. You have truly gone above and beyond.

To Tom Sileo: your relentless efforts helped put this story together in a way that those outside of the military community can appreciate.

To Ryan, Dave, Maggie, and Honor: thanks for all the support and for being there for me. I love you guys!

To Amy, Kevin, Maureen, Steve, Ali, Billy, Morgan, Erin, Bridget, and Kellie Looney: your strength is an inspiration. We will always remember Brendan's life, legacy, and ultimate sacrifice.

To Brendan: no one could ever be a better friend. You are a shining example for generations to come.

To Travis: no son could ever make his dad more proud.

To my dear Janet: finally the book has been written, and my only regret is that you weren't here to share it. I will love you always.

Notes

CHAPTER 1: CALL TO ARMS

9 *covered by a local newspaper:* Hilary Bentman, "Wrestling with Life's Lessons," *Intelligencer*, December 30, 2004.

23 *potential terrorist target:* Childs Walker, "Sept. 11 Changed Destiny for Navy Class of 2002," *Baltimore Sun*, September 9, 2011.

CHAPTER 2: EARN IT

30 *CBS Sports that day, later said: From Philadelphia to Fallujah* (documentary, Sweet Prince Productions, 2012).

38 *486 US service members died:* icasualties.org.

39 *fellow Naval Academy graduates:* Donna Miles, *Myers Girds Naval Academy Grads for Role in Terror War*, report from American Forces Press Service, US Department of Defense, May 28, 2004.

41 *championship game in NCAA history:* Kevin Van Valkenburg, "Syracuse Sinks Navy Bid," *Baltimore Sun*, June 1, 2004.

42 *John Desko admitted:* Frank Litsky, "Navy Has Sentiment on Its Side; Syracuse Has History," *New York Times*, May 31, 2004.

CHAPTER 5: NO GREATER HONOR

87 *fifth anniversary of the 9/11 attacks:* Thomas E. Ricks, "Situation Called Dire in West Iraq," *Washington Post*, September 11, 2006.

CHAPTER 6: THE PIZZA SLICE

110 *the future vice president said:* NBC News, *Meet the Press*, April 29, 2007, http://www.today.com/id/18381961/ns/meet_the_press/t/mtp-transcript-april/#.UlcQUtLNndY.

CHAPTER 12: MISSION 59

215 *Petty Officer First Class Vic Nolan:* The names of certain US Navy SEALs have been changed to protect operational security.

CHAPTER 14: WARRIORS FOR FREEDOM

251 *died in Afghanistan that month:* icasualties.org.

EPILOGUE: MAGGIE AND HONOR'S PLEDGE

257 *op-ed piece published by the San Diego Union-Tribune:* Amy Looney, "Warrior's Compassion Continues to Inspire," *San Diego Union-Tribune*, September 19, 2012.

Index